GEEK GIRLS

Geek Girls

Inequality and Opportunity in Silicon Valley

France Winddance Twine

NEW YORK UNIVERSITY PRESS

New York

NEW YORK UNIVERSITY PRESS
New York
www.nyupress.org

References to Internet websites (URLs) were accurate at the time of writing. Neither the author nor New York University Press is responsible for URLs that may have expired or changed since the manuscript was prepared.

Library of Congress Cataloging-in-Publication Data
Names: Twine, France Winddance, 1960– author.
Title: Geek girls : inequality and opportunity in Silicon Valley / France Winddance Twine.
Description: New York : New York University Press, [2022] | Includes bibliographical references and index.
Identifiers: LCCN 2021031268 | ISBN 9781479803828 (hardback) | ISBN 9781479803835 (ebook) | ISBN 9781479803859 (ebook other)
Subjects: LCSH: Women computer industry employees—California—San Francisco Bay Area. | Computer industry—Employees—California—San Francisco Bay Area. | High technology industries—Employees—California—San Francisco Bay Area. | Women in computer science—California—San Francisco Bay Area. | Women in technology—California San Francisco Bay Area. | Discrimination in employment—California San Francisco Bay Area.
Classification: LCC HD6073.C65222 U589 2022 | DDC 331.4/810040979473—dc23
LC record available at https://lccn.loc.gov/2021031268

New York University Press books are printed on acid-free paper, and their binding materials are chosen for strength and durability. We strive to use environmentally responsible suppliers and materials to the greatest extent possible in publishing our books.

Manufactured in the United States of America

10 9 8 7 6 5 4 3 2 1

Also available as an ebook

For Daily Twine, Sophie Blee-Goldman, and everyone fighting for economic, gender, and racial justice in the technology industry

I'm not a woman at Google. I'm a geek at Google.
—Marissa Mayer, former Google vice president,
San Francisco Magazine, 2011

CONTENTS

Augusta Ada Byron, also known as the Countess of Lovelace, is recognized as the first conceptual computer programmer—a visionary who anticipated the future of computing more than a century before the first electronic modern programmable computer was built. Ada Byron, the only child from the marriage of Anabelle Milbanke and the poet George Gordon Byron, was born on December 10, 1815. Her father, who was commonly known as Lord Byron, separated from her mother when she was four weeks old. Her mother, an educational reformer, introduced Ada to mathematics as a child.[1] During an era when aristocratic women in England were tutored by governesses and barred from attending universities, Ada was tutored in British mathematics by family friends including Augustus De Morgan, a founding professor of computer science at London University (now University College London).[2]

In 1833, the seventeen-year-old Ada Byron met Charles Babbage, an English inventor known as "the father of the computer." A Cambridge-educated mathematician, Babbage designed the first general-purpose computer and became one of Ada Byron's mentors and collaborators.[3] Babbage, who used his inherited wealth to advance British mathematics, hosted a series of salons where leading British scholars discussed the new ideas in British science. In an article describing the early education of Ada Byron Lovelace, Christopher Hollings, Ursula Martin, and Adrian Rice situate her training in a larger historical context: "Lovelace's early mathematical education can be viewed in a broader context of changes in British mathematics. . . . Her later mentors, Babbage, De Morgan, and Somerville, were at the heart of attempts to change it, and to align mathematical education and research with newer more rigorous approaches emerging from Europe. . . . The widespread availability and use of elementary mathematics also led to a surprising familiarity with mathematics in popular culture—young ladies did examples from Euclid for pleasure, periodicals like *The Ladies'*

Diary published mathematical questions and readers' answers, and astronomy was a popular pursuit."[4]

Ada Byron acquired the title of the Countess of Lovelace from her marriage to William King, who became the 1st Earl of Lovelace. In an analysis of Lovelace's mathematical abilities, Thomas Misa argues, "The evidence is reasonably clear that Lovelace created the first step-by-step elemental sequence of instruction—that is, an algorithm—for computing the series of Bernoulli numbers that was intended for Babbage's Analytical Engine."[5] In a review and analysis of pioneering women in computing, Denise Gürer explains the significance of Ada Byron's theoretical contributions to modern computer science: "Her paper . . . discussed the Difference Engine, the first automatic calculating device, and the Analytical Engine, which contained the first set of principles for a general-purpose programmable computing machine. Lovelace's series of notes included a table describing the operations necessary for solving mathematical problems. She therefore became the first conceptual programmer for Babbage's Analytical Engine. In subsequent writings, she developed the 'loop' and 'subroutine' concepts—a century before electronic computing machines appeared."[6]

I begin with the contributions of Ada Byron Lovelace, the daughter of English aristocrats, for two reasons. First, Lovelace was a Victorian mathematician who laid the foundations for modern computing technologies a century before the first electronic computers were built. The Analytical Engine was a forerunner to the electronic calculating computers built in the twentieth century and shares "key design features used in modern computing."[7] Second, until recently, women who were pioneers in the field of computing had been written out of the history of artificial intelligence and computing technologies.[8] Ada Byron's accomplishments during an era when women were excluded from attending universities reveal the ways that class status, social capital, and family support intersected to allow her to pursue the study of advanced mathematics in Britain.

On the other side of the Atlantic, ninety years after the birth of Ada Byron Lovelace, a Cherokee woman, who would cofound the Society for Women Engineers, was born. Mary Golda Ross, a citizen of the Cherokee Nation, was born in 1908 and grew up in rural Oklahoma. Ross taught high school mathematics before she became a statistical clerk for the Bureau of Indian Affairs, in Washington, DC. After earning a graduate degree in mathematics, she was hired for a wartime job at Lockheed Missiles and Space Company (now Lockheed Martin) in Southern California in 1942.

Ross, the first woman to be classified as an "engineer" at Lockheed, cofounded the first chapter of the Society for Women Engineers (SWE) in Southern California and later founded another chapter in Silicon Valley.[9] The Society of Women Engineers is now considered part of an "old girls' network" that has forty thousand members globally. After the war ended, she continued to work for Lockheed and "became the only woman in a forty-person think tank for special projects—'the skunk work'—out of which was born the missile and space division. When the firm launched LMSC in Sunnyvale, she moved to the Valley and worked there until her retirement in 1973."[10]

In 1999, Ross reflected on her career: "You could just practically name what you wanted to do. It was terribly exciting. They'd give us a mission, and we'd figure out how to accomplish it."[11] Lockheed Missiles and Space Company played a key role in the opportunity structure for women engineers in the mid- to late twentieth century. In an analysis of industry archives and interviews with former employees, Glenna Matthews notes, "From about 1960 to the very recent past, Lockheed Missiles and Space Company (LMSC) was the largest private employer in Santa Clara County. At the height of the firm's prosperity, it employed some twenty-five thousand employees, of whom 20 to 25 percent were female, depending on the year. That Lockheed employed a few women in highly responsible positions and that the firm had a ladder for encouraging those in secretarial or other hourly jobs to move into management suggests that LMSC may have inadvertently been a catalyst for social change."[12]

During the mid-twentieth century, women were welcomed into the aerospace industry. Silicon Valley military contractors were pressured to hire talent, and although women were concentrated in nonengineering jobs, they could still "prove themselves". And, if given an opportunity, could remain in their positions after the Second World War ended. But by the end of the twentieth century, the workforce of Lockheed had shrunk dramatically.[13]

Esther Williams, a White engineer and a cofounder of the Society of Women Engineers, was born in 1913 and grew up in Washington, DC.

She earned a degree in engineering at the University of California at Berkeley. During the Second World War, Williams was hired by the Kaiser Shipyards in Oakland. After the war, she secured a job at Douglas Aircraft of Southern California, before going to Lockheed.

Williams organized a meeting while she was working in Los Angeles, and Mary Ross was among the eighteen women who attended. They were both transferred by Lockheed to Silicon Valley, where they established another chapter of the Society for Women Engineers. Both women benefited from labor unions, which played a key role in the development of corporate policies that allowed women to move up the occupational ladder within the firms producing military-based electronics. In the mid-twentieth century, defense contractors like Lockheed recruited, hired, and promoted women in the aerospace industry. Women engineers like Ross and Williams created the first infrastructure of support for women engineers. Mary Ross died in 2008 in Los Altos, California, the heart of Silicon Valley.[14]

Three years before Ross's death, Sarah Lamb, an independent British technology consultant was invited to a "Geek Dinner" in London. As one of the few women at this male-dominated event, Lamb's experience inspired her to organize a dinner for "Girl Geeks" in London. Lamb (now Sarah Blow) recalls, "I'd been in the business world for twelve months when I decided to start up the Girl Geek Dinners, and it all came after going to a Geek Dinner event. . . . The situation there was enough for me to realize how isolated women in the industry were. It also made me understand that some (not all!!) men don't really know how to react to a technical female. . . . I blogged the idea about a Geek Dinner for Girls, . . . which is how the name 'Girl Geek Dinners' came out of it all."[15]

In 2008, Angie Chang founded the Bay Area chapter of Girl Geek Dinners and organized the first Girl Geek Dinner, which was held in San Francisco. Four hundred participants attended. The mission of Girl Geek Dinners includes the following:

- To break down old-fashioned stereotypes
- To identify routes around barriers to entry for anyone to get into technology
- To encourage and nurture women who are interested in technology

- To work with local schools, colleges, and universities to encourage more women to enter the tech industries
- To support women who are currently in the industry and work together to figure out the problems and the solutions
- To include men, women, and children in this journey and not exclude men from Girl Geek Dinner events

These dinners have since developed into a network of sixty-four chapters all over the world, which provides a support structure for women in technology—and inspired the title of this book.

Geek Girls provides the first multiethnic and multivocal sociological portrait of the optimism, opportunities, and obstacles that cisgender and gender-fluid technically skilled women negotiate in their pathways into careers in technology firms in Silicon Valley. Are you a founder, entrepreneur, venture capitalist, engineer, or someone else who wants to enter the technology industry? Do you care deeply about racial, gender, and economic justice? Are you interested in moving beyond "diversity theater" and unconscious bias trainings that have failed to change the status quo? If you want to peak behind the Silicon Valley curtain and learn from technically skilled women working in this industry, this book is for you.

ACKNOWLEDGMENTS

I am grateful to everyone who supported my intellectual life during the research and writing of this book. First, my deepest thanks go to Allan Cronin, whose unconditional support has been central to my ability to complete this book, which was written without any external or intramural grant support. The following friends and colleagues read and provided valuable feedback on earlier drafts of this manuscript, in part or in full: Lamonte Aidoo, Zsuzsa Berend, Kathleen Blee, Lisa Hajjar, Joseph Jewell, Heather Merrill, and Leila Rupp. I thank the women and men in the industry who agreed to share their experiences and provided referrals to their coworkers.

My family has supported me and believed in this book during a time of much loss in my life. This book's publication was delayed and disrupted by the COVID-19 global pandemic. I lost several family members to COVID-19, including my nephew Dominic Twine and paternal uncle Joseph Twine. Family and friends kept me joyful, sane, and spiritually balanced as I completed this book: Lamonte Aidoo, Kathleen Blee, Lane Clark, Donald Carter, Mimi Chung, Allan Cronin, Paul Kwo, Constance Penley, Angela Picerni, Heather Merrill, Kimberly Johnson, Sally Johnson, Stephan Miescher, Selasi Twine, Steve Twine and Amma Amoa.

For friendship, meals, hikes, playdates, and other soulful pursuits, I thank Paul Amar, Trevor Auldrige, Paola Bacchetta, Ingrid Banks, Zsuzsa Berend, Adam Burston, Donald Martin Carter, Sarah Franklin, Cliff Gadsden, Philip Gelb, Bishnupriya Ghosh, Tanya Golash-Boza, Lisa Hajjar, Angela Harris, Annie Hikido, Rhonda Hill, Leslie Hunter-Gadsden, Jonathan Ibarra, Naheed Islam, Joseph Jewell, John S. W. Park, Lisa Parks, Dave Reid, Erik Reel, Sekani Robinson, Deborah Rogow, Leila Rupp, Bhaskar Sarkar, Verta Taylor, Charis Thompson, Howard Winant, and Kim Yasuda.

A number of people provided key introductions to industry insiders, conducted interviews, or contributed in other ways to this research project. In this vein, I thank Lauren Alfrey, Jason Atwood, Tristan Bridges, Lisa Gates, Philip Gelb, Karen Maloney, and Hannah Wohl. Meeta Rani Jha, a London-educated South Asian scholar based at UC–Berkeley, recruited Indian American and immigrant Indian engineers to participate in this study. I presented talks based on earlier versions of book chapters and received feedback from several audiences. I thank the audiences at the Departments of Computer Science, Economics, and Gender, Sexuality & Feminist Studies at Duke University; the Departments of Sociology at the UC–Irvine, Northeastern University, the Colloquium Series in Sociology at the City University of New York (CUNY) Graduate Center, and the Global Media and Cultures Lab directed by Professor Lisa Parks at UC–Santa Barbara.

Ilene Kalish has been a very patient, kind, and enthusiastic supporter of this book from the beginning, and it has been a joy to work with such an insightful, thoughtful, and visionary editor. I am very grateful to the comments of Lynn Chancer, who made herself known to me as a reviewer after the manuscript was accepted. I thank Sonia Tsurouka, Alexia Traganas, and Andrew Katz for their editorial support and guidance during the production process. I am indebted to a number of technology journalists, for their reporting on inequality in Silicon Valley: Katie Benner, Emily Chang, Kate Conger, Will Evans, Mike Isaac, Sam Levin, Claire Cain Miller, Rani Molla, Sinduja Rangarajan, Nitasha Tiku, Daisuke Wakabayashi, and Julia Carrie Wong. Special thanks to Doug Adrianson, whose skillful copyediting strengthened this manuscript, and Andrew Seeber, who created the tables and visual representations of data in this book. This book is dedicated to my niece Daily Twine and the next generation of geek girls.

Introduction

To be a computer geek is to be the ultimate twenty-first-
century entrepreneur, someone who reaps the very tangible
rewards of the most lucrative scientific field of the new mil-
lennium by virtue of being talented, capable and driven.
—Roli Varma (2007)

On July 17, 2012, Marissa Mayer, a, thirty-seven-year-old White, Stanford-
trained computer scientist and Google executive, was hired by Yahoo to
serve as its seventh chief executive officer (CEO). At the time, Mayer was
one of the most glamorous, powerful, and highly visible "geek girls" in
Silicon Valley. When Mayer accepted the position as Yahoo's CEO, "she
was the youngest CEO—male or female—of a Fortune 500 company,
a distinction that placed her at No. 3 on *Fortune*'s annual 40 under 40
ranking."[1] In an industry dominated by Asian and White men, Mayer
stood out as a blond, blue-eyed geek celebrity considered beautiful,
brilliant, and fashion-forward. Her geek girl status and hypervisibility
generated constant media scrutiny.[2]

At the age of twenty-four, Mayer was the first woman engineer hired
at Google. Thirteen years later, she was the vice president in charge of
managing geographical and local search products including Google
Earth for one of the world's most powerful technology firms. When
Mayer joined Yahoo, she was described as "someone who has both business acumen and geek cred at the helm." The *New York Times* described
her as being a member of a "shortlist of women in the technology industry to hold the top spot.[3] At the time, only a handful of White women
including Sheryl Sandberg, chief financial officer (CFO) of Facebook;
Meg Whitman, CEO of Hewlett-Packard; and Virginia Rometty, head of
IBM, enjoyed comparable leadership positions in Silicon Valley.

Mayer's departure from Google was interpreted by some industry
insiders as evidence of the phenomenon known as a "leaky pipeline,"

which refers to the loss of qualified women at a company that had been distinctive for having strong women leaders. Reporting for the *New York Times*, Claire Cain Miller noted,

> Executives have been concerned that too many women dropped out in the interviewing process or were not promoted at the same rank as men, so they created algorithms to pinpoint exactly when the company lost women and to figure out how to keep them. Simple steps like making sure prospective hires meet other women during their interviews and extending maternity leaves seem to be producing results—at least among the rank and file. Still senior women at the company are losing ground. Since Larry Page became chief executive and reorganized Google last year, women have been pushed out of his inner circle and passed over for promotions. They include Marissa Mayer, who left last month to run Yahoo after being sidelined at Google.[4]

Seven months before Marissa Meyer was hired to lead Yahoo, the December 2011 cover of *San Francisco Magazine* featured the headline, "Tech's Femme Boom."[5] Mariam Naficy, a serial entrepreneur and founder of Minted,[6] a stationery website, was featured on the cover as a "Geek Crasher." This celebratory cover story profiled twenty-four women who worked in the tech industry as angels (investors), founders, and connectors. In a section titled "The Strong Suits," Marissa Mayer (then age thirty-six), was featured alongside Meg Whitman, Carly Fiorina, Sheryl Sandberg, and Barol Baartz (former Yahoo CEO). These women had broken what sociologists call "the glass ceiling," an invisible barrier that women bump up against as they seek to advance into leadership and management position.

In spite of the high visibility of a number of high-profile White women in Silicon Valley like Marissa Mayer, men continue to rule in Silicon Valley, and the mythology of the geek male genius remains intact. In a study of women in geek culture, Roli Varma reminds us of the significant role that gendered mythologies play in beliefs about who can be a talented engineer. Drawing on the work of Roland Barthes, Varma notes, "Myths circulate in daily life and once they become established in people's beliefs and values, myths serve the ideological agendas of the dominant classes. . . . Gendered constructions of technology portray women's 'normal' occupations to be in non-computing areas, while men's 'dominant' employment to be in high-computing areas. . . . Geek culture legitimizes men's exclusive claim to computing on the one hand and defuses the power relations between men and women in the high-technology sphere on the other hand."[7]

In an article titled "Where Is the Female Mark Zuckerberg?" in *San Francisco Magazine*, E. B. Boyd begins with this declaration, "For the first time in history, Girl Wonders actually have an edge over the boys. . . . Can the New Femme Entrepreneurs seize their moment?"[8] Later in the article, Boyd argues,

> Four decades into the tech revolution, people are still chafing at the fact that there are so few women in the industry, that the typical startup involves a handful of brash young guys and the occasional geekette. The excuses haven't changed much, either: Women are risk-aversive. Women aren't technical. Women can't figure out the work-family balance. [Venture capitalists] are so besotted with male Harvard and Stanford dropouts that they barely give brilliant female entrepreneurs the time of day. And yet in the New Boom reshaping Silicon Valley, the old paradigms—gender and otherwise—are rapidly shifting. Now there are more female founders than ever before, but for the first time in tech history, women founders in certain types of businesses have an edge over their male peers.[9]

Three years after this optimistic and celebratory special issue was published, a steady stream of blogs, memoirs, lawsuits, annual diversity reports, and investigative reports by technology journalists began to lift the curtain on the "diversity problem," sexual harassment, systemic wage discrimination in Silicon Valley, gender inequality, and anti-Black racism.[10] The rejection of domestic minorities, especially Blacks, Latinx, and Native Americans, remains entrenched in publicly traded technology firms in Silicon Valley, including both American and Indian multinationals with offices in Silicon Valley.[11] While White women have made modest gains moving into management, this has not been the case for Asian American women, Black women, or Latina women.[12] Annual diversity reports, foundation reports, and investigative reporting have all found that the exclusion of Black and Latinx women across all categories of tech employment remains durable.[13] The leadership ranks

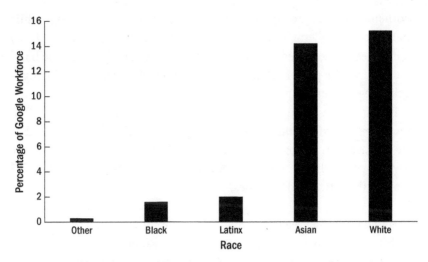

Figure I.1. Women workers by race as a percentage of Google's overall US workforce, 2020. *Note*: Women make up 33.3 percent of the overall Google workforce. (Google 2020)

and decision-makers at the top technology firms remains dominated by Asian and White men.

Hidden Figures: Data Analytics and Inequality

On October 11, 2013, Tracy Chou, a twenty-six-year-old Chinese American engineer at Pinterest, who had formerly worked at Google and Facebook, wrote a blog post on *Medium* titled "Where Are the Numbers?" arguing, "Every company has some way of hiding or muddling the data on women actually in engineering roles. The actual numbers I've seen and experienced in the industry are far lower than anybody is willing to admit. . . . I can't imagine trying to solve a problem where the real metrics, the one's we're setting our goals against, are obfuscated."[14] Three years after Chou's post, 250 companies had submitted data to Chou's repository.

In 2016, women who worked in San Francisco and who had at least ten years' worth of experience responded to a survey, titled "Elephant in the Valley," about their experiences as women in the technology industry. This survey generated a massive set of data and was released on a website. This survey found that "of those surveyed 60 percent reported unwanted sexual advances," while "one in three women" re-ported feeling unsafe at work.[15] Suddenly the media narratives about Silicon Valley shifted from its being a region of opportunities to a bro-topia—a toxic work culture where women endured sexual harassment, systematic pay discrimination, and racism. Articles and discussions on public media about the "diversity problem" became a regular theme.[16]

On May 28, 2014, Laszlo Bock, a Romanian-born businessman who was the senior vice president of people operations at Google, appeared on the *PBS NewsHour* to participate in a discussion on the diversity problem in Silicon Valley. In response to the revelation that only 6 percent of Google's employees were Black (2 percent) or Latinx (4 percent), whereas more than 91 percent were White or Asian,[17] Bock blamed the educational pipeline:

> Part of it is . . . women aren't taking a lot of computer science courses. And the culture of the tech industry at a lot of places isn't that great for women. We have been working on this a lot at Google, and particularly in the last year working on bringing more unconscious bias training to our employees and more awareness of this. For African-Americans and Hispanics, the conditions are even worse. It is a smaller population. Even fewer percentage of people with—from those ethnicities actually earn de-grees in computer science.

In this same interview, Gwen Ifill poses the question, "We have known that the numbers weren't good, even though we didn't have actual num-bers to put to it. Why wasn't action taken before?" Vivek Wadha, an entrepreneur and professor of engineering at Carnegie Mellon, responds to Ifill,

> Frankly, Silicon Valley is a boy's club. It's like a "frat club run wild," is what I often say, because you have young kids hiring other young kids. They don't understand the importance of diversity. They don't understand why they have to be inclusive. . . . Most people are not overtly sexist, racist, or homophobic, but we're human beings. And, as a result, we like people who are like us, who watch the same shows, who like the same food, who have the same backgrounds. So we bring this unconscious bias to every-thing we do. . . . More broadly, though, you have an educational system problem. There is an absolute pipeline problem.[18]

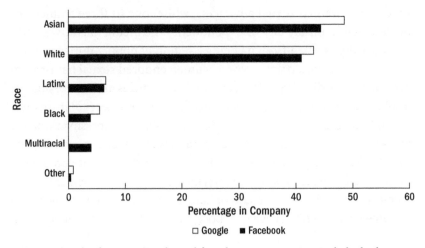

Figure I.2. Facebook versus Google workforce by race, 2020. *Note*: Includes both men and women; Google did not use the multiracial category; Google's "Native American" category is equivalent to Facebook's "Other" category in respective reports; Facebook used "Hispanic" rather than "Latinx"; Google's percentages add to 104 percent. (Statista 2020; Google 2020)

In 2016, only 17.9 percent of university degrees in computer science were awarded to women. Scholars have identified a gender gap in employment in science and technology fields.[19] During the past three decades, employment in STEM fields has grown by 338 percent.[20] The high-technology sector employs 25 percent of professionals in the United States. Jobs in computing have experienced the largest job growth of any sector of the US economy.[21] This job cluster of computing jobs—including software engineers, software developers, mechanical engineers, and programmers—is one of the highest paid and most prestigious fields, yet women, especially Blacks, Latinx, Native Americans, and Pacific Islanders, are being hired at much lower rates than are Asians and Whites in the technology sector.[22] In 2019, the *Los Angeles Times* surveyed tech workers of diverse backgrounds and found that "of the 68 tech workers, who responded to the survey, half said they felt tech was not inclusive to people from diverse backgrounds. . . . People whose identities are underrepresented in their field find themselves judged through a different set of lenses, one that ignores questions of privilege."[23]

Scope of This Study

Geek Girls is an innovative, integrative, and intersectional analysis of inequality and opportunity in Silicon Valley's technology industry—the most economically vibrant sector of the US economy. Silicon Valley is the power center of the "new economy" in the United States. This book provides an analysis of the experiences of technically skilled women who design software, develop new apps, build hardware, write code, and write technical guides. It examines the multiple pathways that women technologists follow into Silicon Valley careers. Technically skilled women working in Silicon Valley are neither a singular nor a homogeneous group with regard to their ranked status and positions in a racialized and class-stratified industry. Yet our scholarly understandings of the occupational experiences of women in the technology industry have been informed primarily by the experiences of middle- and upper-middle-class immigrant Indians, Asian Americans, and White women who have earned degrees in engineering and are presumed to be cisgender and heterosexual.

Geek Girls departs from much of the earlier work that provides intersectional analyses of the US-based high-tech industry in several ways. *Geek Girls* draws on interviews with cisgender and transgender women of diverse ethnic, racial, and class origins. This is also the first intersectional analysis of women in Silicon Valley to include the caste background of the immigrant Indian women who participated in this study.[24] Thus, this study engages and builds on a rich body of data on the South Asian diaspora and the ways that caste-based hiring and merit operate in the global technology market.[25]

Geek Girls sits at the intersection of feminist studies, critical technology studies, and comparative racial and ethnic studies *to provide an analysis of the social, economic, caste, and ethnic dimensions of opportunity structures in Silicon Valley's technology industry.* This book makes significant contributions to earlier studies that examined discrimination in technology markets and moves beyond these by engaging with critical race scholars. Race scholars working in the interdisciplinary field of technology studies have introduced a new set of conceptual tools including *digital elites, digital feminism, digital caste system,* and *digital discrimination.*[26] Research on the IT caste and labor migration has failed to provide analyses of the relationship between Asian Indian migrants and highly educated and technically skilled Black or Latinx employed in Silicon Valley.[27]

I make three central arguments in this book. First, I argue that *the quantity and quality of social and symbolic capital that women possess inform and shape the obstacles and opportunities available to them* as they launch their careers and seek jobs in Silicon Valley. I introduce the concept of *geek capital*, a form of social and symbolic capital that emerged in my analysis of the occupational narratives of women and men in this study. I found that Asian American, Asian Indian, and White women's social proximity to men embedded in the technology industry, with whom they share a caste, class, racial, ethnic, and/or familial relationship, provides these women with privileged access to decision-makers who can offer them entry-level and midlevel jobs.

Geek capital is not simply about technical skills. It refers to networks—social relationships that include membership in exclusive alumni, ethnic, status, or class-based networks that ties one to members of a transnational technocracy. In this study, 40 percent of the White women and 90 percent of the Asian Indian women possessed forms of geek capital as the daughters, siblings, spouses, cousins, domestic partners, former classmates, or friends of men and women embedded in the technology ecosystem. These women were typically from high-caste, middle-class backgrounds and were second-generation engineers. This type of social capital is called "bonding capital,"[28] and connects members of the same exclusive social networks. These networks can include alumni networks, transnational caste-based networks, regional networks, and family networks. Geek capital allows job candidates to be perceived as possessing "merit-based" qualifications. Their abilities and skills are recognized and rewarded by members of the tech ruling class, who attended a small number of US schools and Indian Institutes of Technology and comprise a narrow slice of the university-educated racial and ethnic demographics in the United States. In a study of hiring practices between the 1950s and the early 1970s, Janet Abbate found that "the most popular strategies for recruiting programmers . . . produced contradictory constructions of skill."[29]

My second argument is that an occupational caste system operates in Silicon Valley that consists of layers of discrimination concealed by beliefs in meritocratic recruitment practices. The social discrimination against Blacks, Latinx, Native Americans, and Dalits (members of India's lowest caste) in hiring, recruitment, promotion, and retention is normative and has profound economic consequences for members of these out-groups.[30] The national media covering the technology labor force has reported widely on labor-discrimination lawsuits and investigative reports that have documented systemic employment discrimination against Blacks, Latinx, women, and non-Asian domestic minorities alongside a strong preference for White and Asian men.[31] I argue that this discrimination is a product, in part, of corporate recruitment practices and exclusion from the social networks of members of the dominant ethnic groups in the tech industry.

My third argument is that a persistent belief in and defense of the pipeline myth and the myth of meritocracy has shielded Silicon Valley technology firms and their executives from being held accountable for their role in reproducing structural racism and gender inequality. I identify and analyze the social and cultural mechanisms that reinforce racial, ethnic, and caste inequality among technically skilled women. The use of social referrals and recruitment practices has reproduced structural inequality and left the ethnic, racial, and gender hierarchies in Silicon Valley's workforce intact. CEOs and their representatives continue to place responsibility on the educational pipeline for the dismal numbers of Black, Latinx, Native American, and other underrepresented groups in Silicon Valley.

Research Methods

Geek Girls draws on a total of eighty-seven interviews and surveys conducted between 2015 and 2019 with men and women employed in Silicon Valley. The interviews included sixty-five women and twenty-two men.[32] In addition to interviews, this study draws on blogs, memoirs, surveys, industry-based surveys, Equal Employment Opportunity Commission (EEOC) reports, foundation reports, technology journalism, annual diversity reports released by technology firms, and US Department of Labor investigations. Several research methods were employed to recruit participants, including (1) Facebook postings on a page for women hackers; (2) a key informant at a technology firm

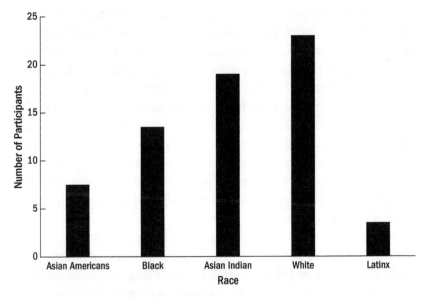

Figure I.3. Female participants by perceived race (n = 65)

headquartered in downtown San Francisco who provided an initial set of referrals; (3) targeted snowball sampling; (4) Tech Inclusion conferences and Lesbian in Tech conferences held in San Francisco in 2015 and 2016; (5) an underground vegan restaurant in Oakland; (6) organizing events for contract workers in Silicon Valley; and (7) referrals from colleagues and neighbors. The interviews ranged from 60 minutes to 120 minutes, and they were recorded and transcribed.[33] Participants and, in some cases, company names have been changed to ensure confidentiality. I employed focused coding to identify recurring themes.[34]

Participants

Geek Girls draws on interviews and survey data from four generational cohorts of women technologists between the ages of twenty and fifty-eight and employed in Silicon Valley. The participants entered the technology industry between 1989 and 2016 and belong to cohorts representing four generations, including Baby Boomers (born between 1946 and 1964),[35] Generation X (born between 1965 and 1980), Generation Y (Millennials; born between 1981 and 1994), and Generation Z (born after 1995).[36] Among the eighty-seven participant-completed surveys, 63 percent were Generation Y (Millennials), 33 percent were Generation X, 2 percent were Baby Boomers, and 2 percent were Generation Z. The technology workers who participated in this study include natives of the United States, foreign nationals, and naturalized citizens from Brazil, Britain, China, India, Germany, Japan, and Mexico.

The technology workers who participated in this study self-identified across a wide spectrum of sexual expressions and gender identity. Among the sixty-seven women in this study, sixty-five completed the biographical surveys. The survey data show that 68 percent identified as cisgender and heterosexual, and 31 percent identified as LGBTQ. White and/or European American women made up 38 percent of the engineers in this study; Asian Indians, 23 percent; Blacks, 16 percent; Asian Americans, 13 percent; Latinx, 6 percent; and multiracial and other comprised, 8 percent. The remaining participants were cisgender men. The participants were employed or formerly worked at start-ups, privately owned companies, and publicly traded companies including Adobe, Airbnb, Amazon, Apple, Autodesk, Cisco, Dropbox, Eventbrite, Facebook, Google, IBM, Indiegogo, Intel, LinkedIn, Lyft, Oracle, Patreon, Salesforce, Square, SurveyMonkey, Twitter, Uber, and Yahoo, as well as more than twenty start-ups.[37]

Three-fourths of the participants in this study were engineers (software, security, front end, back end, or full-stack). The technology workers who participated in this study included entrepreneurs, engineers, founders, graphic designers, technical trainers, technical writers, diversity consultants, digital marketers, and project managers. The sixty-five women in this study worked as engineers, designers, consultants, digital marketers, project managers, technical writers, and customer-support advocates. Slightly more than one-third (n = 27) of the participants identified as LGBTQ, and close to two-thirds (n = 38) identified as cisgender, straight, or heterosexual. Among the women engineers, one-fifth of the White engineers had earned a certificate in a twelve-week accelerated coding boot camp after earning their undergraduate degrees in the arts, humanities, social sciences, or area studies.

Earlier studies of women in science and technology fields have typically employed analyses that flatten the experiences of women and have not included gender-fluid women or those who identify as LGBTQ in

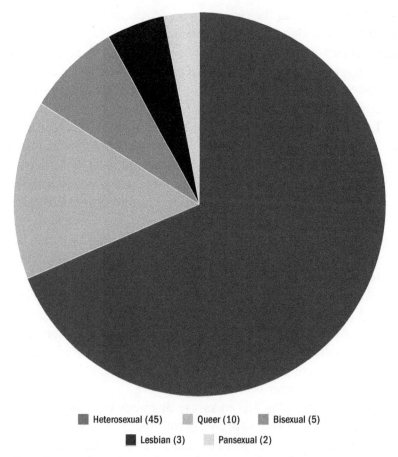

Heterosexual (45)   Queer (10)   Bisexual (5)

Lesbian (3)   Pansexual (2)

Figure I.4. Female participants by sexual orientation (n = 65)

their analysis. One goal of this book is to provide a nuanced analysis that illuminates the differences between women and the mechanisms that sustain ethnic, racial, and gender inequality in Silicon Valley firms. This book contributes a region-specific case study to a growing number of recent sociological studies of women in the technology industry.[38] However, these earlier studies have not provided fine-grained accounts of the complex ways that gender identity and sexual expression operate in concert with race, caste, class background, and marital status to produce barriers to employment in the technology sector for highly educated Blacks, Latinx, and other underrepresented groups.

The women in this study followed six pathways into the technology industry: (1) recruiters, (2) referrals by friends, family, classmates, colleagues, (3) coding boot camps, (4) internships, (5) international visas, and (6) digital/online job boards.[39] The two most common pathways involved social referrals and recruiters. These pathways were followed by women with a wide range of educational credentials and technical expertise. Women who used recruiters often possessed forms of symbolic capital—simply by having a prestigious degree and being embedded in powerful alumni networks associated with one of the "feeder schools" into Silicon Valley, including but not limited to Carnegie Mellon, Harvard, MIT, Stanford, UC–Berkeley, UCLA, University of Washington, University of Texas at Austin, and the prestigious Indian Institutes of Technology (IIT).[40] A third pathway was followed by women who earned degrees in the arts, humanities, or social sciences and who had no technical experiences but enrolled in all-women accelerated skills-based engineering academies (also known as "coding boot camps"). A fourth pathway involved women who were self-taught or who developed technical skills outside of formal classrooms and launched their own businesses before being hired by Silicon Valley firms. A fifth pathway involved women who immigrated from India or Latin America to pursue graduate study in the United States and entered the industry after earning graduate degrees in the United States and working on temporary migrant contracts before going into a full-time contract.[41]

The Research Site: Silicon Valley

Silicon Valley is a region in Northern California that is the epicenter of the North American technology industry. The City and County of San Francisco form the northern boundary of Silicon Valley, which extends south for thirty-five miles along the San Francisco Peninsula. The geographical boundaries south of San Francisco include all of Santa Clara County and San Mateo County and the cities of Fremont, Newark, and Union City in Alameda County. Silicon Valley is the global epicenter of the technology industry and the home to more than two thousand startups and technology firms including Alphabet (parent of Google), Apple, Autodesk, Cisco, Eventbrite, Facebook, Oracle, Salesforce, Twitter, Uber, and Zendesk. It is the economic engine of the largest state by population in the United States and a vehicle for upward mobility, financial stability, and economic growth. It is also an industry that has generated vast wealth and opportunities in a region of stark inequalities where local residents who are Black, Latinx, or Native American remain virtually invisible in executive boardrooms and in technical positions in the technology sector of the economy.

According to the 2010 US Census, Silicon Valley's ethnic composition is 35 percent Asian, 33 percent White, 25 percent Hispanic/Latinx, 2 percent Black, and 5 percent other/multiethnic. Foreign-born residents make up 39.1 percent of the population, with China (18 percent), Mexico (16 percent), and India (13 percent) accounting for 47 percent of the foreign-born, followed by Vietnam (10 percent), the Philippines (10 percent), Europe (8 percent), and other countries in Asia (12 percent). Among the residents, 25 percent have earned a graduate or professional degree, 28 percent have a bachelor's degree, 22 percent have some college, 14 percent are high school graduates, and 11 percent have some high school.

On January 10, 1971, Don Hoefler, a technology journalist, used the term "Silicon Valley" in a three-part series of articles on the "men, money, and litigation" behind the semiconductor business.[42] Writing for the *Electronic News*, a now-obscure industry trade journal, Hoefler was the first to popularize that term. When Hoefler used that term, most local papers referred to this region as the "Santa Clara Valley electronics industry."[43] Today the term is used to refer geographically to this area south of San Francisco and metonymically to refer to the entire technology industry based in Northern California.

Silicon Valley takes its name from the main component in semiconductors. Before the production of silicon chips, software, cloud computing, and information technologies replaced plums, prunes, apricots, and other agricultural products as one of the dominant industries, this region was called the "Valley of the Heart's Delight." Timothy Sturgeon argues that the Silicon Valley technology industry is "nearly one hundred years old and grew out of a historically and geographically specific context that cannot be re-created" and that its roots can be traced to the early electronics industry that emerged in San Francisco Bay in its "early days of experimentation and innovation."[44]

Between 1909 and 1960, a series of technological innovations and commercial products in wireless communication technologies and military electronics used by the aerospace industry and the US Navy, consumer electronics (microwave ovens), and commercial radios were developed in the larger San Francisco Bay Area. These innovations, networks, and military financing laid the foundation for many new industries including radio, telegraph, telephone, film, hi-fi stereo sound systems, public broadcast, and radar systems for the military.[45] Radio waves and telephone and telegraph communications, with military applications, were the new technologies of the late nineteenth and early twentieth century.

A decade after Hewlett-Packard was founded, the transistor was invented at Bell Laboratories in New York by William Shockley. A Stanford graduate and native of Palo Alto, Shockley returned to his home region and set up the Shockley Transistor Corporation after leaving AT&T's Bell Laboratories. In October 1957, eight engineers who had been hired by Shockley established the Fairchild Semiconductor company in Palo Alto, with financing from the Fairchild Camera Shop in New York. Historians of Silicon Valley have described Fairchild as the single most important firm because of the number of companies that it spun off.[46] Between 1959 and 1961, research teams at Fairchild and Texas Instruments independently developed the integrated circuit. Another decade would pass before Intel was founded in 1968. Intel was a small firm that invented the microprocessor, called a "computer on a chip," a breakthrough invention that followed the microchip. This invention laid the foundation for a new generation of personal computers that followed.[47]

A Region of Stark Inequalities

On June 23, 2020, the San Jose State University Human Rights Institute held a press conference outside the Dr. Martin Luther King Jr. Library in downtown San Jose. It released a report authored by Scott Myers-Lipton, titled the "Silicon Valley Pain Index," the first of planned annual reports on racial discrimination and income inequality in Silicon Valley.[48] Myers-Lipton, an activist and sociologist at San Jose State, drew on sixty-five different data points to analyze racial and income inequality

TABLE I.1. Silicon Valley Pain Index: Income and Wealth Inequality in Santa Clara County

0	Number of Black women employed by ten large Silicon Valley tech companies
1%	Percentage of venture capital (out of $19 billion) that went to Black start-up firms
3%	Percentage of large Silicon Valley technology firms that have no Black employees
3%	Percentage of Black employees in the top seventy-five Silicon Valley technology firms
31%	Percentage of large technology firms that have no women of color executives
46%	Percentage of employees at Google, Hewlett-Packard, Intel, LinkedIn, and Yahoo who are White (but Whites hold 80% of executive positions)
47%	Percentage of employees at Google, Hewlett-Packard, Intel, LinkedIn, and Yahoo who are Asian and Asian American (but they hold 25% of executive positions)
6	County's rank among US counties in income inequality
5.6%	Percentage of Whites in county who are living in poverty
11.8%	Percentage of Latinx in county who are living in poverty
12.7%	Percentage of Blacks in county who are living in poverty
61%	Percentage of homeless population that is Black and Latinx
74	Number of billionaires who live in Silicon Valley
$28,960	Average per capita income for Latinx
$40,886	Average per capita income for Blacks
$63,136	Average per capita income for Asian Americans
$82,810	Average per capita income for Whites
$117,000	Yearly income for family of four to be considered low income in Silicon Valley
$1,200,000	Median home price

Source: San Jose State University Human Rights Institute 2021.

in the Silicon Valley. Myers-Lipton concluded that White supremacy is operating in most of the institutions and systems in Silicon Valley.

In Silicon Valley, residents who earn less than $82,000 per year or $117,000 for a family of four are considered low income. The city's minimum wage is $15.59 per hour, which means a minimum-wage earner working forty hours per week with no vacations will gross $32,427.20 per year—far less than the median rent for a one-bedroom apartment. Many homeless (unhoused) residents in the San Francisco Bay Area who sleep in homeless shelters are employed full-time during the day.[49] Since 1970, "real income" in the United States, that is, income adjusted for inflation, has been nearly flat. But the cost of major purchases (houses, cars, education) has increased ahead of inflation.

Scholarship on the experiences of working-class immigrant workers in Silicon Valley's electronics industry have examined the unequal labor conditions of low-wage workers in the technology industry. Scholars have argued that Silicon Valley technology firms have reinforced local and global inequalities.[50] Focusing on low-wage immigrant Asian and Latina women, David Pellow and Lisa Park identified stark inequalities in exposure to chemical toxins, access to health care, and the precarious job situation they endured: "Power, privilege, and wealth are relational, which often means that one person's riches and leisure time are derived from another's impoverishment and hard labor; one socioeconomic or racial/ethnic group's access to safe, high-salary jobs and clean neighborhoods is frequently linked to another group's relegation to dangerous, low-wage occupations and environmentally contaminated communities."[51]

The South Asian Diaspora in Silicon Valley

Silicon Valley is home to the largest diasporic Indian population in the United States. Indians are the second-fastest-growing immigrant group in the United States after Mexicans.[52] The four states that have the largest numbers of Indians include California (21 percent), New York, New Jersey, and Texas. Asian Indians are 1.42 percent of the California's state population and are concentrated in the highest paying and most lucrative job in the technology industry.[53] Workers on the H-1B visas comprise about one-sixth of the total IT workforce in the United States.[54] Between 1990 and 2000, the number of Indian workers on H-1B temporary work visas grew by 113 percent. During this same decade, an estimated nine hundred thousand skilled workers entered the United States on H-1B visas. According to the *Institute of International Education Report*,[55] students born in India were the second-largest group of international students in US universities enrolled in STEM majors, after China.

Three immigration acts have played a role in transforming the ethnic structure of Silicon Valley's labor force. The H-1B nonimmigrant visa program for temporary workers was created by the Immigration and Nationality Act of 1952. This act allowed United States employers to hire foreign workers on a temporary basis, with an annual cap of sixty-five thousand. This act was amended by the Immigration Act of 1990, which allows employers to hire skilled foreign workers for speciality occupations on a temporary basis. Payal Banerjee describes the changes introduced by the 1990 act: "A speciality occupation is defined as one that 'requires theoretical and practical application of a body of highly-specialized body of knowledge' and a bachelor's degree or its equivalent. . . . The H-1B visa, classified under the non-immigrant category, is considered a temporary work visa that can last for up to six years. Changes enacted in 1990 made it possible for immigrant workers on the H-1B visa to have the dual intent of working on a temporary basis and adjusting their status to permanent residency."[56]

Scholars studying the labor migration and occupational experiences of IT workers have provided a rich body of literature on what scholars call the "IT caste," which refers to workers described as urban, highly educated, high-caste, and middle-class Indians who are employed in the global IT labor force in Australia, India, Europe, and North America.[57] This research has provided important insights into the challenges, negotiations, and successes of Indian transnational IT workers who have migrated on student visas or temporary employment visas.[58] Scholars have argued that Asian Indian migrant workers are "racialized" when employed on temporary work visas and before they secure permanent residency in the United States. In a study of temporary workers employed on H-1B visas, Renee Reichl Luthra argues, "Many H-1Bs later transfer to permanent residency status so the disadvantages posed by the visa are seen as a temporary tradeoff for longer-term entrance into a labour market with high rewards for H-1B skills. . . . Once they transfer to a permanent residency status, their high skill levels should enable them to compete in H-1B occupations."[59]

Sociologists have produced a wealth of literature on employment discrimination and specifically on the way that status or group membership structures the hiring process.[60] Most of the India-born women in this study had family members who immigrated to the United States in the 1980s. They described a highly organized and well-positioned transnational network of support that helped immigrant Indians get settled and secure jobs and sponsorship in the United States. Today there are Facebook groups and other online communities that provide a road map to jobs, permanent residency, and eventually naturalized citizenship in the United States.

Shiva, a thirty-something India-born woman who immigrated to the United States to pursue a graduate degree and moved with her husband, an engineer, to the Bay Area, described the Indian version of the American Dream.[61] She recalls a how-to manual that her uncle consulted; it provided detailed information on the steps to follow on his migration pathway to the United States:

> My uncle came here in 1981 or so. . . . At his school . . . [the use of these manuals] is very well known. I think [this manual] still exists. They used to have this thing called ROTGAD. It's an acronym . . . "Realization of the Great American Dream." Basically, in this manual, it provides details for when you apply [for an immigration visa], . . . when you go to the interviews, what kind of answers, what kinds of questions can be expected. What kinds of answers do you give? What re: the different schools? What are they good at? Your multiple entry visa, all this kind of thing, . . . navigating the US border. . . . It's a minutely calibrated system. They've figured out the system, and they play the system well. That all translates to when you come to the US with so much social support.

Indians constitute the largest group of immigrant engineers in Silicon Valley. As a result, immigrant Indians possess an important form of capital called *bonding capital*. Bonding capital is a form of social capital that operates within groups and creates network closure. This form of social capital is distinct from *bridging capital*, which is capital that provides resources that are not available within one's group—it is an inclusive form of social capital based on weak ties between groups.[62] Compared to US domestic minorities who remain underrepresented in technically skilled positions—Black, Latinx, or Native Americans—immigrant Indians and their US-born children possess higher quantities of bonding capital. They hold a disproportionate number of the technically skilled jobs, and recent lawsuits have alleged discrimination against non-Asians and a preference to hire Asian immigrants for technical positions.

Theoretical Concepts

Beginning in the 1970s, sociologists studying gender inequality in organizations generated a cluster of new concepts that illuminated how structural inequality operates in the workplace. These include *tokenism,*[63] *labor queues,*[64] and *inequality regimes.*[65] Joan Acker introduced the concept of inequality regimes to describe the "loosely interrelated practices, processes, actions, and meanings that result in and maintain class, gender and racial inequalities in all organizations."[66] In other words, even organizations that have explicit egalitarian goals tend to develop inequality regimes over time. These regimes do not exist in a vacuum, Ackers says, but are built from "inequality in the surrounding society, its politics, its history, and culture."[67]

In *Men and Women of the Corporation,* a foundational sociological study of women in a New York corporation, published in 1977, Rosabeth Moss Kanter provides a trenchant analysis of the mechanisms that reproduce gender inequality in a corporation. Kanter introduces a number of new concepts, but her most significant is "a theory of tokens." Kanter argues that "the life of women in the corporation was influenced by the proportion in which they found themselves." Defining a token, Kanter writes, "Those women who were few in numbers among male peers and often had 'only woman' status became tokens: symbols of how-women-can-do, stand-ins for all women. Sometimes they had the advantages of those who are 'different' and thus were highly visible in a system where success is tied to becoming known."[68] As a pioneer in the study of gender in organizations, Kanter's analysis preceded the emergence of intersectionality in studies of employment discrimination in the field of sociology. Today gender organization theory has developed, and there are studies that employ a more intersectional analysis that considers LGBTQ women and Black women negotiating multiple axes of difference.[69]

Geek Girls introduces several concepts including *geek capital, glass walls* and *first- and second-generation* technology workers. These concepts build on earlier sociological literature on employment discrimination, gender inequality, and racial inequality in the US labor market. This book is in conversation with an interdisciplinary body of research on gender, labor, technology, and employment discrimination. *Geek Girl* engages with debates in several research streams including (1) gender inequality in organizations,[70] (2) women in computing and engineering,[71] (3) labor-market discrimination,[72] and (4) caste, class, gender, and migration.[73]

Geek Capital

Geek capital is a form of social capital that does not require one to have technical experience or even a degree in engineering or computer science.[74] This form of capital is produced, in part, by a matrix of advantages including class or caste privileges that facilitate movement into the technology sector. What is significant about geek capital is that it illuminates the way that symbolic capital (Whiteness, family occupations) is intertwined with ethnic, caste, and class background to enable gatekeepers to "interpret" the applicant as an "ideal" worker in "cultural" terms, in addition to any specific technical skills that they may have. An example of how geek capital operates can been seen in the experience of Giselle, the sister of a Silicon Valley technology executive.

Giselle: Sister of a Tech Titan Drifts into the Industry

Giselle's career trajectory represents one pattern found among the White women in this study, who began their careers in nontechnical careers such as high school teachers, administrative assistants, or marketing and drifted into the industry through their familial relationships with a White male family member who was employed in the technology industry. Family members and friends provide social referrals to jobs, which represents a significant form of geek capital that has been undertheorized in studies of women working in nontechnical positions in Silicon Valley. These women possess an important form of geek capital: their social relations with White and Asian men who are gatekeepers— executives, founders, directors, or other positions that enable them to secure crucial introductions.

Giselle, a twenty-seven-year-old White woman who earned a degree from an Ivy League university, drifted into the technology industry via her relationship with an older sibling, who is an executive at one of the top technology firms in Silicon Valley. Giselle's brother provided her with a social referral to his company's director of hiring. She is now employed as a recruiting coordinator for this San Francisco–based technology firm. She was not vetted through a competitive interview process and recalled not being able to answer basic questions that were asked during her interview. Before entering the technology industry, she worked as a high school teacher.

As the daughter of a financially secure middle-class family of professionals, Giselle possessed several forms of geek capital. She had attended an exclusive high school and had earned a degree at an elite university. A native of California, she also had an organic network of family support in Silicon Valley. Describing the events that led to her employment at a major technology firm, Giselle identified her brother as the central player in her ability to secure her current job as a recruitment coordinator. She recalled a particular visit with her brother during a time when she described feeling lonely and bored with her career. Giselle's brother encouraged her to move to San Francisco and build a new life. He set up an interview for her at his company, which included a conversation with his boss, who was the CEO. With an older sibling who had worked at three of the top technology firms and held a leadership position in his firm, Giselle was hired, despite having done poorly in her interview. When asked, "What was appealing to you about working for a tech company?" she replied,

> My brother worked there, so that's a more comfortable environment to get started in. . . . I had been to visit [my brother] once before and had . . . seen the office and seen that it had a very fun vibe. And, you know, they give you meals. . . . A lot of the stupid stuff that had been hard about living alone in [name of state] would be made a lot easier by joining a tech company. . . . I was like, "Oh, I need new friends, and so this would be a great way to have a job that pays reasonably well and have friends."

Giselle's experience is representative of roughly half of the White women in this study, who had secured their first position or their current position through a social referral from a family member or close friend. Family members employed in the industry provide a form of "dynastic" privilege, which can be converted into geek capital. Having a family member employed as a tech executive embedded Giselle into the tech system without her having to invest much effort. She moved across the country and secured a six-figure job with no coding experience, no previous internship experience, and no real passion for the field. In the following chapters, we will meet a number of Asian and White women who use social referrals as a form of geek capital that provides greater access to employment than earning a degree in computer science or completing an internship does for Black women in this study (see chapter 3).

Social referrals constitute a significant form of geek capital possessed by many White and Asian women in this study. They are also an expression of class, caste, and racial privilege. In other words, members of the groups that are overrepresented in technology in the executive suites and leadership positions have a built-in advantage. In Giselle's case, we see that her brother essentially gave her a social referral to his boss, who is also a friend, and she did not have to endure rigorous recruitment process common in Silicon Valley firms. And the company created a position for her. This is not unique to the company that hired her but reflects a side door into the industry, the opposite of what I call "glass walls," which I will introduce next.

Glass Walls

I now introduce the concept of *glass walls*, which are *social and cultural barriers to employment that confront qualified job applicants from underrepresented groups even when they possess the educational credentials and/or technical expertise to do the job well.* Glass walls are produced by corporate recruiting policies and social referrals that privilege nonmeritocratic factors. They block access to entry-level positions as well as horizontal mobility into full-time permanent positions for employees on short-term contracts.[75] Like glass ceilings, glass walls are often barriers that are invisible until you hit them. They are only evident when you are unable to move further and enter the industry. Glass walls sort or stratify workers into a two-tier system in which some workers are hired on temporary contracts and treated as disposable. Glass ceilings differ from glass walls in that glass ceilings block upward mobility or advancement within an organization for those who are already employed.

The concept of glass walls illuminates the ways that corporate hiring and recruitment practices can create obstacles to employment for qualified job applicants and reproduce the racial, gender, and class status quo. Glass walls are produced by recruitment practices such as *social referrals* and related policies that restrict information about jobs and access to gatekeepers and permanent employment for job applicants including those who possess the education, experiences, or technical skills through extensive prior work experience. Glass walls reinforce social closure and enable groups that are dominant in the industry to hoard opportunities for members of their own group—in other words, job candidates or applicants who share the age, race, ethnicity, caste background, cultural tastes, leisure interests, and national origins of the managers, teams, and other gatekeepers. Recruitment practices can include a series of interviews with members of one's potential team and can take months. This process can become a barrier to employment for job applicants who cannot afford to wait months for a job offer that may not materialize. Thus, Black and Latina women who lack the economic resources are not able to convert their educational credentials into employment as easily as can their peers who possess racial privilege.

Due to intersecting forms of discrimination and forms of capital (economic, residential, educational, social, marital), the Black women in this study experienced more "social closure" than did their Asian and White peers employed in the technology sector. Sociologists refer to this as "network distance"—that is, one's social distance from founders, decision-makers, and gatekeepers in the industry. In other words, the Black women typically lacked friends, family, spouses, siblings, or former classmates who were in the tech industry.

First- and Second-Generation Geeks

The third concept that I introduce is first-generation and second-generation technology workers. Women, who are the first generation in their family to work in the technology industry, face different challenges and encounter different barriers as they enter the industry than do second-generation technology workers—that is, women whose parents, siblings, aunts, uncles, older cousins, or other family members tended to follow a well-worn pathway. These second-generation women had more family support and often economic capital, which prepared them for entering the industry. In this study, roughly 40 percent of the White American women and 90 percent of the Asian Indian women who were engineers identified as the daughters or younger sisters of engineers. The second generation were the daughters, cousins, nieces, and younger siblings of technologists, usually engineers who were embedded in a global and local technology ecosystem, which provided these women with family mentors and other cultural advantages when they entered the job market.

Mimi: A Korean American Technical Writer

Mimi, a twenty-six-year-old Korean American technical writer, is a first-generation geek girl who earned her degree at Carnegie Mellon, one of the top engineering schools and a feeder school into Silicon Valley.[76] Her degree from a prestigious feeder school into Silicon Valley is another form of geek capital that the small number of Asian American and White women of working-class origin in this study possessed. Although Mimi is the first member of her family to work in the technology sector, she possesses an educational credential that positioned her at the top of the educational caste system and allowed her to gain access to a lucrative career in Silicon Valley. Describing the way that she ended up moving to San Francisco at the age of twenty-one, immediately upon graduation, and working in her first job for Salesforce, she recalled, "What got me into tech is I've always been writing my entire life, and I wanted to be a writer. And I had gotten to the point where I was enjoying my technical classes, . . . but I still didn't feel at all like it was a place I belonged, until I found this one little spot where I felt like I could fit, and that was technical writing, which is the career that I'm in now and the one that I pursued." Not initially drawn into engineering or computing and not passionate about technology industry, Mimi described her transition into science and technology.

> When I was accepted to CMU, I was accepted into this . . . program for students who were interested in the humanities and the sciences both, and so it was this program that allowed you to kind of merge those two interests and kind of explore other majors in a way that most—and so I actually didn't have much of an extensive math and science background. Actually, when I was growing up, I went to this tiny rural public school in a poor part of the country, and my math and science background was actually abysmally behind when I got to college. That was really, really difficult, but when I got into this program, built into this program were a lot of courses in math and science and computer science and some engineering courses and things like that, so I was taking them whether I liked it or not.

Here, Mimi described her initial struggles in her classes because her exposure to computing and engineering had been very limited compared to her more economically privileged classmates. Recounting the economic and regional factors that she had to overcome, she recalled,

> I found computer science really, really overwhelming, so . . . my relationship with tech has been mostly around coming from sort of a depressed socioeconomic background and from a rural background. So where I grew up, we didn't have computer scientists. We didn't have programmers. No one did that. No one knew what it was. Basically my computer class in high school was like a typing class, and I learned how to type and print things and scan a document. So that was my experience with business and computers before I went to school. And so when I was in my first programming class, it was really interesting because it was obvious that they assumed that everyone knew what computer programming, and I had literally no idea. . . . I probably spent the first two months in that class just—the questions I would ask of my professors and my TAs were so elementary that no one knew how to answer them.

Ultimately, Mimi was able to convert her interdisciplinary degree from Carnegie Mellon into a six-figure job in in Silicon Valley. Describing her pathway from school to her first Silicon Valley job, she recalled, "Carnegie Mellon has a huge recruiting base with [. . .] technology companies in the industry. And so I basically heard about it on a college job board, and I sent in an application and heard back." Mimi's degree from Carnegie Mellon provided her with geek capital, precisely because CMU is celebrated for its engineering curriculum and has become one of the feeder schools into Silicon Valley. This, combined with stereotypes about Asian Americans in science and technology, enabled Mimi to move out of her natal family's class position and join the labor aristocracy in the technology sector.

When Mimi's experiences are compared to those of some of the Black women in this study, who had more technical experience and also possessed university degrees, it is clear that they lacked the geek capital that Mimi possessed. Their racial position required them to compensate for their Blackness. Their skills were questioned, and they had to repeatedly perform and demonstrate their skills prior to being hired, in ways that Mimi did not report. They did not describe a smooth process into the industry (see Maya in chapter 3). Geek capital is enhanced when one is "similar" to people who are already dominant in the industry—Asian Indians, Asian Americans, and Whites. While job interview protocols can be brutal for everyone, the difference for those with geek capital is that they can employ social referrals or alumni networks or other pathways if they fail to get through the front door. There are many what I call "side doors" into the technology sector.

Feminist Critical Technology Studies

In the 1980s, a new subfield emerged that reframed the study of technology by asking new questions that synthesized the concerns of scholars working in the fields of gender studies, labor studies, and technology studies. Gender scholars reframed earlier research on technology and challenged the notion of "technological determinism." The centrality of gender to the definition of technology became the focus of feminist scholars of technology and especially in critiques of science. Susan Harding, Cynthia Cockburn, Sally Hacker, and Judy Wajcman, foundational scholars in the intersecting fields of gender studies and technology studies, posed important questions about the relationship between gender, power, and technology.[77] These questions included "How do social factors shape technological changes?" and "How do technologies become gendered as masculine?"[78] The relationship between gender and technology became a rich area of research and developed into what is now known as feminist technology studies and sociology of technology. Another stream of research in technology studies focuses specifically on women who worked in engineering.[79]

Feminism Confronts Technology, a groundbreaking book by the Australian sociologist Judy Wajcman, challenged the idea that technology is gender-neutral and that it would liberate women. Adopting a sociohistorical analytical framework, Wajcman critiqued gender-blind historical accounts of the impact of technological innovations. She identified several layers of the meaning of technology:

> Firstly, "technology" is a form of knowledge. . . . Technological "things" are meaningless without the "know-how" to use them, repair them, design them and make them. That know-how often cannot be captured in words. It is visual, even tactile, rather than simply verbal or mathematical.

But it can also be systematized and taught, as in the various disciplines of engineering. . . . "Technology" also refers to what people do as well as what they know. . . . A computer without programs and programmers is simply a useless collection of bits of metal, plastic and silicon. . . . And finally, at the most basic level, there is the "hardware" definition of technology in which it refers to sets of physical objects, for example, cars, lathes, vacuum cleaners and computers.[80]

During the first decades of the twenty-first century, a new field of study emerged. It brought science and technology studies, and critical race studies into dialogue. Critical technology scholars have generated a new set of concepts, methods, and theories that examine the intersections of racism, artificial intelligence, and social inequalities on digital platforms and in hardware, software, online, and applications.[81] Scholars at the forefront of this intellectual movement in science and technology include Ruha Benjamin and Safiya Umoja Noble. *Geek Girls* is inspired by and in dialogue with research by Black critical technology scholars who have generated new questions, new methods, and new concepts. The women in this book include Black, Asian, and White women engineers who are the creators, innovators, and architects of digital platforms play a central role in the racial dimensions of technology, including what Benjamin calls "The New Jim Code."

Gender Symbolism

In 1955, Cambridge University created the first computer science program in the world. At that time, the computing field was still perceived as gender-neutral by many observers.[82] Three years later, in 1958, Andrina Wood traveled around the world to introduce, demonstrate, and provide training on a new general-purpose electronic computer built by British Tabulating Machine. An early electronics computer expert, Wood played a central role in the international transfer of technical knowledge in the post–World War II era. The British historian Marie Hicks clarifies Wood's historical significance: "Wood's importance therefore lies not in being exceptional, but in being representative of the vast, largely hidden store of women's labor and expertise in early computing. The fact that there were many more women performing jobs like her—operating early electronics computers, teaching others how to use them, and convincing companies to buy them—literally defined the progress of computerization."[83]

In the 1950s commercial computing industry, computer programmers were "envisioned as little more than glorified clerical workers." This changed as the computer market grew and the coding of computers was no longer viewed as a "relatively simple process of translation that could be assigned to low-level clerical personnel."[84] The computer historian Nathan Ensmenger argues in his analysis of the "computer revolution," "It is the history of computer software and not of the computer itself that is at the heart of the larger story of the great computer revolution of the mid-to-late twentieth century. What makes the modern electronic digital computer so unique in all history of technology—so powerful, flexible, and capable of being applied to such an extraordinarily diverse range of purposes—is its ability to be reconfigured via software, into a seemingly infinite number of devices. . . . Software transforms the latent power of the theoretically general-purpose machine into a specific tool for solving real-world problems."[85]

Gender is a set of ideas, discourses, and a cultural system. The gender system creates social and symbolic distinctions and assigns roles to individuals on the basis of their sex assigned at birth and gender expression. The feminist philosopher Sandra Harding argues that gender consists of three dimensions: *gender identity* (how an individual identifies, feels, and expresses their gender), *gender structure* (the sexual division of labor), and *gender symbolism* (the meanings, representations, and value assigned to jobs, tasks, occupations, and skills).[86] When there are technological innovations, jobs often become gendered as masculine. An example is clerical work, which was gendered as male in the nineteenth century, only to become regendered as female at the turn of the twentieth century.

Before computers and computing became a "specific brand of masculinity," there had been optimism about the ability of the computer to change gender relations.[87] The British sociologist Ruth Woodfield identifies three waves of optimism in computing culture. The first wave emerged in the 1970s, when what Woodfield describes as the "myth of the neutral computer" was dominant in commentaries about the computer as a machine that had an "indeterminate gender." During this first wave of optimism, when computer science was a new academic discipline, it was perceived by women as offering a gender-neutral technical arena, in contrast to physics and engineering. Woodfield writes, "[the computer's] future trajectory as equally masculine could not be assumed, and the field of computer science need not be littered with the same obstacles that had hampered previous female forays into scientific and technical areas."[88] In the 1960s and '70s, women were welcomed into the computing industry, as reflected in magazine articles that targeted women readers.

In 1967, *Cosmopolitan* magazine published an article titled "The Computer Girls." This article reflected the optimism of an era when women were welcomed into the booming, gender-neutral commercial computer industry. Written for female readers, this article encouraged women to enter this new field. The article reflected the promise and hopes that women had for computing as a gender-neutral field. It also represented a paradox for women at a moment when "vertical mobility" was available to women in computer programming. Describing this moment, Ensmenger argues that the *Cosmopolitan* article "captured perfectly the promise of opportunity available to women in the early decades of computing."[89] Janet Abbate writes, "The 1968 guidebook *Your Career in Computers* suggested that readers who enjoyed 'cooking from a cookbook' might have a natural aptitude for programming. Grace Murray offered her own domestic metaphors in a 1980 interview: 'I think that it's always been true that women were more willing to finish the job. They'll stay with it; tie up the loose ends. . . . Then I always said that the concept of getting the data all together so you could operate on it was the same thing as getting a dinner ready.'"[90]

In the mid-to-late twentieth century, computer programming became a new discipline, and the gender of this new field changed.[91] In the early twenty-first century, computer science and engineering are occupations and forms of knowledge that have become gendered as masculine—and thus symbolize masculinity. In a discussion of the "subjective and symbolic significance of technology," Fergus Murray writes, "In arguing that technology is a core domain of a socially constructed masculinity I want to suggest that it plays an important role as a boundary marker; what is perceived to be technology is perceived to be masculine. That is, masculinity claims for itself an exclusive control of the technological and when masculinity fails to control or loses control of technological practices those practices then lose their status as technological practices."[92]

Historians have shown how the gender symbolism of the computing industry changed and masculinity became symbolic of the new discipline of computer programming. Describing this process of *regendering* the computing industry as masculine, Ensmenger argues that professionalization implied masculinization. Most significantly, professionalization "requires segmentation and stratification": "In order to elevate the overall status of their discipline, aspiring professionals had to distance themselves from aspects of their work that were seen as low-status and routine."[93]

A Gendered Technocracy

Historians of computing technology have documented how a gendered technocracy assigned women to computing roles but feminized these roles.[94] These roles were feminized by assigning them a lower value and lower status than tasks performed by men. Before mechanical or electronic computers, women who worked as "human computers" were placed under the supervision of a "cadre of elite men" and given job titles that did not accurately reflect their skills. Hicks has argued that the labor of university-educated women was "formative to the project of computing and the twentieth century technological state in a way that remains understudied."[95]

The historian Thomas Haigh documents the gender flipping of occupations in administrative computing:

> Punched card machine operation . . . was a tiny island of male craft work in a sea of low-status female office labor. Operation of other administrative machinery such as typewriters, bookkeeping machines, dictating machines . . . and of course keypunches was already women's work. Beginning with new occupations, such as typist, one clerical job category after another had flipped from male to female. Historians have a rich literature on this topic from the 1870s, when clerical work was an overwhelming male activity seen as a good starting point for the apprentice businessman, to the 1920s when most clerical jobs were low-paid, dead-end positions filled with women.[96]

In the aerospace and military-intelligence fields, women were also employed as "operators" (now called programmers). Jobs as "programmers," which are now perceived as "masculine," developed out of feminized clerical labor.[97] Jennifer Light, a historian of science, builds on the earlier research of gender scholars and labor historians to recognize and honor the role that women played in ballistics computation during World War II.[98] Light argues, "Ballistics computation and programming lay at the intersection of scientific and clerical labor. Each required advanced mathematical training, yet each was categorized as clerical work."[99]

Occupational segregation by sex and race—that is, the assignment of women and men as well as racialized groups to different jobs, tasks, and job titles on the basis of social characteristics—has been a consistent feature of the US labor market. The technology labor market is no different. In the twentieth century, as jobs became professionalized or more desirable in administrative computing, commercial computing, and scientific computing, White women were pushed into gender-segregated occupations and lower-paying, lower-status jobs. In an analysis of the archives of commercial firms that relied heavily on keypunch operators (later called "data entry"), historians have documented the process by which jobs that were previously perceived as low skill and low paid— and thus appropriate for women—were professionalized and redefined as masculine. This process involved changes in perception.

Organization of the Book

Chapter 1 details the ways that top technology firms in Silicon Valley can best be understood as an occupational caste system in which Asian Indian, Asian American, and White men occupy the higher-wage, higher-status, higher-tier technical, management, and leadership positions. The occupational caste system in Silicon Valley restricts and denies economic opportunities to Blacks, Latinx, Native Americans, Pacific Islanders, and other underrepresented minorities. Studies have documented the ways that White women have been allowed some limited mobility up the corporate ladder, while Asian women remain blocked by a "bamboo ceiling."[100] This chapter draws on blogs, memoirs, and court cases to examine routine practices that have reproduced structural racism and gender inequality—the foundations of an occupational caste system fueled by ideologies and mythologies about who has the skills and talents to work in the industry.

Chapter 2 draws on interviews with Asian Indian, Asian American, and White technology workers in Silicon Valley to identify the dominant ideologies and mythologies that support the status quo. Technology workers employ and recycle the myth of meritocracy and others that shift the responsibility for the racial disparities onto underrepresented racial minorities. These beliefs are held by women and men from diverse national backgrounds and locate the "diversity problem" outside the technology firms. These mythologies include (1) the myth of meritocracy, (2) the pipeline myth, (3) the myth of biological essentialism, and (4) the skills gap myth. These myths support and normalize the over-representation of Asians and Whites and the virtual absence of Blacks and Latinx in the industry. The applicant pool is identified as the cause of racial and ethnic disparities in hiring, recruitment, and outcomes that have resulted in the underrepresentation of Blacks and Latinx in proportion to their numbers among the college educated.

Chapter 3 focuses on the experiences of technically skilled Black women, who make up 1 percent of the Silicon Valley technical workforce. In this chapter, I discuss the concept of glass walls, a barrier to employment that roughly half of the Black women in my study encountered. The career trajectories and experiences of technically skilled Black women varied based on their class background, social capital, and regional background. The Black women who possessed a degree from an Ivy League or Ivy-equivalent school (e.g., Stanford) or a public Ivy (UCLA, UC-Berkeley) shared some of the same advantages as their non-Black peers, such as privileged access to alumni networks that can generate interviews and job offers in Silicon Valley.

Chapters 4 and 5 discuss the concepts of first- and second-generation technology workers and shift the focus to a comparative analysis of Anglo-American, Chinese American, and Indian immigrants who belong to the second generation of technology workers in their families. These chapters draw on the occupational narratives that emerged in interviews with Asian American, Asian Indian, Black, Latinx, and White women from impoverished, working-class, and middle-class backgrounds. First-generation technology workers have different challenges and different forms of geek capital from second-generation workers—that is, women who are the family members (daughters, nieces, cousins, or younger siblings) of technology workers. Women who are the first generation in their family to work in the industry tend to lack "built-in mentors"—that is, family members who can provide them with access to knowledge and resources that help them enter the technology sector.

Chapter 6 examines the experiences of transnational middle-class migrants from Colombia, Mexico, and India who arrived in the United States as foreign nationals on student visas to pursue graduate education, remained in the United States, and secured jobs after completing their degrees. The occupational trajectories narrated by the India-born women in this chapter support earlier research on migration studies that showed the portability of caste privilege. Caste privilege is portable and can be converted into educational credentials, economic capital, and citizenship rights in the United States for highly educated and mobile IT workers from India.

Chapter 7 examines the career trajectories of White women who had earned degrees in the arts, humanities, and social sciences and moved from nontechnical positions to technically skilled careers as software engineers. They transitioned into technically skilled positions after completing an accelerated and immersive ten- or twelve-week skills-based engineering curriculum at all-women coding boot camps. I analyze the mechanisms and forms of capital including "marital capital" that allowed women who had no prior work experience or training as engineers to secure full-time positions as software engineers.

In the conclusion, I discuss emerging forms of collective mobilization among women in Silicon Valley, who are innovators, investors, connectors, and founders who seek intersectional justice in the technology sector. I examine strategies employed by women to move beyond "discursive diversity" and take actions to challenge the caste system in Silicon Valley. Women in Silicon Valley are creating social and economic infrastructures that provide opportunities for women across generations to connect, network, fund, and launch their own start-ups and to empower women who have been excluded or underfunded by angel investors. Women are building intergenerational networks and mentoring relationships. It is too early to know how this emerging intersectional movement for labor equality will take shape, but we are witnessing the beginning of a new social movement in the most powerful economic sector in North America.

1

The Silicon Valley Caste System

Silicon Valley tells an imaginary story about itself. It is a story about a utopic space—a region where Ivy League dropouts, male geniuses, and model minorities have built an innovation economy that benefits everyone. Before 2014, the media and CEOs of technology firms celebrated Silicon Valley as a place where anyone with a laptop could build their dreams and launch a start-up (with the help of an angel investor). Yet between 2014 and 2018, a different story began to disrupt this fable of tech utopianism. Silicon Valley's caste-like structure of gender, racial, and caste inequality became more transparent. Between 2014 and 2019, a series of investigative journalistic reports began to expose the various forms in inequality among Silicon Valley workers.[1] Blogs, interviews, memoirs, and lawsuits by women engineers, venture capitalists, and company cofounders exposed a culture of workplace retaliation, sexual harassment, and anti-Black discrimination. Women began to come forward and share their experiences on their blogs and in court cases.[2] A growing cohort of women began to challenge the gender caste system, if not the ethnic and racial one, in Silicon Valley.

In this chapter, I map the contours of the racial, ethnic, and gender hierarchies that shape what can best be characterized as an occupational caste system in Silicon Valley. I detail how an ethnic structure shapes the "inequality regimes" and opportunity structure in Silicon Valley.[3] Inequality regimes are a durable feature of Silicon Valley technology firms and represent a central feature of an *occupational caste system*. I employ this term to refer to an occupational structure in which individuals are rewarded, recruited, and disciplined based, in part, on factors unrelated to merit, such as their race, gender, caste background, national origins, and the ranking of their school in a prestige system. In interviews, a number of White women acknowledged that in their firms highly qualified Black and Latinx applicants were often not given serious consideration. In addition, job candidates are recruited and sorted into job categories on the basis of alumni networks, their social capital, and their similarity (age, race, alumni networks) and cultural ties to gatekeepers in the industry.

Structural Racism in Silicon Valley

Blogs, memoirs, lawsuits, and interviews with women employed in the industry suggest a troubling pattern of racism and sexual harassment in the organizational culture in Silicon Valley's technology sector.[4] Racism and casteism are endemic in Silicon Valley. In a series of articles, technology journalists have documented the caste discrimination and anti-Black racism in Silicon Valley. The representation of Black employees in the technology industry varies by region in the United States. The American Community Survey (2016) found that the technology hubs in Atlanta, Houston, Miami, New York, New Jersey, and Washington, DC, employ 1.5 times to 3.3 times the number of Black and Latinx tech workers as Silicon Valley does.[5] This is striking when compared to Atlanta, where Blacks represent 20.6 percent of the technology workforce, and in Houston 11.9 percent. Silicon Valley has the worst record of hiring Black technology workers when compared to other regions in the United States, as measured by the numbers of technically skilled Black workers in the labor force.

In 2014, Facebook (changed its name to Meta on October 28, 2021) reported that it had hired 7 Black people out of a total of 1,231 people hired globally the previous year.[6] In 2013, Facebook had only 10 Black women and 28 Black men in its global workforce. Between 2014 and 2018, the percentage of Black employees at Facebook grew from 1 to 3 percent. As its US employee base grew more than sixfold to 27,705, Facebook hired fewer than 1,000 Black people, according to the EEO-1 reports that the company files each year with the federal government. Black employees' share of the company's workforce during a period of rapid expansion rose to 3.7 percent.[7]

According to Google's 2020 *Diversity Report*, the numbers of Black and Latinx employees remained flat, with little change during the past five years.[8] Reporting for the *Los Angeles Times*, Sam Dean and Johana Bhuiyan write, "The industry, which prides itself on agility, has failed to move the needle on workplace diversity. The net result of an entire sector of the economy—the sector that has created the most wealth in California in the last 10 years, minted billionaires, and reshaped the San Francisco Bay Area in its own image—that is functionally barely open to Black and Latino people."[9]

University-educated Black and Latinx women are hired at much lower rates than one would expect given their percentage of the university-educated population. In this study, the university-educated and technically skilled Black women described having little or no access to the mentors, money (funding), or coethnics in management or leadership positions described by their Asian and White peers in the industry. While there was one exception, this was the pattern for technically skilled women. When compared to their Asian and White peers, they lacked the same quantity and quality of social ties to the industry. In other words, they did not have family members embedded in the tech ecosystem. A degree in computer science or engineering did not protect them from patterns of rejection that have been documented by technology journalists and sociologists.[10]

Writing for the *San Jose Mercury News*, Priya Anand and Sarah McBride report that working while Black in Silicon Valley is humiliating because of Black people's differential treatment. In the article, "For Black CEOs in Silicon Valley, Humiliations Is Part of Doing Business," Anand and McBride write, "Black entrepreneurs say they are encouraged by the movement but deeply skeptical that the industry will change. . . . Black CEOs describe a career of subtle slights or outright discrimination in which they face regular inquisition about their credentials and peculiar suggestions to hire a White business partner to make investors more comfortable. One says he carries around a notebook emblazoned with the logo of his alma mater, Stanford University, to fit in."[11] Interviews with Silicon Valley gatekeepers who participated in this study confirm that Blacks are relatively invisible and that one reason may be anti-Black stereotypes by immigrant Indians.

Raihan, a forty-nine-year-old Indian entrepreneur and vice president of a technology firm, was born in Mumbai. After earning a bachelor's degree in engineering in 1991, he migrated to Barbados, where he worked for several years before getting a job in the United States through his Asian Indian networks. He has worked in Silicon Valley for more than two decades and is the founder of several start-ups. He described Silicon

Valley as "generally quite inclusive." When asked to explain why Blacks and Latinx were severely underrepresented in his company and in Silicon Valley, Raihan identified racial stereotypes that technology workers hold about Blacks and Latinx and their exclusion from Indian social networks and social referrals. He confirmed that social networks play a key role in the inability of job applicants to secure positions in Silicon Valley start-ups and publicly traded technology firms:

> You need to know someone in the company. . . . Because, you know, again, if 50 percent of the company is just Asian—the likelihood that . . . How many of their contacts would include non-Indians? . . . That's the way the Valley works. . . . It's very rare that you get a job by just applying online or sending in your resume. Beyond a certain point, you only get a job based on who you know at the company. . . . I think it's also perceived that, from an aptitude level, from a technical aptitude perspective, Hispanics and African Americans don't have the aptitude. That's a perception. . . . You know, again at a technology company, the roles that are filled are not just technical roles. You have HR and GNA and administration and finance. There are a lot more roles. There's marketing, so a company can make a conscious effort to at least fill those these roles [with Blacks and Latinx].

Raihan was unable to identify a single Black or Latinx whom he had hired or mentored during his two decades of working in Silicon Valley. Immersed in Asian Indian networks, Raihan embraced ideologies of meritocracy that conceal layers of discrimination that circulate in immigrant and second-generation Indian American communities. The absence of Blacks and Latinx was so normative that it was not mentioned unless specifically asked about. This is an example of how the pipeline myth can operate against the hiring of Blacks and other underrepresented groups. If Asian Indians and Asian Americans in a position to hire and mentor embrace this myth, then the logical conclusion is that if Blacks do not show up in the "pipeline," it is because they do not possess the academic qualifications and/or are disinterested in these positions. The pipeline myth operates in concert with the meritocracy myth.

When Raihan was asked if he had experienced discrimination in the industry, he replied that his national origins and strong Indian accent had not been a barrier to his upward mobility or professional success in the technology industry. In the firms that had hired him and where he spent his early career, he recalled that Asian Indians constituted between 30 and 50 percent of all of the engineers. They were not only highly visible but in many cases were the founders or cofounders and managers of start-ups that became successful companies in Silicon Valley.

Anand and McBride write, "The roots of racism extend deep in Silicon Valley. Leland Stanford, the founder of the area's preeminent university, ran for California governor in 1859, just before the dawn of the Civil War, declaring 'I prefer the White man to the negro.' More than a century later, in 1974, the founder of one of the valley's seminal tech companies, William Shockley of Shockley Semiconductor, appeared on a television show *Firing Line*. There he asserted that African Americans were socially, intellectually and genetically inferior to White people."[12]

A 2014 report published by the US Equal Employment Occupation Commission found that when the high-tech industry is compared to overall private industry, it employs a larger share of Whites (68.5 percent) and Asian Americans and a smaller share of Blacks, Hispanics, and women. This report also argued that "Whites are represented at a higher rate in the Executive category (89.3 percent)."[13] According to this report, Blacks and Latinx represent only 6.9 percent of Silicon Valley's tech workforce, while they make up 16.9 percent of US citizens in California with at least a bachelor's degree. Investigations by technology journalists reveal a persistent pattern of discrimination in hiring and recruitment of women and non-Asian minorities in Silicon Valley.[14]

The Quiet Racism of Silicon Valley: The Black Experience

In a 2016 article titled "Why Doesn't Silicon Valley Hire Black Coders?," Vauhni Vara profiles a cohort of Black students working toward their degrees in computer science at Howard University, the oldest historically Black college in the United States. Vara writes, "From

2001 to 2009, more than 20 percent of all Black computer science graduates attended an historically black school, according to federal statistics—yet the Valley wasn't looking for candidates at these institutions." After visiting for the first time, a Black student described Silicon Valley as "a startling homogeneous culture made up of Asian and White people."[15]

In 2021, Nitasha Tiku interviewed current and former Google employees and former faculty members and reviewed planning documents, emails, and performance reviews. Her reporting confirmed that a gap exists between the public discourse that Google embraces and its actual investments in Black graduates of HBCUs. The prestige system used in its rankings placed HBCUs at the bottom or the hierarchy of desirability. "But one category of higher education that was missing from Google's ranking system, according to several current and former Google employees involved in recruitment, . . . [was] historically Black colleges and universities, also known as HBCUs."[16]

Summarizing a 2016 EEOC report that found that the technology industry is underutilizing a diverse talent pool, Megan Rose Dickey writes, "Of the people graduating from top engineering programs, 9% are Black and Latinos but representation at tech firms typically falls around 5% according to the EEOC's recent analysis of the EEOC data."[17] Since 2015, millions of dollars have been spent on diversity initiatives, which have failed to increase the numbers of Black and Latinx employees in Silicon Valley's firms.

In interviews with technology workers, technology reporters have identified a pervasive pattern of sexist, racist, and misogynistic behavior, as well as the rejection of qualified Blacks as job candidates, as a normative part of the "bro" occupational culture. Erica Joy Baker is a Black engineer who formerly worked for Google and cofounded Project Include with Ellen Pao, Tracy Chou, and others.[18] Joy worked for Google for more than a decade in three of its regional offices. Joy described job-hopping between three different Google regional offices, in Atlanta, New York, and finally the San Francisco Bay Area. In all three cases, she experienced the same forms of discrimination. Job-hopping does not always resolve the problems for Black women because, as gender and racial tokens, they can encounter the same labor conditions, including having to manage the same set of ideologies and cultural practices that marginalize and disempower them. Joy was transferred to the New York office after she complained about what she called microaggressions at the Atlanta office but what I view as racial abuse. She described how she encountered the same hostile climate in the New York office:

> On the team in New York, I was once again the only Black women. I did what I thought I had to do survive in the environment. I once again donned the uniform to fit in: jeans, "unisex" T-shirt, Timbuk2 messenger bag. I stayed late playing multiplayer Battlefield; I quickly learned a bunch of classic rock songs so I could play Rock Band and Guitar Hero with the team. I don't like beer, so I went out to beer taverns and drank water. . . . We worked a lot then, so my team became my social life, and I never hung out with many others.

What Joy described here is what the sociologist Karyn Lacy refers to as "social unity." Joy described her adoption and performance of a cultural style that created a bond with her White and Asian peers. This is a form of *cultural literacy* employed by Black professionals to negotiate and minimize the cultural distance between themselves and non-Black workers with whom they share a class status. This is also an example of "boundary work."[19]

After leaving the New York office and transferring to Google's Silicon Valley office, once again Joy found herself in the same racially homogeneous workplace. Although she liked her work, she continued to have to deal with the stress of having no coethnics in her work environment. Joy detailed the emotional cost of working in the tech industry as a Black woman. In her analysis of her situation, it is clear that there has been a long-term impact on her mental, emotional, and physical health from working in the tech industry for thirteen years. Here are just a few of the issues that Joy detailed:

- "I feel alone every day I come to work despite being surrounded by people, which results in feelings of isolation."
- "I am constantly making microevaluations about whether or not my actions will be attributed to my being 'different.'"

- "I feel like there isn't anyone who can identify with my story, so I don't tell it."
- "I feel like I have to walk a tightrope to avoid reinforcing stereotypes while still being heard."
- "I feel a constant low level of stress every day, just by virtue of existing in my environment."

In Joy's blogs and other writings about the ideological variety among technology workers and the ways that racism is allowed to thrive in Silicon Valley technology firms, she has called for racism to be a fireable offense.[20] Black men have also described the feeling of isolation and compared it to being in a "parallel universe." Mark Karake, the founder and CEO of Impact Africa, describes the limits of diversity discourse in this way: "Diversity was an academic concept, something they had encountered only on screen as part of a soon forgotten college lecture, an abstraction they would never have to deal with in their lives. . . . So many arrived from Boston that at some point you could pick them out right away. . . . San Francisco felt like an annex of Boston. . . . The mono culture was suffocating, the social rejection painful, and the isolation crushing.[21] The isolation that Black technologists described in interviews in this study echoed those published in media reports.[22]

The IT Caste: The South Asian Experience

Indian women employed in the Silicon Valley technology sector belong to a "transnational class" of knowledge workers. These workers have been described as a highly educated, skilled, and mobile transnational professional class that is part of a "flexible" labor system.[23] Indian IT workers occupy what has been described as a "specialized, privileged segment of the global economy,"[24] and Indian engineers have been described as knowledge workers who are located at the upper end of the global economy.

In 2010, there were an estimated 3.2 million people of Indian origin in the United States, making them the third-largest Asian group. In 2016, Indians were the top recipients of high-skilled H-1B temporary visas and were the second-largest group of international students in the United States. Studies of IT workers in India have shown that what are referred to in India as the "forward castes" or privileged castes dominate this employment sector.[25] Indian immigrants are likely to be young, be Brahmin, have a bachelor's degree, and have excellent English-language skills due to the legacies of British colonialism as well as the Indian government's investment in Indian technical universities that provide courses in computing, engineering, and science as well as English literacy. In a study of Indian IT workers, Deepthi Shanker found,

> Data reveals that most women professionals in the IT industry belong to the forward caste. . . . Nearly 73% of the total workforce belongs to the privileged caste groups. . . . When only engineering staff was examined, it was found that 82.5 percent of the software engineers have a privileged background. . . . This suggests that technical education and emerging modern professions in the IT field have largely been the monopoly of certain segments of the population. The social attributes of professionals, such as caste, have significance in understanding the implications of the IT industry on social structure. . . . It suggests that caste silently operates in society, linking status with modern jobs. The new dimensions of occupational structure in society, currently through the IT industry, only reflect and reinforce the continuing influence of caste, in which privileged groups dominate over the less privileged. Surveys indicate the predominance of forward caste individuals, especially Brahmins, in the IT work force.[26]

In an ethnography of the "new middle class," Smitha Radhakrishnan discusses the material and symbolic privileges of Indian transnational technology workers as a group: "What are the various layers that comprise the privilege of India's transnational professional class? What does it mean to call them an elite? As in all situations of privilege, that of IT professionals is relative and does not extend to every circumstance. Still, their position of privilege is derived not only from their dominant position in the worldwide story of globalization . . . but also in their ability to represent 'everyman' in India, thereby disguising their eliteness."[27]

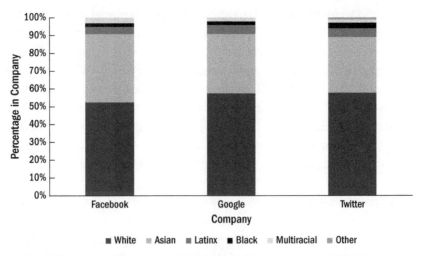

Figure 1.1. Racial demographics of employees at Facebook, Google, and Twitter, 2016. *Note*: "Other" includes Native Hawaiian or Pacific Islander and American Indian or Alaskan Native; figures may not add up to 100 percent as a result of rounding. (Evans and Rangarajan 2017)

Scholarship on the experiences of the IT caste has argued that a key dimension of caste and class privilege is the ability to be mobile—to possess the resources to migrate to Australia, Canada, the United States, and Europe as technology workers.[28] Merit in India is defined by and produced by caste, urban residence, educational credentials, language skills, and occupation. Indians evaluate one's linguistic skills (English fluency without a "village" accent), dress (Western clothing as opposed to traditional Indian clothing), and access to economic and social resources.[29]

Ethnographic studies of transnational Indian IT workers have found that they belong to a class that symbolically and materially represents the "new Indian middle-class." Writing about workers who move between Silicon Valley and India, Radhakrishnan calls attention to the continuities in the forms of privilege that they possess:

> Educational credentials and the subsequent professionalization of personal identifications serve to mask the continuity of class dominance; such credentials came to be viewed as evidence of personal "merit."

Merit then becomes a powerful, benevolent-sounding feature of up-wardly mobile work culture, but its allure masks the continued inequal-ities that it justifies. . . . Transnational Indian IT professionals transform a previously existing middle-class category by associating it with par-ticular kinds of work and lifestyle patterns. This transformed category is more exclusive and yet appears more accessible. In practice, however, clear limitations on mobility remain, and despite the exuberance of this class, few readily accept that anyone in India can gain access to it, as the divisions between this class and the marginalized majority remain striking.[30]

Of the immigrant Indian women who participated in this study, all shared the social characteristics of members of the IT caste documented in earlier research by South Asian scholars studying labor migration and globalization. Like many of their Asian American and Anglo-American counterparts who attended top universities, many took for granted their economic and social privileges.

Caste Discrimination in Silicon Valley

In the summer of 2020, the issue of caste discrimination in Silicon Valley gained national attention when a lawsuit was filed by an Indian engineer against Cisco. Writing for the *New York Times*, in an article titled "The Specter of Caste in Silicon Valley," Yashica Dutt, the author of a memoir, reported on the experiences of a Dalit, called "John Doe" in this employ-ment discrimination lawsuit.

> The lawsuit accuses Cisco, a multibillion-dollar tech conglomerate based in San Jose, Calif., of denying an engineer, who immigrated from India to the United States, professional opportunities, a raise and pro-motions because he was from a lower caste, or Dalit, background. The lawsuit states that his Indian-American managers, . . . who are described as high-caste Brahmins, harassed the engineer because of their sense of superiority rooted in the Hindu caste system. . . . Caste prejudice and discrimination is rife within the Indian communities in the United States and other countries. Its chains are even turning the work culture within multibillion-dollar American tech companies.[31]

The lawsuit filed against Cisco and Sundar Iyer and Ramana Kompella, Indian managers at Cisco, argued that John Doe was blocked from pay raises and promotions on the basis of his caste background. "Unlike Doe, most Indian immigrants in the United States are from upper castes. For example, in 2003, only 1.5 percent of Indian immigrants in the United States were Dalits or members of lower castes. More than 90 percent were high or dominant castes. . . . Doe worked with a team of entirely Indian employees. . . . As beneficiaries of the caste system, Doe's higher caste supervisors and co-workers imported their discriminatory system's practices into their team and Cisco's workplace."[32]

The experiences of this Dalit engineer can be compared to those of Blacks, who also represent roughly 2 percent of employees at Silicon Valley's technology firms and face discrimination, both overt and subtle. I follow Isabel Wilkerson's use of the term *caste* and bring the research of sociologists who study gendered processes in organizations into dialogue with the research of sociologists and gender scholars who study race, racism, and racial discrimination.[33] A body of literature on the sociology of discrimination in employment, housing, and consumer markets describes a system that operates against Blacks and Latinx. Discrimination in hiring remains a durable part of systemic racism in the United States and suggests that Blacks are treated by many organizations as members of a "caste."[34] Sociologists have documented the systematic racism against Blacks in education, access to in employment, housing, and all aspects of social life.[35]

A global movement for the rights of Dalits, the lowest caste group in India, has grown and has arrived in the United States. Recently, Asian Indian women are coming forward to share their experiences of caste-based discrimination. In the *Washington Post*, Nitasha Tiku, a technology reporter, wrote about this growing movement against caste discrimination in Silicon Valley:

> And a group of 30 female Indian engineers who are members of the Dalit caste and work for Google, Apple, Microsoft, Cisco and other tech companies say they have faced caste bias inside the U.S. tech sector. . . . The women, who shared the statement on the condition of anonymity for fear

of retaliation, argue that networks of engineers from the dominant castes have replicated patterns of bias within the United States by favoring their peers in hiring, referrals and performance reviews. "We have also have had to weather demeaning insults to our background and that we have achieved our jobs solely due to affirmative action. It is exhausting. . . . We are role models for our community and we want to continue to work in our jobs. But it is unfair for us to continue in hostile workplaces, without protections from caste discrimination."[36]

Equality Labs, a nonprofit advocacy group for Dalit rights, received complaints from nearly twenty-six US tech workers in June after the Dalit engineer filed his lawsuit against Cisco and the two Indian managers. The issue of caste discrimination in the United States has been neglected by sociologists studying the new economy and organizations in the technology sector. In 2018, Equality Labs released *Caste in the United States: A Survey of Caste among South Asian Americans*, the first report on caste discrimination in the United States. This report, which was endorsed by all major anticaste groups, is based on a survey that included forty-seven questions administered to fifteen hundred respondents; 33 percent of the respondents identified as Brahmin. A primary goal of this report was to provide "insight into how the South Asian community balances the experiences of living under white supremacy while replicating Caste, anti-Dalitness, and anti-Blackness." What is caste? Equality Labs describes caste this way:

Caste is a structure of oppression that affects over 1 billion people across the world. It is a system of religiously codified exclusion that was established in Hindu scripture. At birth, every child inherits his or her ancestor's caste, which determines social status and assigns "spiritual purity". . . . There are four main Caste groups. Those at the very top are Brahmins, who have traditionally been priests, scriptural knowledge-keepers, and legislators. Below them in status are the Kshatriyas, who were kings and warriors. They are followed by Vaishyas, or the merchant classes. People in these three Caste groups are often referred to as the "upper castes." . . . Those at the bottom of the Caste hierarchy are Shudras or traditional peasants. . . . Outside of the 4-Caste group structure are people considered lower than the lowest of Castes. They go by the term Dalit meaning "broken but resilient," formerly known as "untouchables" and the Adivasis, or the indigenous peoples of South Asia.[37]

In Silicon Valley, technology journalists have reported on the intersecting forms of anti-Black racism, caste-based discrimination, and gender discrimination.[38] Here I will use the term "caste discrimination" to refer to both anti-Black racism and discrimination against Dalits. There are some parallels between the system of White supremacy and the segregation and brutal treatment of educated Black citizens in the United States and the treatment of Dalits in India.[39]

Caste discrimination is not recognized in US law, in part, because South Asians were not a segment of the US labor force when the country was founded. The system of racial capitalism in the United States was organized as a slave republic based on an economy that relied on the enslavement and forced labor of Africans and Native Americans and, later, indentured servitude and the semibound labor of US-born Blacks and immigrants from China, the Philippines, Mexico, and parts of Europe.[40] Racial classifications used today, such as the term "Caucasian" were introduced by Europeans like Johann Blumenbach in the eighteenth century. Race is a powerful idea invented by Europeans that gave Europeans and others who were classified as "White" or eligible for "Whiteness" access to opportunities and resources (jobs, education, land, rights) that were until recently denied to Black citizens, Native Americans, Asian immigrants, and others.[41]

The complex occupational trajectories of Black, Latinx, and Native American women employed in the Silicon Valley technology industry have been understudied in sociological studies of elite labor markets and of women in the "new economy."[42] Their experiences are flattened and buried in macro-level studies of women in STEM fields. A focus specifically on Silicon Valley is important given its significant role as an economic engine and a vehicle for upward mobility for women from working-class backgrounds.

In *Caste*, a comparative and historical analysis of inequality in India, Nazi Germany, and the United States, Isabel Wilkerson argues for the use of the concept of caste in understanding how structural racism operates in the United States:

> Caste . . . predates the notion of race and has survived the era of formal, state-sponsored racism that had long been openly practiced in the mainstream. The modern-day version of easily deniable racism may be able to cloak the invisible structure that created and maintains hierarchy and inequality. But caste does not allow us to ignore structure. Caste is structure. Caste is ranking. Caste is the boundaries that reinforce the fixed assignments based upon what people look like. . . . Caste is the granting or withholding of respect, status, honor, attention, privileges, resources, benefit of the doubt, and human kindness to someone on the basis of their perceived rank or standing in the hierarchy.[43]

In this book, I employ the term "caste" to refer to an occupational structure that is an expression of durable labor-market inequalities in the US technology sector that are produced by intersecting racial, gender, and economic inequalities. To many technology workers in Silicon Valley who belong to the dominant groups, these inequalities may be invisible or at least "taken for granted." The uneven and unequal distribution of women, Asians, Asian Indians, Blacks, and Latinx across occupational categories is a stark expression of an occupational caste system.

The annual diversity reports and EEOC filings released by some technology firms confirm that their workforce consists almost entirely of Asians, Asian Americans, and Whites. Asian and White men are concentrated in the executive, leadership, and gatekeeping positions as founders, CEOs, CTOs, and CFOs. With regard to immigrant Indians who are prominent CEOs, in those cases where their caste is acknowledged, they typically identify as Brahmin. A prominent example is Sundar Pichai, born as Pichai Sundararajan in Chennai, the CEO of Google. A Stanford-educated engineer, Pichai has a background that resembles that of most of the immigrant Indian women in this study, who were born in the state of Tamil Nadu and identified as Brahmin.

While immigrants from India employed on temporary work contracts negotiate unique challenges, the demographics of the Silicon Valley workforce suggest that Asians and immigrant Asians are favored over domestic workers who are Black or Latinx. Asians constitute one of the dominant racial and ethnic groups in Silicon Valley firms, along with Whites. In this study, immigrant Indian technology workers were successfully recruited into the industry, and most had achieved their goals of securing permanent residency or citizenship and getting promoted. The US government has failed to regulate the technology sector and has not protected US citizens and others who belong to groups that are underrepresented in this industry from systematic discrimination. As a result, a form of economic and social injustice operates in which CEOs and managers have not been held accountable for the denial of opportunities in hiring, recruitment, promotion, and retention in the industry.[44]

An analysis of the annual diversity reports released by selected Silicon Valley firms reveals a troubling pattern of the absence of Blacks, Latinx, Native Americans, and Pacific Islanders, who have been excluded from and denied opportunities in an industry that is the economic engine in California. Technology firms do not specify the caste origins of their immigrant Indian or Indian American employees and do not release this data because the US government does not require it, but other data points suggest that more than 95 percent are probably from the upper-caste groups.[45] In the United States, there has been a retreat from racial justice, and affirmative action in education has been abolished, leaving structural racism and the US caste system intact.[46]

Race and Color-Evasive Discourses

Among the participants in this study, race- and color-evasive discourses recurred as technology workers defended their companies and argued that they were diverse, based on the recruitment of Asian nationals and the regional diversity among East and South Asians. A race-evasive and color-evasive ideology, combined with a belief in meritocracy, was repeated among the majority of Asian American, Asian Indian, and White technology workers.[47] The narrative that we are "hiring the best" was expressed by non-Black technology workers—even as they admitted that they had secured their position through exclusive ethnic-based networks, family, friends, or recruiters whom they paid. These ideologies include the belief that Silicon Valley is a utopia where diversity and innovative companies flourish for anyone with an idea and a laptop. When asked to define "diversity" and to explain the near invisibility of Blacks and Latinx, the technology workers in this study employed discourses that reflected their belief in a number of mythologies.

In an analysis of the postracialism discourses and the strategies employed to "mask" the racism of technological elites and employment discrimination against Blacks, Latinx, and women in Silicon Valley, Safiya Noble and Sarah Roberts argue,

> There is disproportionate representation of East Asian and South Asian employees and leadership, which often confuses and masks the hostile disposition of Silicon Valley toward historically underrepresented minority communities in the United States that fall into federally protected classes. This is no mistake; a fundamental part of the logic of postracialism is that it refuses to deal not only with the realities of race in American society but also with the more than three hundred years of legal discrimination and disenfranchisement of African Americans, Latino/as, and Native American Indians, while pointing to the increasing numbers of South Asian, East Asian, and South Asian Americans participating in the tech sector labor force as evidence of success in diversifying across racial lines.[48]

Postracial discourse and global metrics erase or elide discrimination against non-Asians, particularly US nationals. The obstacles and opportunities that women navigate differ based on their ethnic status, caste background, class background, and national origins. For example, the Black women in this study who had earned engineering or computer science degrees were not able to convert them as easily into jobs and were not the primary beneficiaries of the diversity initiatives that have successfully recruited and increased the numbers of Asian and White women in Silicon Valley. Structural racism and a lack of bridging capital have created barriers that Black and Latinx women described even when they demonstrated technical expertise, educational credentials, and a job history that reflected their skills.

Britney: A Chinese American Perspective

Britney is a twenty-eight-year-old US-born daughter of Chinese immigrants who currently works for a start-up founded by Chinese Americans in Silicon Valley. She works on a team of thirty people, which she described as being composed mainly of Asians. She was not able to identify a single Black or Latinx who worked at her start-up. When asked to describe the racial and ethnic demographics of her team of coworkers, she described a workplace that was overwhelmingly Asian, with a few "Whites" of US, Israeli, or European origin:

> We are mostly Asian: Chinese, Indian, Vietnamese, Korean. The remaining [employees] are White. And then, there's like one or two group fallouts in that category. I would say that . . . I think it's interesting that we actually have a fair mix of like immigrant Asians and American Asians, people who essentially spent their whole lives here. And I think if you take the American born and raised people as their own type of group, it becomes a lot more diverse feeling. . . . I don't know how that happens. Maybe people refer people whom they know and like working with, and those people tend to be similar to them. I think that's definitely true. Or people who are even related to them. We have a couple of people who are cousins. There is a father and a son who co-own the company. And like, clearly, they are going to be of the same ethnicity.

As Britney explained why her company is "diverse" when the demographics are heavily skewed in favor of Asian immigrants and Asian Americans, she carefully and precisely described the cultural differences within the Asian diasporic community. The cultural distinctions that Britney identified are significant and reflect a common measure of diversity among technology firms. Britney's definitions of diversity reflect the global demographics of Silicon Valley's technical workforce as well as established discourse in which numbers of foreign nationals have replaced numbers of domestic groups in calculations of diversity in everyday speech. This metric erases and normalizes the glass walls that continue to systematically exclude non-Asians, particularly US-born Blacks and Latinx, from equal access and participation in Silicon Valley's technology sector. This exclusion is particularly striking when Silicon Valley is compared to other regions of the United States. It also perpetuates the idea that Asians are somehow more suited for skilled technical labor.

Britney did not identify or consider social referrals and related hiring practices at her firm that privilege the Asian friends and relatives of current employees. Yet she identified a number of employees who were biologically related to the Asian male founders and CEOs of the company. After Britney struggled to explain how she measured diversity on the basis of immigrant versus nonimmigrant Asians, she returned to the pipeline. Her argument shifted to a discussion of the cultural differences between immigrants and nonimmigrants as a definition of diversity. In her narrative, we see a recurring pattern among non-Black technology workers: the "human capital" theory, which comes out of economics and corresponds to logic employed in much of the quantitative data on pathways in the sociology literature and which assumes that if an individual earns a degree in computer science or engineering, they will be hired in STEM fields.

Gatekeepers: Social Closure and Homophily

Sociologists have documented the way that social similarity in age, race, education, and occupation, along with social capital—that is, *nonmeritocratic* qualities unrelated to the skills required for the job—shape recruitment, promotion, and retention.[49] Social closure—that is, the distance (racial, ethnic, class) from social networks—advantages the in-group and structures access to gatekeepers including recruiters, managers, directors, and those who could provide social referrals in Silicon Valley. The issue of homophily and social closure is not unique to the technology sector. In Silicon Valley, qualified candidates are routinely rejected on the basis of "cultural fit," a code that can justify the exclusion of qualified applicants who do not share the caste, class, or ethnic background of the gatekeepers or hiring teams. In the technology sector, individuals are often required to participate in off-site as well as on-site team-building activities that include drinking alcohol, playing specific games, and other activities that reflect class markers. These activities are defined by the dominant group members and reflect the cultural tastes, including musical tastes, food preferences, and drinking behaviors, embraced by members of the dominant groups in technology.[50]

Sociologists use the term "homophily" to describe the tendency of individuals to form associations, friendships, and relationships with those who share their social characteristics (age, race, religion, class background, leisure interests). In other words, social networks tend to be composed of people who are similar to each other on one or more dimensions. Miller McPherson, Lynn Smith-Lovin, and James Cook have studied homophily and have found that race and ethnicity constitute one of the strongest areas of similarity.[51]

Lata is a twenty-five-year-old Indian American and native of California who has been employed as a product engineer for four years. The US-born daughter of an Indian engineer who immigrated to the United States in the 1970s, Lata earned her bachelor's degree in engineering in 2015. A religious outlier among the Indians in this study, she identified as a Christian, rather than a Hindu. Her description of her coworkers followed a pattern among most of the Anglo-Americans and Indians interviewed: they typically worked with people who shared their age and race, and the dominant groups were Asians and Whites (from the United States, South Asia, and Europe).

In Lata's description of her workplace, she commented on how everyone assumes she is working on an H-1B visa because most of her coworkers are what she called "immigrant Indians." As a US-born citizen, she is a minority among the Asian Indian women in this study. When asked to describe the demographics of her workplace, she said, "Actually most of the people who work with me are immigrants." She later clarified that 70 percent of the workers (out of two thousand) at her location were Indian immigrants. Her description of the demographics of her workplace confirms the job segregation by occupation, with Asian Indians being overrepresented as engineers and with a near absence of Blacks, whom she referred to as "Africans," except in nontechnical positions in marketing and human resources.[52]

Inequality Regimes in Practice

In December 2016, a lawsuit was filed in San Francisco Superior Court against Google. Google was asked to hand over salary histories that included data from 19,500 employees located at its headquarters in Mountain View. Google denied this request and refused to hand over the job and salary history to the Department of Labor (DoL).[53] Marc Piltoni, a DoL attorney, argued that "Google wanted to hide pay-related information."[54] The DoL is engaged in ongoing gender and racial discrimination cases that allege what the DoL calls "systematic" and "extreme" wage disparities that operate against women and minorities. Google, Oracle, Microsoft, and Twitter are among the companies that have been accused by current and former employees of systematic gender discrimination in salary and pay.

Four months after the Google lawsuit was filed, Janet Herold, a DoL regional director, testified in a San Francisco court, "We found systematic compensation disparities against women pretty much across the entire workforce." Herold continued, "'The government's analysis at this point indicates that discrimination against women in Google is quite extreme, even in this industry.' . . . The explosive allegations against one of the largest and most powerful companies in Silicon Valley comes at a time when the male-dominated tech industry is facing increased scrutiny over gender discrimination, pay disparities and sexual harassment."[55] According to the DoL's lawsuit, Google, in violation of its contract with the US government, initially refused to turn over its employment data.[56] In August 2017, Qichen Zhang quit her position at Google, saying, "I was invisible." In an interview published in the *Guardian*, Zhang is quoted as saying, "I didn't see a lot of women, especially Asian women, black women or other women of color in the executive ranks. I didn't see any opportunities there for myself. . . . The culture there was really discouraging, and that's ultimately why I left."[57]

One month later, in September 2017, three women sued Google in San Francisco Superior Court on behalf of all women employees for violating the state of California's Equal Pay Act. Kelly Ellis, a software engineer; Holly Pease, a manager; and Kelli Wisuri, a communications specialist filed a legal suit alleging that Google had kept them in "job ladders" that had lower compensation than those for male employees. This practice of "occupational segregation," that is, assigning women and restricting them to lower-paid career tracks, has long been documented across many industries and produces a "glass ceiling" that limits the economic and career mobility of women professionals in organizations. Describing the legal significance of this complaint, which could affect as many as eighty-three hundred workers, writing for the *Guardian*, Sam Levin reports, "The complaint, filed on Thursday on behalf of all women employed by Google over the last four years, provided the most detailed formal accounts to date of gender discrimination and pay disparities at the company after months of criticisms and a growing chorus of women publicly speaking out."[58]

Almost one year after this complaint was filed, this discrimination lawsuit moved forward in court. The US Labor Department performed a statistical regression analysis of the pay for twenty-one thousand Google employees at the Mountain View office in Silicon Valley for the year 2015. Its analysis found "systematic compensation disparities against women pretty much across the entire workforce." In interviews with tech workers, Levin writes, "Several former and current employees spoke in interviews about the ways in which they believe minorities, particularly women of color, are denied opportunities and equal pay. They described a culture that tolerates racism and sexism, where white male managers frequently support and promote employees who look like themselves."[59]

Joan Acker pioneered the study of gendered processes in organizations and generated a number of new concepts that were foundational to gendered organization theory.[60] She coined the term "inequality regimes," which she defines this way in her foundational research on gender inequality in organizations: "Systematic disparities between participants in power and control over goals, resources and outcomes; workplace decisions such as how to organize work; opportunities for promotion and interesting work; security in employment and benefits; pay and other monetary rewards; respect; and pleasures in work and work relations. Organizations vary in the degree to which these disparities are present in how severe they are."[61]

A series of high-profile discrimination cases in Silicon Valley exposed a pattern of gender-based and racialized discrimination that exemplifies

Acker's inequality regimes. On January 18, 2019, a class-action motion was filed in San Francisco Superior Court on behalf of more than forty-two hundred women employed at Oracle. The DoL lawsuit against Oracle, a leading Silicon Valley technology firm, alleged that the company had engaged in "a systematic practice" of paying White men more "than their counterparts in the same job title."[62] This lawsuit also documented that Oracle, a recipient of $1 million in government contracts, expressed a strong preference for hiring Asian students with visas, whom they could pay less (and thus discriminates against US nationals who are Black, Latinx, Native American, and Pacific Islander). Oracle was found to have underpaid women and minorities by at least $400 million over a four-year period.

Nitasha Tiku reports for *Wired* magazine, "Oracle's suppression of pay for its non-White, non-male employees is so extreme that it persists and gets worse over long careers; female, Black, and Asian employees with years of experience are paid as much as 25 percent less than their peers."[63] In an analysis of Oracle's pay data, David Neumark, a professor of economics at the University of California, found that women were paid $13,000 less than White men were, which is a violation of California's Equal Pay Act. This analysis was submitted in support of a class-action lawsuit on behalf of the female employees: "An analysis of payroll data found disparities with an 'extraordinarily high degree of statistical significance,' the complaint said. Women made 3.8% less in base salaries on average than men in the same job categories, 13.2% less in bonuses, and 33.1% less in stock value. . . . The case against Oracle . . . resembles high-profile litigation against Google, which has also faced repeated claims of systematic wage discrimination."[64] This suit also challenges Oracle's "systemic practice of favoring Asian workers in its recruiting and hiring practices for product development and other technical roles, which resulted in hiring discrimination against non-Asian applicants."[65] According to the DoL, "Out of roughly 500 people hired into technical jobs over a four-year period, only five were Hispanic and only six were African-American."[66]

The wage discrimination at Oracle is one expression of a gendered and racial caste system in which women, Blacks, and Latinx tend to be segregated into lower-status and lower-paying nontechnical job categories. Silicon Valley has been described as a caste system in which women, Blacks, Latinx, and other non-Asian minorities are concentrated in nontechnical positions, remain underrepresented in leadership positions, and occupy the bottom rungs of the pyramid at major technology firms. Whether the absence of Black women and men from technical positions and leadership positions, which also lowers their pay, is intentional or not, they have been excluded. After the murder of George Floyd by the White police officer Derek Chauvin, Blacks began to speak out about the racism and toxic workplace culture at Facebook, Google, Twitter, Refinery29, and other technology firms. Black workers interviewed by technology journalists and in their tweets have described a culture that does not protect them from ongoing racism, not only microaggressions.

The Sexual Predation of Women

On February 19, 2017, Susan Fowler, who had recently left her position as an engineer at UBER, published a blog post in which she detailed her experiences of sexual harassment and a toxic masculine culture in which the human resources (HR) department defended the predatory behavior of Fowler's boss. A native of Arizona and the second eldest of seven children, Fowler grew up as the poor daughter of an evangelical preacher. After earning a degree in engineering, she was hired by Uber in 2009. Six years after Uber was founded, Fowler was hired as a site-reliability engineer. She was not prepared for the culture of discrimination, harassment, and retaliation that she encountered.

In the blog post, Fowler recounted how she had been sexually harassed on her first "official day" on the job in 2015. She was propositioned for sex by her male manager. Instead of holding her manager responsible, the HR department defended him, lied about his past, and forced Fowler to find a new work team. Fowler writes, "Over the next few months, I began to meet more women engineers in the company. As I got to know them, and heard their stories, I was surprised that some of them had stories similar to my own. Some of the women even had stories about reporting the exact same manager I had reported, and had reported inappropriate interactions with him long before I had ever joined the company. It became obvious that HR and management had been lying about this being his first offense and it certainly wasn't his last."[67]

The day after Fowler's blog went viral, Uber hired Eric Holder, the former attorney general in the Obama administration, to conduct an independent investigation into the workplace culture. Four months after Fowler published her blog post, Holder reported that his investigation found widespread sexual harassment and gender discrimination at Uber.[68] This report called for the CEO, Travis Kalanick, Uber's founder, to be reviewed and released. One week later, Kalanick, one of the most powerful CEOs in San Francisco's tech community, was forced by Uber's investors to resign.

On May 15, 2018, Uber announced a radical reversal in its policy on forced arbitration agreements, which obscured the degree of sexual assault and harassment in the company. In other words, legal agreements that prevented transparency no longer fit the company's efforts to clean up its image. However, this policy did not address structural racism or racial discrimination cases. Reporting for the *New York Times*, Daisuke Wakabayashi writes, "That new direction includes ending the use of forced arbitration agreements. The practice—common to many industries—has been denounced for allowing companies to keep sexual misconduct claims out of the court system and away from public view. Because the claims are kept under wraps in confidential hearings, critics say bad behavior is allowed to perpetuate without warning to future victims."[69] Uber's policy change and new direction, although significant, is a small step that does not make trends of racial discrimination, pay disparities, or other inequities transparent. Furthermore, this policy does not allow individual women to join class-action lawsuits. This reversal of the forced arbitration policy is narrowly focused on sexual assault and sexual harassment and is designed to prepare the company to become publicly traded.

The legal cases currently being waged against several tech giants including Google, Facebook, Oracle, and Uber are evidence of growing recognition that the technology industry has continued to engage in forms of employment discrimination that have produced durable inequality regimes. We see that women and underrepresented minorities are treated differently from Asian and White men, in pay, promotions, recruitment, and retention. The Department of Labor is engaged in an ongoing investigation of these disparities in pay, power, and leadership positions and the failure to hire non-Asian domestic minorities in technical positions. At this time, there have been no structural changes and no meaningful measures of accountability.

Techno-utopianism, a dominant discourse in Silicon Valley, refers to the belief that Silicon Valley is a utopian space where the digital economy and high-tech firms have provided opportunities that benefit everyone. In an analysis of this Silicon Valley ethos, Marina Levina and Amy Hassinoff note,

> This dream, which is often wholeheartedly and sincerely believed in Silicon Valley, emerges in part out of the area's history of libertarianism and techno-utopianism. The key idea is that technological innovations are the best way to provide efficient solutions to structural problems of inequality and access. For example, UBER offers a cheap and convenient alternative to public buses, trains, and taxis. . . . The promise that capitalism raises all boats and benefits everyone has long provided a powerful justification for an economic system that depends on the exploitation of wage labor and results in increasing economic disparities. Silicon Valley's specific promise is that technological progress driven by capitalism not only provides personal convenience and raises the standard of living but also spurs social change. Such celebratory claims about social change are not limited to hashtag activists and philanthropists running campaigns on social media; indeed ideology is commonplace in Silicon as a social, political and economic enterprise. . . . Because Silicon Valley is both a technology industry and a cultural force, there is a need for a systematic critique of the discourses and practices that emerge out of and about the Valley because they influence the way people think about technology, political change and economic development.[70]

In chapter 2, I analyze the ideologies and mythologies that naturalize and rationalize the current racial structure, which leaves structural racism intact. Asian, Latinx, and White technology workers in this study embraced color- and race-evasive discourses that do not acknowledge structural racism or hold companies responsible for the underrepresentation and near exclusion of Black and Latinx workers from technical positions. When they were asked to describe their workplace and to explain the "diversity problem," a pattern emerged in which roughly 90 percent of the technology workers in this study argued that their firms were diverse while also being unable to identify a single Black or Latinx employee on their team or in their firm. They expressed beliefs in mythologies that normalize and justify the exclusion of Blacks, Latinx, and other underrepresented groups.

2

Ideologies, Mythologies, and Realities

Despite an avalanche of rigorous data to the contrary, the belief in pure meritocracy persists.
—Freada Kapor Kein, interview in *New York Times*, 2016

I grew up firmly believing the world was a meritocracy.
—Ellen Pao, interview in *New York Times*, 2016

I've sat on both sides of this table; this game is rigged.
—Lydia Fernandez, a transgender technologist[1]

The technology workers in this study often used discourses that reflect dominant ideologies and myths that normalize the racial and gender status quo, in which White and Asian men dominate the leadership, technical, and managerial positions. In this chapter, I consider the ideologies expressed by technology workers when they were asked to explain the "diversity problem" in the Silicon Valley technology industry. I argue that the discourses presented by the Asian and White technology workers reflect mythologies that sustain, normalize, and rationalize the exclusion of Blacks, Latinx, and other underrepresented groups. An analysis of the arguments presented to explain "diversity" reveals why non-Black technology workers do not always perceive structural racism or do not consider it a major problem at their start-up or firm and may not hold their corporate leadership responsible for the exclusion of Blacks, Latinx, and other underrepresented groups on their teams or at their companies.

When technology workers described their coworkers and explained the "diversity problem" in Silicon Valley firms, I found several recurring mythologies in their discourses. Among roughly three-fourths of the Asian and White technology workers in this study, the absence of Black and Latinx women and men in technical and nontechnical positions

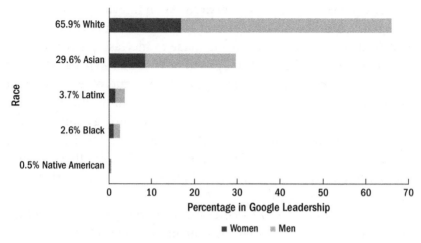

Figure 2.1. Google intersectional leadership representation, 2020. *Note*: "Native American" includes American Indian or Alaskan Native and Native Hawaiian or Pacific Islander EEO-1 categories. (Google 2020)

was normative and unremarkable unless they were directly asked about it. Two-thirds of the Asian and White technology workers in this study did not directly challenge corporate practices that privilege and reinforce the position of Asian and Whites in leadership and gatekeeping positions. These ideologies support recruiting practices that produce glass walls that block Blacks, Latinx, and other underrepresented non-Asian candidates from entry-level jobs in publicly traded firms and start-ups.

In this chapter, I draw on interviews with technology workers with origins in China, India, and the United States between the ages of twenty-four and fifty. A pattern emerged in the narratives of technically skilled workers in which, with a few exceptions, they drew on ideologies and mythologies that rationalize the exclusion of Blacks, Latinx, and the underrepresentation of women in their firms. While several White or multiracial gender-queer or nonbinary trans women spoke about the anti-Black discrimination they witnessed in hiring, most White and Asian technology engineers did not identify, remark on, or consider the exclusion of non-Asian workers as a problem at their firm or start-up. Technology workers, with a few exceptions, avoided terms like "racism," "structural racism," or "systematic discrimination."

The vast majority of Asian American, Asian Indian, and White technology workers described their companies and workplaces as "diverse" and argued that efforts were being made to increase the recruitment of underrepresented groups. They used metrics that were based on the global recruitment of Asian, European, Israeli, and other immigrant workers. A race-evasive discourse and a belief in meritocracy were repeated among the majority of non-Black technology workers. The narrative that "we are hiring the best" was repeatedly expressed in the narratives used by these workers—even those who admitted that they had secured their position through ethnic networks, family, friends, or recruiters whom they paid.

These ideologies reinforce cultural stereotypes and produce unique challenges that differ for women on the basis of their racial and ethnic status, caste background, class background, and national origins. For example, the Black women in this study did not benefit from diversity initiatives in the ways that Asian and White women reported because "global" diversity was used as a metric, which often distracted attention away from the lack of diversity among US-born workers.

Four mythologies were repeatedly expressed in discourses used by the technology workers who participated in this study. These mythologies form part of a larger belief system that normalizes and rationalizes the absence of Blacks, Latinx, and Native Americans from the industry. These ideologies are not unique to Silicon Valley and can be found in other corporate environments.[2] The discourses and narratives that emerged in interviews with male and female technology workers reflect the dominant mythologies that circulate in Silicon Valley, including (1) the pipeline myth, (2) the meritocracy myth, (3) they myth of biological determinism, and (4) the skills gap myth. Two-thirds of the non-Black participants in this study used discourses that expressed one or more of these mythologies. They used them to explain, justify, or normalize the exclusion of non-Asian domestic minorities. These discourses shifted the responsibility away from corporations, recruiters, and the failure of diversity initiatives and instead placed responsibility on Blacks and Latinx for their underrepresentation in Silicon Valley.

The Pipeline Myth

A key claim in this book is that the pipeline model does not explain the dismal and relatively static numbers of Black, Latinx, and other underrepresented groups in technical and nontechnical jobs in Silicon Valley firms. The pipeline myth argues that the women and underrepresented minorities are responsible for their own exclusion because they have not earned degrees in science, engineering, and mathematics or related fields. In other words, it is their limited human capital that is the problem, rather than discrimination in hiring, recruitment, and retention.

In a trenchant critique, Heather Metcalfe argues that the pipeline model is deeply flawed and fails to account for varied career paths into the technology labor market.[3] This model has been used for the past three decades to predict labor shortages. Metcalf explains that this mathematical model continues to be used despite its repeated failure to account for nontraditional pathways into technology careers. In an analysis and critique of the historical origins of the pipeline model, Heather Metcalf writes,

> The pipeline model based on supply-side economics, flow modeling, and social engineering was designed by engineers and the National Research Council's Committee on Educational Utilization of the Engineer. Depicted as a balanced equation, the model describes the linear sequence of steps necessary to become a scientist or engineer that would be needed to maintain national competitiveness. . . . Since its inception, researchers have used the model repeatedly to predict labor shortages in the workforce supply and to focus on key populations and points along the pipeline.[4]

In a mixed-methods sociological study, Yingyi Ma and Yan Liu conclude that the pipeline metaphor does not accurately reflect the pathways into technology careers. They argue that the social controls that prevent women from entering math and science fields during the precollege years may ease up in college, which may help to account for the influx of women into STEM later in college. "As the metaphor of the pipeline indicates, the process is characterized by uni-directional rigid steps in choosing a college major and then persistence in attaining the degree.... The pipeline imagery is grounded in the framework of cumulative disadvantage theory, ... which posits higher attrition rates among traditionally under-represented groups, such as women and racial minorities."[5] Ma and Liu conclude that non-Asian students, in particular, are disadvantaged by their family backgrounds and class. They note that "black and Hispanic students, in particular, are disadvantaged because they disproportionately derive from low-income households. Underrepresented racial minorities are less likely to be (registered) in courses than their white and Asian peers."[6]

The educational pipeline is routinely blamed by CEOs, chief technology officers (CTOs), and diversity officers at technology firms in defense of their company. An example of this strategy is evident in an interview with Maxine Williams, the chief of global diversity at Facebook. Hired in 2013, Williams is a Black native of Trinidad, a former soap-opera actor, and a Yale-educated lawyer. In a 2016 interview, Williams defended Facebook's dismal numbers of Black, Latinx, and other underrepresented groups by pointing to the educational pipeline. She argued, "It has become clear that at the most fundamental level, appropriate representation in technology, or any other industry, will depend more on people to have the opportunity to gain necessary skills through the public education system."[7] The Facebook blog post, which presents a sanitized and optimistic progress report by Williams, is an example of how diversity representatives "deflect" away from corporate responsibility for institutional racism and instead blame the educational pipeline. In an analysis of the language of diversity, Sara Ahmed considers diversity as an "institutional speech act." Ahmed describes a "speech act" as "if that person is speaking for or even as the institution. An institutional speech might make claims *about* an institution, as well as on *behalf* of an institution." In her analysis of institutional power, Ahmed is interested in the gap between what institutions "say" and what they actually "do" with regard to diversity.[8]

During Williams's tenure as the chief diversity officer at Facebook, the numbers of Blacks have remained flat, while the numbers of Asian and Asian American employees and women have increased. In 2018, Maxine Williams was one of only nine Black females among Facebook's top 1,053 executives. Diversity officers like Maxine Williams routinely engage in what technology workers call "diversity theater"—a reference to executives releasing annual diversity reports, which are accompanied by statements from a chief diversity officer (often a Black or other "person of color") to manage the corporation's public image. Annual diversity reports have to be "spun" and interpreted for the public in ways that minimize the gap between corporate rhetoric about their commitment to diversity and the reality of anti-Black racism, gender discrimination, and a leadership structure that excludes women and particularly Asian and Black women. Diversity officers routinely argue that while their numbers of women and non-Asians are low, this is not an expression of their corporate values. The belief that the technology industry is meritocratic and that the issue is the "educational pipeline" remains a dominant discourse in the technology industry.[9] One goal of this book is to provide empirical data that challenges the pipeline model that continues to be employed to rationalize the underrepresentation of Blacks, Latinx, and women in the tech workforce.

The pipeline myth is constantly recycled by male CEOs and their female proxies when they are asked why the numbers of Black and Latinx employees remain so low and have remained relatively flat or statistically insignificant. Three-fourths of the participants in this study argued that the educational pipeline is responsible for the underrepresentation of women, Blacks, Latinx, and Native Americans in the tech industry. CEOs and apologists for big technology firms continue to identify the educational pipeline as primarily responsible for the exclusion of Blacks, Latinx, and women from proportional representation in the industry. By framing the structural exclusion of Blacks and brown Latinx and the underrepresentation of women as a "pipeline" issue, rather than focusing on the social mechanisms by which White and Asian men control the industry, a type of consensus is produced. Furthermore, in much of the discussion about the "diversity" problem, there is careful avoidance of terms such as "racism," "sexism," and "power." Instead, terms like "implicit bias" are used.

Female founders and technically skilled insiders in Silicon Valley have directly challenged the myth of the pipeline. Elissa Shevinsky, a White technologist and veteran in the technology industry, argues,

> Putting the blame on the pipeline problem is good for PR and shareholder value because it shifts blame away from tech companies' leadership and HR departments, and onto women. This is a way for big tech companies to avoid hard conversations about fixing broken recruiting practices

and fixing work environments that are hostile to women and people of color. . . . I take their descriptions of tech problems with a grain of salt. When I see a video of YouTube CEO Susan Wojcicki describing the pipeline problem, I see a representative of YouTube (which is owned by Google). Her problems are not the problems of most women in technology. Her problems are those of shareholders and board directors charged with optimizing quarterly revenues. The "pipeline problem" narrative is a double win for big tech companies. It absolves them of responsibility for their faulty hiring practices and problematic work environments. It sweeps these issues under the rug.[10]

The pipeline myth was identified by Asian Americans and Asian Indians in this study, across age, gender, and regional origins, when asked to explain the gender gap in the computing industry and the absence of Blacks and Latinx. Saraswati is a forty-year-old India-born entrepreneur who immigrated to the United States with her family as a child. After earning a degree in engineering at a private university, she held several internships before becoming an entrepreneur. When asked to explain the gender gap in Silicon Valley, she pointed to the educational pipeline:

> I think first—certainly there's a pipeline problem. Right? There's just not enough emphasis in elementary school, middle school, high school. . . . A lot of that is based in the education system, family values, and general awareness. . . . A lot of my friends were dropping out of math and science. It's very hard to get someone into it, beyond high school and certainly at the college level, because a lot of it's like foundational work. . . . But I think that high school is a pretty critical period that feeds people into college and what they decide, um, but then there's certainly a secondary drop-off in—you know, I saw this happen a lot in engineering school, where it's kind of funny—a lot of freshmen would drop out but then would go into premed, which is fine, you know—you're not going to be an engineer but a doctor!

Saraswati's belief in the pipeline is troubling, not because there is inequality of access to science and math education for children living in poor school districts. The bigger issue is that her perception avoids a reality described by Asian and White technology workers of a persistent pattern of *dynastic hiring*—especially in start-ups. Dynastic hiring is a process by which people are hired on the basis of their relationship to a company's founder or a friend of the founder. This reproduces a racial and ethnic caste-like system in which members of the dominant groups continue to refer friends and family who typically share their caste, class, and ethnic identity. The use of social referrals establishes and reproduces systematic discrimination and inequality, as reflected in the workforce demographics of those companies that have released their numbers.

Although a growing number of industry actors are challenging this mythology of the pipeline, which is intertwined with myths of meritocracy, Saraswati's analysis represents the position of the majority of non-Black women in this study, whose parents were engineers and who were from middle- and upper-middle-class backgrounds. To some extent, like other middle-class and upper-middle-class Americans who reside in socially and racially segregated communities, they are living in a "bubble," where the pipeline myth remains a powerful ideology. This belief that the pipeline is to blame is partially responsible for the failure of companies like Google, Facebook, Twitter, and other major firms to increase the numbers of Blacks and brown-skinned Latinx in their workforce.

The Myth of Meritocracy

The *myth of meritocracy* is one of the most powerful ideologies that circulated in the discourses of the technology workers in this study. This belief in "pure merit" is dominant in India and the United States among technology workers. In the United States, this myth has existed alongside slavery and racial capitalism since the founding of the nation. The myth of meritocracy asserts that everyone has access to the same opportunities and that the groups that dominate the corporate leadership have earned their status and have not benefited from cumulative advantages related to nonmeritorious factors such as their race, class, caste, and cultural background or parental resources but have achieved their positions on the basis of individual merit.

This myth conceives of workers as if they exist isolated from networks and that job applicants operate in a social vacuum and that their "human capital" rather than economic, cultural, and social capital is primarily responsible for their situation. This myth places the responsibility on underrepresented groups—primarily Blacks and Latinx—for their failure to get hired, rather than considering larger structures and the ways that "skill is a social construct."[11]

The meritocracy myth is an enduring and resilient myth that continues to be embraced, even though it is undermined by observations that contradict it. For example, Ellen Pao recalls in her memoir, "About four hundred employees were working there when I started, and the three cofounders were creative, smart, and professional. . . . I don't think I worked with a single Latinx or Black employee the whole time I was there. The three cofounders were white men; most of the managers were, too. My group—business development—had three women in it, including one manager. To me, at the entry level it was fine and fair enough."[12] Among the eighty-seven technology workers who participated in this study, only a small minority (fewer than 10 percent) directly challenged the myth of meritocracy, even after describing being passed over for promotions. The people most likely to challenge it were Black women, gender-queer women, and people from working-class backgrounds. Indian women who reported having experienced discrimination and having witnessed men being promoted over equally qualified women adhered to a belief that these men had secured their position through a meritocratic system.

In an analysis of the discourse of "pure merit" versus "caste merit: in India, Marilyn Fernandez found that the IT industry in India is an "ironic vehicle for the reproduction of caste hierarchies in the IT occupational world. The seemingly caste-neutral merit construction project has turned discriminatory of the lowest castes while privileged the dominant cases and classes."[13] Fernandez explains how the notion of "merit-based" hiring is compared to and perceived as the opposite of the "nepotism of old industries," where personal ties came first, family second, and caste third.[14] In India, the Mandal Commission created a system that reserved a quota of positions in government and public industries for the "Scheduled Castes" (SC) and the "Backward Castes" (BC). The IT industry is seen as an industry in which jobs are secured based on merit, yet Fernandez argues that "merit" is the product of caste and class privilege.

If "pure" merit is primarily accessible to the dominant castes and classes,
it stands to reason that caste privileges are reproduced in the new IT

sector. Caste privileges percolated into the preparation of "pure" merit and in its application in the recruitment and promotion structures in the IT workplace, set the stage for diffusion and replication of caste hierarchies in the IT workplace structure and practices. . . . *Pure merit*, to many Indians from dominant castes and class backgrounds, is also the opposite of reservation merit. . . . Caste, to them, stands for SC (Dalits) and for the reservation merit gained by Dalits and other minorities through the social justice programs. . . . It is the caste-embedded merit, hidden and normalized, that offers clues into the caste diffusion and replicating potential in Indian IT. . . . "Pure" merit is just a "code" word for caste advantage fiercely defended, to the point of turning the competition into a "blood sport."[15]

In a context in which IT workers belong to a global labor force, it is important to understand how the elites and dominant classes from in the United States and India understand the meaning of "merit" in ways that reinforce structural inequality. The dismantling of "affirmative action programs" in the United States and resistance by upper-caste Indians to the Mandal reservation system in India demonstrate a transnational form of solidarity that supports discriminatory policies disguised as merit-based.

Farshid: A Persian Perspective

A thirty-one-year-old Persian engineer, Farshid was born in China and speaks four languages including English, Farsi, and Mandarin. Farshid has worked in the Silicon Valley technology sector for seven years. When he was asked to describe the demographics of his firm, his description echoed that of the Asian Indian and Asian American technology workers in this study. He described a racial and gender hierarchy dominated by Asian and White men: "It's definitely skewed towards Whites, East Asians, and South Asians—definitely—predominantly. I think that definitely management skews more male. . . . I don't think I've seen any Black managers." Describing the absence of Black managers, which has also been documented in a growing number of lawsuits against companies like Facebook,[16] he shifted to a discussion of the ideological climate and the power structure. Farshid explained that among his peers, there is a lack of awareness of structural barriers and racial patterns that privilege non-Blacks. He noted that a toxic environment exists for underrepresented groups and that his White and Asian coworkers respond negatively to initiatives to increase the numbers among underrepresented groups. After describing his colleagues' indifference to diversity initiatives that would increase inclusion, he commented on their arguments. He argued that his colleagues embrace a belief in meritocracy and that they are not aware of structural barriers to underrepresented minorities like US-born Blacks, indicating that they lack knowledge. In his words, they have "no kind of idea of structural barriers that are in place or any kind of nuanced view."

Farshid's analysis is remarkable in that he is an outlier among the Asians, Asian Americans, and White cisgender participants in this study. He argued, like many of the Black technology workers, that the diversity initiatives and hiring programs are cosmetic only and leave the current racial hierarchies, reward structure, and power structure intact. In contrast to many of the Asian Americans and immigrant Indians in this study, Farshid identified an ideological climate in which his coworkers remain indifferent to diversity initiatives designed to increase the numbers of underrepresented groups such as Blacks, Latinx, and women. Like a number of the Black women and many White LGBTQ technologists, he identified a need to change the toxic culture:

> It's not just about hiring these people and getting the numbers up. We should make them feel comfortable being here and not be a terrible environment for them. . . . I think that ultimately we need to get to the point where we realize all of these systems . . .—the way we reward people, all of our incentives. Who gets promoted? All of these decisions are being made by people at the top. If you look at corporate America, they're White males. All of these systems, all of these processes, all of these structures are created by a small, narrow set of White men. These decisions are being made without anyone else in the room.

In contrast to Farshid's analysis, most technology workers tended to blame Blacks and Latinx for their absence. With a few exceptions, non-Blacks minimized or denied the role that their race, ethnicity, and class advantages plays in their possession of "merit." It is a convenient fiction that relieves individuals of any responsibility for their role in perpetu-ating structural inequality—even as they recommend or "refer" their friends, family, and others from their social networks for jobs at their current firms.

With the exception of Farshid and several LGBTQ technology workers in my study who identified as White or multiracial, a pattern emerged in which technology workers held Blacks and Latinx respon-sible for their underrepresentation at technology firms and exclusion in the industry. The participants in this study employed discourses that shifted responsibility away from the CEOs and corporate practices and instead recycled and resurrected the pipeline myth, the meritocracy myth, and the model minority myth. The absence of Blacks and Latinx was so normative that it was unremarkable. Unless directly asked, the participants did not even mention knowing a single Black person hired by their manager or on their team when discussing diversity.

The Myth of Biological Essentialism

The biological determinism myth refers to the belief that an individu-al's sex assigned at birth (which may not match one's gender identity, a social role) and one's racial classification (a sociolegal category) are responsible for and determine one's intellectual capacities. In inter-views with roughly two-thirds of the technology workers in this study, a belief in innate abilities (and inferiorities) emerged, often cloaked in the language of "cultural" differences to explain the absence of Blacks and Latinx in the hiring pool and among their coworkers. This belief in bio-logical essentialism and determinism was rarely explicitly stated but was often revealed when respondents were asked to explain the absence of Blacks, Latinx, and other underrepresented minorities at their firms. In analyzing the exclusion of non-Asian domestic minorities, particularly Black and Latinx employees, technology workers would reference the applicant pool and offer essentialist arguments that located the problem outside of their firm and in the cultural preferences and abilities of these underrepresented groups.

Taxonomies of racial classification employed in the United States today were developed and introduced by Europeans in the eighteenth century during colonial expansion, transatlantic slavery, and genocide.[17]

During this period, Europeans invented a new "racial science" and created the first racial classification systems, including the term "Caucasian." This term refers to people from the Caucasus region of Russia. Johann Friedrich Blumenbach, a German physician and naturalist, created a racial classification system in the eighteenth century that included five human races, with Caucasians being at the top of the hierarchy. The term "Caucasian" is still used as a self-identifier today by people of European ancestry. Human beings were classified and measured by skin color, hair texture, shape and size of skull, and deviations from Caucasians, who were defined as the "ideal" group. Blumenbach asserted that physical characteristics reflected innate intellectual abilities. This idea was widely taught and became accepted doctrine in the United States.[18]

This mythology is reflected in a controversial memo written by James Damore, a White male engineer formerly employed by Google. The controversy generated by Damore's manifesto revealed that at Google, there was an enduring belief among a segment of the White male engineers that biological essentialism, rather than structural racism and inequality regimes, is responsible for the overrepresentation of White men in leadership and technical positions. The evidence that others agreed with him includes the fact that several other White men joined his legal discrimination suit against Google.

On August 7, 2017, James Damore, a twenty-eight-year-old, White, cisgender male software engineer, was fired by Google for writing a ten-page memo that he posted on an internal message board for Google employees before it went viral a month later. Damore, a native of Chicago's suburbs who has been diagnosed with a form of autism, fits the stereotype of the awkward White nerd engineer. After he was fired by Google, he quickly became an "internet hero" for the right-wing conservative movement[19]. White male conservative supporters were quoted in the *Washington Post* as calling Damore's firing representative of an "alt-tech revolution," "an uprising of conservative Silicon Valley workers against the tech world's left-leaning culture."[20]

Google's management had been divided on whether to fire Damore over his memo.[21] This document, which has been called a manifesto, was titled "Google's Ideological Echo Chamber." Damore wrote and posted it after attending a voluntary diversity training session. After circulating for a month on various internal message boards at Google, in August it was leaked in tweets by Google employees and became public on the technology blogs.

On August 4, three days before Damore was fired, the memo, which Damore had reposted on August 3 to Liberty, an internal message board for libertarians at Google, was published on the tech blog *Motherboard*.[22] Damore argued in his manifesto, "At Google, we're regularly told that implicit (unconscious) and explicit biases are holding women back in tech and leadership. . . . It's far from the whole story. On average, men and women biologically differ in many ways. These differences aren't just socially constructed. . . . I'm simply stating that the distribution of preferences and abilities of men and women differ in part due to biological causes and that these differences may explain why we don't see equal representations of women in tech and leadership."[23] This echoes the statements made by Lawrence Summers, former president of Harvard University (and a mentor of Sheryl Sandberg), almost a decade earlier, when he explained why women were "poor at science."[24] In 2013, Damore dropped out of a Harvard PhD program to join Google's "army of 23,000 mostly male engineers."[25] Within two years, he was promoted to senior engineer and led projects related to Google's search engine. It has been estimated that with stock options, he was earning $300,000 per year.

According to media reports and tweets from Google employees, Damore had supporters within Google who shared his views that diversity programs for women and minorities should be eliminated in favor of "ideological diversity." In Damore's view as a White conservative man who had watched documentaries such as *The Red Pill* about men's rights and read *The Myth of Male Power*, he had been silenced by Google's corporate practices and policies designed to increase the representation of women and underrepresented minorities. He alleged that "Google's left bias" had harmed him by creating a politically correct monoculture that maintains its hold by shaming dissenters into silence.

It is worth taking a moment to consider the main arguments that Damore made in his memo. Damore argued that one reason women remain underrepresented in leadership and technical positions is due to "men's higher drive for status" and to their biology. His main arguments, cloaked with scientific references, were that women have innately different traits and personalities that make them biologically ill suited for certain types of technical jobs. According to Damore, these innate differences between men and women "explain why women relatively prefer jobs in social or artistic areas." Damore then argued against mentoring programs, classes, or initiatives that provide support for "people with a certain gender or race." He concluded by stating, "Philosophically I don't think we should do arbitrary social engineering of tech just to make it appealing to equal portions of both men and women."[26]

After the memo went viral and the tech media began reporting on it, Google fired Damore for "violating company code of practice," and the same day, Damore filed a complaint with the National Labor Relations Board (NLRB) for "political discrimination," which is not covered by the First Amendment but is covered by California state law that protects political speech. In 2018, when Damore filed his lawsuit, Google's leadership was 75 percent male and 68 percent White, while its technical employees, which includes engineers, was 80 percent male and 53 percent White. Its overall workforce is 69 percent male. Google was and is currently facing a Department of Labor investigation claiming that it discriminates against women in pay and promotion.

On February 16, 2018, Jayme Sophir, the attorney for the NLRB, ruled that Damore's firing by Google was legal and that his statements about women in his memo "were discriminatory and constituted sexual harassment, notwithstanding efforts to cloak comments with 'scientific' references and analysis, and notwithstanding 'not all women' disclaimers.'"[27] The controversy generated by Damore's manifesto revealed a toxic culture in which a segment of the male engineers and others at Google embrace some version of the idea of biological determinism as an explanation for the small number of women in leadership positions and were offended by any efforts to provide support for women and underrepresented minorities.

The Skills Gap Myth

The skills gap myth is the idea that there is a shortage of skilled workers in the US technology sector. This myth obscures the actual local markets as well as the training that many individuals receive on the job. The skills gap myth, which is intertwined with the pipeline myths, distracts attention away from two realities that have been documented in gender discrimination lawsuits, media reports, and EEOC reports provided by Silicon Valley technology firms: the failure of Silicon Valley to recruit and retain US Blacks and Latinx job applicants in proportion to their numbers in the college-educated US workforce, including those who have earned degrees in computer science.[28] In 2015, Silicon Valley firms (Google and Pinterest) hired only two out of a total of twenty-eight Black graduates who had earned degrees in computer science from Howard University.[29]

In a report on the recent closures of coding boot camps, Audrey Watters argues that the skills gap narrative does not reflect reality at the local level. She challenges conventional wisdom and dominant narratives about skills gaps in the media:

> Industry groups have suggested that there are currently some 500,000 unfilled computing jobs. . . . That number is more invention than reality, a statistic used to further a particular narrative, about the failure of schools to offer adequate technical training. That 500,000 figure, incidentally, comes from a Bureau of Labor Statistic's projection about the number of computing and IT jobs that will be added to the US economy by 2024, not the number of jobs that are available—filled or unfilled—today. . . . There isn't really much evidence of a "skills gap"—there's been no substantive growth in wages, for example, that one would expect if there was a shortage in the supply of qualified workers. . . . It's important to remember that the job market isn't national; it's local.[30]

In this study, half of the university-educated Indian women who immigrated to the United States as foreign nationals described skills that they developed after immigrating to the United States. Even women who had prior work experience described being sent to the United States by their companies in India to learn technical skills and then returned to India before immigrating on either a family visa or an H1-B visa.

In a study of technology executives in leadership positions, Alison Wynn found that they rarely engaged in attempts to change the structure of their company.[31] Wynn identified five ideological dimensions regarding the sources of gender inequality that are the foundations of current diversity approaches. She argues that "organizational initiatives designed to achieve equality are limited in their reach and effectiveness because they remain anchored to individualistic gender ideologies, and in doing so, such programs reinforce the status quo rather than challenge it."[32]

Conclusion

In this chapter, I have identified four mythologies expressed in discourses used to explain the absence of Blacks and Latinx in the technology industry. These mythologies inform corporate recruitment and hiring practices that establish glass walls. These resilient mythologies, or belief systems, reinforce the racialized and gendered structures of power that have closed the door to many Black and Latinx applicants. These discourses represent ideologies that reproduce and rationalize a caste-like structure in Silicon Valley in which Asian and White men are concentrated at the top of the corporate hierarchies.

Moreover, Asian American, immigrant Asians, and White technology workers placed emphasis on gender inequality and used global metrics when defining diversity. A neglect of underrepresented Black and Latinx domestic minorities distracts from and carefully elides the ethnic rankings and unequal distribution of geek capital among applicants and employees with different racial, caste, and class backgrounds. These dominant mythologies fail to acknowledge the ethnic and racial hierarchies in Silicon Valley that differentially advantage, reward, and promote women who belong to the dominant caste, class, and racial backgrounds.

The dominant mythologies in Silicon Valley reinforce the discourse of utopianism and individualism. The technology workers in this study also reported that their firms use social referrals to hire between at least one-third to one-half of their employees. The use of social referrals is even higher at start-ups, where virtually everyone is recruited through personal networks that are, in many cases, ethnic-based, kin-based, or alumni-based. The routine use of social referrals by technology firms represents a nonmeritocratic recruitment tool that rewards and reproduces gender inequality and structural racism. This was rarely defined as a problem by the workers in this study. Social referrals are not meritocratic and directly shape one of the pipelines into the industry. They also reproduce the exclusion of women and ethnic minorities who are underrepresented and sustain the occupational segregation that characterizes the industry because technology workers, like other occupational groups, tend to socialize and know people who share their age, race, ethnic, class background, and educational status.

3

Black Geek Girls

Silicon Valley's 1 Percent

People like to mentor people who look like them, and there's nobody in tech who looks like me.
—Erica Joy Baker, former Google employee and cofounder of Project Include

I didn't have many students who looked like me. I didn't have a support system and I didn't know how to create one.
—Kimberly Bryant, CEO of Black Girls Code

I always feel that I have two lives. . . . When I am in a corporate world, or predominantly White world, I'm a certain way. . . . And if I'm in an African American community, I have to go back and be able to be relatable. Being able to compartmentalize—those things are really hard for a lot of people.
—Maya, Black tech worker

In February 2015, Angelica Coleman, a twenty-five-year-old Black woman, left her position at Dropbox. Coleman had been hired in 2013 as an administrative assistant. During her time at Dropbox, she had taught herself to code Python and several programming languages through a "learn to code" club that she launched. She understood that she would be able to move into another role on the team that her administrative job supported. This did not happen. Negotiating a hostile work environment, Coleman found it increasingly difficult to relate to her coworkers, with whom she shared neither an ethnic, racial, or class background. Describing her year at Dropbox, Coleman summarized it as "death by a thousand cuts."[1] In a Facebook posting, Coleman detailed the hostility that she endured during her final months as one of a total of eleven Black employees in Dropbox's global workforce:

> After spending months apologizing for being me, and after a white manager sat me down, looked me in the eye and told me, "If you ever want to be anything other than an admin, you need to go somewhere else" . . . Nobody can ever tell me what I can and can't do. I decide my own life, and if I want to code, then I'll fucking do it. I left Dropbox because, as a black woman, working on bettering myself, the tech industry doesn't give a shit. Even with the skills to do more, if I had stayed at Dropbox, I would have always had the submissive role of serving others and never calling the shots. Why? Because a white manager didn't want to see me do it.[2]

Coleman had been hired in a nontechnical role and had learned to code, yet there appeared to be no meaningful attempt to retain her or to promote her to a technically skilled position. Coleman's departure from Dropbox reflects a contradiction between the stated diversity initiatives of major technology firms and the realities that Black women face. Moreover, the segregation of Black and Latinx employees demonstrates that they remain concentrated and segregated by function and prestige into the lower-status and lower-paying jobs. The segregation of Black women and men into lower-status jobs is supported by data from foundations, demographic data released by technology firms, and memoirs.[3]

A study conducted in the summer of 2017 by the Pew Research Center found that Blacks employed in STEM fields reported the same forms of discrimination that they had reported four decades earlier. And on the basis of the survey data, they perceived the STEM field to be a hostile and alienating workplace due to their race and ethnicity. In other words, their exposure to discrimination resembled studies that had been conducted in the latter half of the twentieth century. In a summary of the Pew report, Monica Anderson writes, "Roughly six-in-ten black (62%) STEM workers say they have experienced any of eight specific forms of racial or ethnic discrimination at work, from earning less than a coworker who performed the same job to experiencing repeated, small slights. . . . One of the most common forms of race-related discrimination reported in STEM fields is being treated as not competent. Among STEM employees, 45% of blacks say they have had this experience because of their race or ethnicity, compared with smaller shares of Hispanics (23%), Asians (20%) or whites (3%)."[4]

I begin this chapter with the case of Angelica Coleman because her experiences are an example of the glass walls that block technically skilled Black and Black Latinx women from moving into technically skilled entry-level positions in Silicon Valley. Glass walls are formal corporate policies and informal social practices that block horizontal access to entry-level positions for technically skilled workers employed on short-term contracts for a particular job. Coleman represents the 1 percent of Silicon Valley's technical workforce—a small cohort of "invisible" Black women who barely register in the demographic data released by technology firms. Although Coleman's description of her experiences at Dropbox represents an example of blatant racism and may not reflect the technology industry as a whole, the demographic data released by technology firms strongly suggest that the technology industry has not welcomed Black women.[5] Dropbox denied that Coleman's experience reflected a pattern of blatant racism at the firm. And her case may be exceptional.

In a cover story titled "Why Is Silicon Valley So Awful to Women?," published in the April 2017 issue of the *Atlantic*, Liz Mundy interviewed dozens of women in Silicon Valley about their experiences. A recurring theme in interviews with women of diverse racial and ethnic backgrounds is the amount of emotional labor required daily to negotiate a racial and gendered caste system that has been called a "brotopia." In a profile of a Black woman in Silicon Valley, Mundy shows the ways that race structures the experiences of Black women and the daily assaults they report: "Stephanie Lampkin, who was a full-stack developer (meaning she had mastered both front-end and back-end systems) by age 15 and majored in engineering in Stanford, has been told when applying for a job that she's 'not technical enough' and should consider 'sales or marketing'—an experience that many white women in the field can relate to. But she has also . . . been told by a white woman at a conference that her name ought to be Ebony because of the color of her skin."[6]

This chapter has two goals. First, I demonstrate that the experiences of Black women in the technology industry are shaped by *social closure* and, in some cases, by anti-Black racism. "Social closure" refers to the exclusion of Black women from social networks that include technologists employed in Silicon Valley. In contrast to their Asian and White female colleagues, Black women rarely, if ever, work with Black coethnics—especially if they are working on teams with engineers. I also show how the career trajectories of Black women are shaped by the quantity and quality of the social and economic capital they possess.

Second, I examine the strategies used by Black women who are racial, gender, and class tokens to break through glass walls and to manage anti-Black racism, their hypervisibility, and a toxic workplace. I introduce six Black technology workers between the ages of twenty-eight and forty-eight, from diverse ethnic backgrounds (Caribbean, North American, and Native American) and employed in Silicon Valley. Some of these women were able to break through these glass walls, but not without a friend in the industry who could provide introductions to recruiters or the founders of start-ups. While there are variations in their career trajectories, their experiences differ significantly from their Asian and White peers. This chapter builds on earlier research on race, gender, and Black professionals.[7]

I build on Adia Harvey Wingfield's concept of *gendered racism* in my intersectional analysis of the experiences of Black women technology workers in the Silicon Valley labor system.[8] In a series of case studies that focus on the experiences of Black professionals, Wingfield has revised and renovated theoretical concepts produced by gender scholars studying discrimination in organizations, including *tokenism* and the *glass escalator*.[9] Wingfield has generated a new cluster of concepts including *racialized feeling rules*, *racialized glass escalator*, and the *theory of racial tasks*.[10] These concepts are central to the analysis of Black women's experiences in the technology sector but have not been applied to their experiences in the technology industry.

Black women in this study described facing more barriers to employment than their non-Black peers do. Their educational credentials or technical expertise do not protect them from structural racism or what has been called the "quiet racism" in Silicon Valley. Black women negotiate being a racial, gender, and class outsider in an industry in which Whites and Asians hold the gatekeeping, decision-making, and managerial positions. The Black female technology workers in this study had to turn for support to managers who did not share their race, gender, and in many cases class origins with them.

Half of the Black women who participated in this study described having to manage a persistent pattern of racial abuse and having been disciplined when they refused to accept this treatment and did not adopt a pleasant and obedient public persona. In this study, eight out of twelve Black women reported experiencing microaggressions, overt racial abuse in the form of jokes, comments, or being disciplined after taking additional time to fix a problem they found while completing an assigned technical problem. They employed a range of strategies to manage this treatment, including being silent, carefully curating their appearance to minimize clothing and hairstyles that could be interpreted as a "Black" aesthetic, and generally trying to "fit in." They also engaged in what Johanna Shih has found to be a common strategy among technology workers who are negotiating discrimination: they left their jobs.[11]

Declining Numbers of Black Women in Silicon Valley

In 2016 Reveal's Center for Investigative Reporting analyzed the diversity reports of Silicon Valley technology firms. Reveal found that Black employees made up no more than 2 percent of the companies that released their figures.[12] Eight of the twenty-three companies that provided data, including Google, Twitter, Square, and 23andMe, did not report a single Black woman in an executive role.[13] At the executive level, Black women were almost completely absent. The numbers of Black and Latinx women in Silicon Valley has declined between 2014 and 2017.[14]

In a study of Silicon Valley technology executives and an analysis of more than eighty meetings, Alison Wynn identified ideological barriers to organizational change. Wynn argues that executives differed in their understandings of the sources of gender inequality. Their understandings of the sources shaped their approaches. Wynn does not address race or racism in her analysis, but she provides important insights about the lack of efficacy of diversity initiatives. "Executives tend to limit their efforts to individualistic and/or societal types of change rather than organizational change. Such approaches have implications for the way equality initiatives are implemented and likely contribute to their lack of effectiveness. . . . The structural ideologies supported by decades worth of gender scholarship are rarely the ideologies that executives tend to endorse. . . . Organizational initiatives designed to achieve equality are limited in their reach and effectiveness because they remained anchored to individualistic gender ideologies, and in so doing, such programs reinforce rather than challenge it."[15]

In 2020, Google employed 741 Black women, which represents 1 percent of its global workforce. Black women make up slightly more than 1 percent of the women in technically skilled positions in Silicon Valley. In a 2016 report, the Ascend Foundation, a pan-Asian organization, published a report that analyzed EEOC data for the period 2007–15. In a detailed analysis of professionals at the managerial and executive level—those employees who held leadership positions and who possessed the power to implement changes—this report found that there had been no meaningful progress for racial minorities in reaching management and executive positions. The report concluded that efforts at diversity had produced measurable results for White women, while Asian women faced a "bamboo ceiling" and Black women lost significant ground in an industry where they are barely visible. At every level of the tech ladder, Black women are doing poorly, as a group. The Ascend report found an 18 percent decline in the number of Black managers and a 13 percent decline in Black professional women in the Silicon Valley workforce. Using an intersectional lens that addressed race and gender, the report notes, "In general, although minority women faced both racial and gender gaps, . . . race, not gender, was increasingly the more important factor in limiting minority women in the pipeline. The data show that for Black women, the racial gap was 5.35× the gender gap in 2014; for Asian women, the racial gap was 2.91× the gender gap in 2015."[16]

In the following sections, we will meet six Black women between the ages of twenty-eight and forty-eight who are employed in Silicon Valley's technology sector. The experiences of these women show the ways that Black women employed in Silicon Valley's technology sector have been denied opportunities for employment through informal and formal recruiting processes. Furthermore, in contrast to the Asian Indians and Asian Americans in this study, who had parents and extended family employed in the tech industry and thus followed a well-worn pathway into the industry prescribed by their parents, Black women were occupational renegades. They also differed from non-Black women in that half of the Black women in this study developed their coding skills and technical competence before securing a full-time job at a Silicon Valley technology firm. Thus, in general, the Black women had more technical experience than did the White and Asian women, who typically were hired after one or two summers as a student intern. Three of the fourteen Black women had been self-employed entrepreneurs prior to securing a full-time job at a technology firm.

Although these Black women have had a range of experiences, five out of the six described experiences that range from microaggressions to verbal abuse to workplace sabotage, which illuminates the ways that Black women negotiate what is often a toxic workplace. Their experiences highlight the ways that Black women must continue to perform and often outperform their White and Asian colleagues while being disciplined as racial and gender tokens on the job. We see the role that racial status, class background, marital status, and elite educational credentials play in shaping their occupational pathways in Silicon Valley.

Maya: An Entrepreneur Breaks through Glass Walls

Maya is a twenty-nine year-old, Black, technically skilled program manager, with more than a decade of work experience. She is employed at one of the most powerful technology firms in Silicon Valley. A native of Baltimore, Maya grew up in a working-class family. She took online courses and taught herself to code while working full-time and running a consulting firm. Maya never formerly studied engineering or computer science as a university student. Maya's entrée into the Silicon Valley technology workforce was a dynamic and nonlinear path that involved a decade of working full-time jobs in marketing, building websites, doing social media, and doing systems analysis. She secured her current job through the help of a recruiter after having run a consulting firm. After attending a historically black college (HBCU) for a year, she left without completing her degree to marry her husband, who was on active military duty. When she moved to California with her husband, she enrolled in university courses.

At the age of twenty, Maya launched her own consulting business and taught herself how to build websites, while working full-time at a day job. The White women who were interviewed for this study typically acquired these skills through formal courses in school, boot camps, or being coached by their boyfriends or significant others. Without a partner or family member employed in the industry, Maya did not possess an organic alumni network of support like her Asian and White peers who possessed degrees from institutions like Carnegie Mellon, Harvard, MIT, UC-Berkeley, Stanford, or Indian Institutes of Technology. Instead, she had to work hard to develop technical skills and networked constantly to accumulate geek capital without any familial support. Describing her childhood, Maya recalled,

> I grew up in Baltimore in a poor neighborhood. My mother was a single mom and worked two jobs. I'm the oldest of six kids. . . . I didn't have any computer classes or anything like that until the sixth grade. I left Baltimore in the sixth grade. . . . But the crazy part is that I didn't have computer classes either. . . . I didn't get into my Excel class until I moved in my senior class in high school, when we moved to Delaware. And I only spent one year there. And in that one year, I had Microsoft Excel classes. Everything else I learned on my own.

While living on a military base, Maya took a series of exams that allowed her to test out of several courses and earn her bachelor's degree in one year instead of two years. Maya paid for her education without taking out any student loans. Being debt-free laid the foundation for her to be able to launch her own consulting business. After leaving college, she went to work full-time for a marketing company. She started out in marketing because the marketing classes she had taken in high school enabled her to secure a job in this sector. That led her to move to Los Angeles, as a sales rep, to open a new sales office.

By the time Maya was twenty-three years old, she had cultivated a skill set that prepared her for a position in the technology industry. She had taught herself to code and built websites while working two full-time jobs. She started a consulting business with another self-employed Black professional woman. They built websites and developed social media strategies for female authors and entrepreneurs in the online publishing industry. Maya recalled, "I didn't have any web-development experience so I had to go and learn. So that's the self-taught web development. Because work wasn't consistent, I also had a day job as well."

Although Maya had continued to learn new coding languages and taught herself to build a website, her technical competence was not enough to secure a full-time position in the high-technology section until a Filipina American friend introduced her to a recruiter. This recruiter helped May to secure a three-month contract for a project-based position at a top technology firm. This three-month contract position marked a turning point in her career. Describing how she helped her Asian friend better market herself to Google and secure a job, Maya recalled,

> I just took [her résumé] from her and just rewrote it. . . . Two weeks later, she comes back to the office and says, "You have to listen to this." And I go, "Okay." And it's a voice mail from a recruiter that says, "Hey [name of friend], we saw your résumé. We think that you would be perfect for this position. By the way, the company is Google." And I freak out. . . . But she is actually really bad at her job. And I was really good at my job. And I had all of these other qualifications. I had an internet consulting business online. . . . And she got a phone call to work at Google.

After Google hired her friend, Maya, who recognized that she had skills superior to those of her friend, devised a plan. She asked her friend for the recruiter's contact information so that she could contact him directly. She phoned him every day until he helped her to land a part-time position on a temporary contract at a major technology firm. Describing how much work she invested in preparing for her interviews, which gave her a foot in the door at her current firm, she recalled,

> But I studied, and I studied, and I studied, and I studied. And I literally searched for everything. And there was one question that [the interviewer] asked me. She said, "How would you rework our community website?" And I'm sitting in my car in a parking lot looking at a computer. . . . I guess I sounded like I knew what I was doing. . . . They put me to the next step, where I had to do an on-site interview. I Googled 150 interview questions in every possible category: behavioral, analytical, conflict-management. Every question I had answers to.

Maya practiced her answers to 150 questions every day. She was overprepared for her interview. She explained, "All they really want is to see your train of thought. They don't care about the right answer. I practiced out loud my answers every waking moment that I had. I had a week before my on-site interview. Every moment that I wasn't working, I practiced all 150 questions. . . . I had the interview, and [the interviewer] asked me, 'So, come up with a social media strategy right now.'" She impressed the interviewer and secured a temporary contract job. She described the challenges that she faced as a temporary worker on a three-month contract:

> When you're a contractor, it's incredibly hard to get converted into a full-time position. . . . I kept asking questions about getting converted every week. I kept, like, trying to network my way around [the barriers to full-time employment]. About a month in, they had told me that there was no head count for me.[17] If I wanted to stay at [the company], I had to find a job on another team. . . . I basically networked and went to every possible event that I could. I volunteered at everything. . . . I asked full-time [tech workers at the company] to help me with jobs. If you're a contractor, you can't see the internal jobs board. You have to . . . ask a full time [employee] to look at the internal board—which is breaking all the rules—and help you to reach out to the hiring manager. I also went to outside networking events. I think that I went to a networking event at least three times every week. And I then was going to internal events and meeting people all the time. I had a lunch appointment every day with someone. . . . And then I finally started getting traction. I interviewed for four different teams, internally. I had performance reviews. I had all of those things. And I still had fifteen interviews.

In *Blue-Chip Blacks*, a study of the status distinctions negotiated by Black middle-class professionals, Karyn Lacy introduces two important concepts: *script-switching* and *improvisational processes*.[18] Maya's description of the strategies she employed to navigate around company rules that erected glass walls between employees working on short-term contracts and permanent workers is an example of what Lacy conceptualizes as an *improvisational practice*. Lacy writes, "When these middle-class blacks employed improvisational strategies, they left the impression that they were obeying the rules, when they were, in fact, circumventing rules and established practices."[19]

The number of additional meetings and network events that Maya described is an example of an improvisational practice. Maya invested three times the amount of energy to cultivate social capital and tech networks and to secure additional positive performance reviews. Maya networked nonstop for four months. She spent every waking moment setting up meetings, volunteering, and taking on extra work so that she could generate positive performance reviews.

As a first-generation technically skilled Black woman from a working-class family, Maya did not possess geek capital, that is, family members (or coethnics) to provide her with introductions or social referrals. Instead, lacking an organic network of support or alumni networks, she had to work nonstop to cultivate a network of White and Asian techies who could serve as social referrals. They did this by authorizing, validating, and testifying to her performance on projects that demonstrated her technical skills. Despite her technical competence and wealth of experience, she was not offered a full-time position at a major technology firm until a White technology worker with whom she had previously worked as an unpaid volunteer on a project vouched for her technical fitness.

Maya's career trajectory and learning experiences differ from those of the middle-class Asian Indian and White women in this study. When Maya was a military wife while she was completing her education near the base, she was socially and spatially isolated from technology networks. In contrast to 40 percent of the White women in this study and 95 percent of the Asian Indians, Maya did not have family members employed in the industry who served as "built-in-mentors."[20] Maya did not possess any of the social, class, or racial privileges that provided invisible benefits to many of the non-Black women who participated in this study.

Maya had earned a bachelor's degree at a school that was not distinguished for its curriculum and did not belong to the group of feeder schools privileged in the tech industry. She did not have access to alumni networks embedded in the technology ecosystem. Thus, in contrast to her peers who had earned their degrees at Carnegie Mellon, MIT, Harvard, Stanford, UC-Berkeley, or equivalent universities, she did not have easy access to job fairs where she could meet industry recruiters.

Maya's experiences as a contract worker before securing a full-time position illuminate the precarity of her status as a technically skilled Black woman working on a temporary contract. In contrast to her Asian

American and immigrant Indian peers, she did not have the support of a prominent and powerfully placed network of coethnics who could help her secure a permanent position through their closed networks. Despite her many talents, Maya lacked crucial forms of geek capital—including the possession of a degree from the small number of feeder schools—and she was not embedded through family in the technology ecosystem. Maya shared some of the same vulnerabilities of workers on H-1B visas described by Payal Banerjee because she was employed on a three-month contract.[21]

Although Maya carefully avoided the term "racism" and never acknowledged that she experienced racial discrimination, she had observed that there was a strong preference for Asian workers, as reflected in their dominance in the leadership, managerial, and technical positions. Maya, like many workers on short-term contracts, was disposed of when her contracts ended. In addition, she lacked even the basic protections and benefits of an employer-sponsored multiyear contract that could be renewed. Black women also face more challenges when they try to job-hop.[22] The barriers that Maya had to overcome represent a pattern among first-generation Black and Black Latina technology workers who were born in the United States. Even if they secure an internship in Silicon Valley, they are rarely offered full-time positions at these firms at the conclusion of the internship.[23]

In Maya's case, we have seen how the use of social referrals and standard recruiting practices at her firm set up barriers to her becoming eligible for a full-time job. Glass walls are corporate policies and practices that block horizontal access to entry-level positions rather than upward mobility on a career ladder for people already employed in the industry. Glass walls are the product of recruitment policies such as social referrals and other practices and processes that block access to information about jobs, access to gatekeepers, and permanent employment for job applicants, including those who have either earned degrees in computer science, engineering, or mathematics or possess the technical skills through extensive prior work experiences.

The glass walls that Maya broke through were produced by restricting the flow of information between contract and permanent workers on the same teams. Information about job openings is not available to contract workers, so they are segregated and kept on a parallel track without opportunities for horizontal mobility. In order to get information about job openings, Maya violated company policies—rules that denied access to the internal job board to contract workers. She benefited from the fact that her teammates may not have been aware that sharing information about job openings with her was a violation of company policies. This is an example of a corporate policy that reproduces an internal caste system and denies experienced and technically skilled workers the ability to move into a full-time position without a social referral.

Camille: From the Ohio State Legislature to the Digital Economy

The forty-four-year-old Black daughter of blue-collar workers in Ohio and the divorced mother of two teenage sons, Camille earned a bachelor's degree in political science from Bowling Green State University. Her route to a technology career was improvisational, rather than linear. Camille is a digital marketer who has worked on a series of temporary contracts in both technical and nontechnical roles at companies such as Autodesk and Adobe, among others. After working for many years as a contractor for a number of larger technology firms and nonprofits, Camille is now building a consulting business in the San Francisco Bay Area.

Camille's work as a contractor is precarious because she does not have security of employment or long-term job benefits. After leaving politics, Camille bounced around between a number of jobs including working at a homeless shelter for women. Her most recent job was working for a company that is testing self-driving cars. Describing her first job out of college and what led her to leave a career in Ohio state politics, she recalled,

> What I thought my career was going to be was a legislative aide on the state level. So I got my degree. And then I did a pretty prestigious internship in Ohio, which led to me getting full-time employment [at the Ohio State House]. The internship was paid. . . . After the internship, I ended up working for the minority whip of the Senate of Ohio until Ohio changed—the leadership changed from Democrat to Republican. . . . This was a long time ago, in 1996–97. I was working for a high-profile senator on the state level, and then literally overnight—with the

elections—everything changed. . . . It was an eye-opener as far as political really is. I had grown up with rose-colored glasses as far as politics. My dad was in the union. My parents always voted. They always voted Democrat. And I went into [politics] . . . wanting to be the voice of social change, wanting to be the voice of the common—common working men and women because my parents were blue-collar. Looking back on my childhood, we led very successful, very privileged lives being blue-collar workers. I'm like, "I can't do this"—especially losing power, because the same lobbyists who were our best friends last week would not even speak to me in the hallways. We couldn't get bills passed. . . . I got married. And I had kids. I was a stay-at-home mom. And we moved to California. That was the end of my political career.

Camille's career trajectory has been shaped by her disillusionment with her first career as a legislative aid. This was followed by her transition from a stay-at-home mother to the working mother of two young children. Her experiences working with a wide range of companies also demonstrate the critical role of recruiters in connecting experienced, self-taught women to part-time jobs in the tech industry. Camille possessed transferrable skills but did not possess the alumni networks and *marital capital*, that is, the economic and social support provided by a spouse that enabled some of the White and Asian women in this study to "choose" to temporarily opt out of full-time employment.

After Camille left her position as a legislative aide, she got married, became the mother of two children, and built a life in San Francisco with her then-husband, who was a critical care nurse. After Camille gave birth to her second son, she became a full-time stay-at-home mother. When her sons were two and a half and four years old, a girlfriend offered Camille an opportunity to work on a marketing project. Describing her pathway into a career in marketing, she recalled her friend's offer: "I had a friend who was an event marketer, and she had a contract . . . ABC TV had offered her a contract, but she was doing something else. She said, 'You are perfect for this! Why don't you try!' It was working with college campuses, and ABC was trying to promote a TV show. So that was my foray into marketing as a whole."

This job helped Camille to develop her digital marketing skills. She started doing digital marketing on her own as marketing moved from physical marketing (fliers, print ads) to online marketing (emails, blog-ging, social media). After her divorce in 2008, Camille began blog-ging and writing and slowly developed an online presence. Camille established her internet presence four years after the birth of Face-book (2004) and three years after the birth of YouTube (2005). Camille launched her career as a blogger during the birth of social media. In the early days of social media, the term "digital marketing" had not yet been invented. Describing the beginning of her digital marketing career, she recalled,

> My digital marketing career began as a creative endeavor. It started out with blogging. It started out with me writing. And then in order to market better, I started to blog. And that turned into email marketing and social media marketing, Facebook marketing, YouTube marketing. Working for the digital marketing firm in Ohio gave me credibility to get digital marketing contracts when I came back to the Bay Area. And then those digital marketing contracts with the nonprofits opened up the door to tech. Because at that point, I had had so much experience in marketing with physical marketing—like event marketing, which led me to digital marketing. And so—and then having that first tech company on my ré-sumé opened me up to the next company.

But it was a recruiter who opened new doors into jobs. Camille's experi-ences as a digital marketer were not sufficient to secure her jobs in the tech industry—she also needed an intermediary, and recruiters serve as bridges to entry-level jobs. After returning to Ohio for a time to get back on her feet after her divorce, Camille returned to the Bay Area.

> And then, when I was [back in the San Francisco Bay Area], I would do contracts with nonprofits—very small companies. A recruiter just happened to see my résumé on a job board. . . . And she called me and said, "Do you want to apply for this job?" And that job happened to be a month-long job contract with Autodesk. . . . It's very technical—like for engineers and engineering students. It's an amazing company. A lot of 3-D printing. . . . And that was my foray into tech. Somebody was on maternity leave, and her replacement couldn't start until a month. So they just had me fill in until her maternity leave replacement came.

Camille's labor as a contract worker supports the generous maternity leave polices of the full-time workers, which is one part of the Silicon Valley caste system. Since her return to California, she has worked for a series of companies but has not managed to secure a full-time job with benefits. As a contract worker, Camille is involved in precarious work, which has not led to a full-time position. Describing the emotional costs of working as a contract worker, she recalled one experience: "It was an entry-level position. . . . I actually drove the self-driving cars—the workplace was absolutely toxic. We didn't get the same benefits, and I kinda had an epiphany. I'm not quite sure I want to be the catalyst to bring Black people into tech—this tech workspace—because I have had so many issues. I have some trepidation about working in tech. . . . I have had a lot of toxic experiences—a lot—a lot of microaggressions."

Two years ago, Camille returned to school and earned a master's degree in anthropology and social change, with the goal of consulting "with tech companies on how to bring more Blacks into tech." While working for a company that makes self-driving cars, Camille began to rethink this goal and has shifted her position. She has now moved into a different kind of consulting, including developing "self-care" workshops for Black professionals. At the time she was interviewed, Camille was shifting her energies toward organizing these self-care workshops because she is challenging the idea that Blacks are resilient and can tolerate this toxic culture.

In striking contrast to Maya, and in spite of her transferrable skills, Camille was not able to break through the glass wall that stigmatized her labor and separated her from the full-time workers whose labor she supported. Camille continues to be a contractor and remains locked out of long-term stable employment. Like a growing number of technology workers, she moves from one short-term contract to another. She is one of what some writers have called the "ghost workers," those who belong to the flexible, temporary economy of disposable workers in Silicon Valley.

Yvette: A Case of Workplace Sabotage

Yvette, a twenty-eight-year-old Black engineer, is actively searching for her next position—referred to as "job-hopping" and one way that technology workers negotiate discrimination or unsatisfactory work conditions.[24] Describing her current situation as the sole Black engineer at her company, she identified a common structural theme among technically skilled Black women—working with no coethnics and being racially isolated from other Black employees: "Here, I got [hired] to do an interactive developer role under the pretense that I would be in a small team. My senior developer up and left. . . . I am the sole engineer at this company. I am the sole Black person at this company. I had no idea that it was lacking in diversity when I came in, because I couldn't see the company profile. I couldn't see the people. . . . I just assumed my engineering team would be White."

One of the struggles that Yvette identified was the lack of transparency in the metrics used in performance reviews. This confirms the findings of earlier research on racism and the experiences of Black middle-class professionals.[25] As Yvette reflected on her earlier experiences with overt racism, she recalled her efforts to get precise details on the metrics that would be used to evaluate her performance:

> I've been unethically fired before. Looking back on that experience, I asked [the company], "Do you have a performance improvement plan with HR? So I can be on base with what you want. So we can all be on the same page, because I'm doing this ambiguous shit.
> "Oh, we don't have those."
> "Oh, really? You don't have improvement plans?"
> "No. We just play it by ear, you know?"
> That's when I was like, yep, the storm is coming. I don't know when, but it's coming.

After Yvette was removed from the project, she described being given vague reasons for being taken off her job. She recalled, "I told my husband that day that they're going to fire me. . . . They're not following HR procedure. They are giving me vague expectations. . . . Everybody thought I was being paranoid. I was like, 'No, I'm a Black woman that works in engineering. I know the game by now.' Three days later, I took two days off after I finished all my tickets. I took two days off because they had unlimited vacation at my job." A "ticket" refers to a specific assignment, a job or technical problem that has to be solved. Once that job is done, the ticket is completed. Yvette had completed her assignments (tickets) and thus decided to take some time off. It is not clear how the hierarchy operated at her job, but it is possible that there is an informal system in which there are unwritten rules about when and how many days one can actually take off without being punished by management. "You know, anytime a job is like unlimited vacation, . . . they work you like a dog. Any tech company that does that, with benefits, just look at their company. If you have excessive benefits, no one takes them because they work them like a dog. That's a guarantee, especially if you're a Black person or a woman. . . . They are not even able to take advantage of those perks." After returning from Miami two days later, she was asked to account for being away. The storm that she was waiting for arrived. She was given no warning. Recalling how she was fired, she noted,

> Thirty minutes before this regular meeting on my calendar, one of the partners of the company gets in on the Gmail invite, and also the director of HR gets in on the Gmail invite. I see them get in thirty minutes before the meeting—no email contact, no one gives me a pre-rec, no one says anything to me. And so I'm like, here comes the bullshit. It's the storm. I can see it. I start prepacking my things. . . . I'm like already packing. I get in the room. [They tell me], "You're still not performing to our expectations."
>
> "I asked you all for a PIP plan three weeks ago. You said you didn't have one. . . ."
>
> They gave me two options. Go in this PIP or take severance pay and leave. . . . So I just took the month's severance pay and walked out happily. I let myself chill for a couple of days. I did some job searching. And I ended up accepting this job here at [this company]. This job itself has provided some very common challenges that I just keep coming across over and over.

Describing how the company set her up to be fired or to leave voluntary with severance pay, Yvette recalled how she was lied to about the process that led to her taking more time to complete an assignment:

> They cite some ticket that I apparently took a long time on with the next client they put me on. Mind you, the project manager that apparently told

them I was being a burden on that ticket, . . . he green-lighted me to have more time on that ticket that should have just taken an hour. But I caught some problems. So I rewrote the file, which took a little longer. It took a few more hours. I made sure I tested it properly, everything. They cite that same ticket and say that I was taking too long. I was like, "This is the setup." . . . I was being a good developer, and I was punished for that. They said I was taking too long and that it should have taken twenty minutes. . . . The project manager gave me the green light to rewrite the file.

This form of workplace sabotage is not unique to Black women but was also identified by White and Latina women. In this case, we see that Yvette was punished for expressing her feelings and calling out the White men for their refusal to provide her with a transparent mentoring plan that would help her improve her performance. A recurring theme among Black women was the lack of a mentor who was in a position to advise them and perhaps offer protection. This appeared to be less of a problem for second-generation technology workers or for first-generation Asian and White in this study women who were married to an engineer or had family members in the industry because they had "built-in mentors."

Black women repeatedly described the emotional costs of being a racial and gender token and working on a team with no coethnics or family members in this industry. A pattern emerged in which Black women described being the sole person of their racial background for most of their career, and this pattern was confirmed in interviews with Asian and White women. Writing in the 1970s about the strategies employed by numerical tokens in a New York firm to manage a toxic workplace, Kanter argues,

The choices for those in token positions were either to over-achieve and carefully construct a public performance that minimized organizational and peer concerns, to try to turn the notoriety of publicity to advantage, or to find ways to become socially invisible. The first course means that the tokens involved are already outstanding and exceptional, able to perform well under close observations where others are ready to notice first . . . but also able to develop skills in impression management that permit them to retain control over the extra consequences loaded onto

their acts. Such dexterity requires both job-related competence and political sensitivity that could take years to acquire.[26]

In the case of Yvette, because of the fluidity in the Silicon Valley
technology industry and the common practice of job-hopping or "job-
shopping," she found another position.[27] Some women choose to directly challenge their managers and then to leave for another position
rather than engage in the emotional labor required to remain in a toxic
workplace.

Black and brown-skinned Latinas in this study reported having to
constantly manage their emotions and the feeling of "not belonging,"
alongside stereotypes that position them as less technically competent.
Although White LGBTQ women also described similar feelings, they
were able to identify coethnics and other LGBTQ women in their firms,
or in the larger industry, to whom they could turn for support. In contrast, Black women are unlikely to have a Black supervisor or a Black
woman in middle management who can advocate for them.

Many scholars and policy makers have accepted the argument that
the pipeline problem is a result of a lack of STEM education and that if
Blacks, Latinx, and other underrepresented groups earned degrees in
computer science and engineering, their numbers would increase at top
technology firms. However, Yvette's experiences represent one pattern
found among employed women. Workplace sabotage is not unique to
Black women, but if most Black women have fewer, weaker contacts
who are not well positioned to hire them, the cost of resistance to workplace abuse is high. Yvette has few options other than leaving the industry or job-hopping to another company, where she may find similar
dynamics. The focus on STEM education cannot capture the forms of
occupational discrimination that push Black women out of their jobs
and out of the industry.

Vanessa: Impression Management and "Surface Acting"

A thirty-eight-year-old Black entrepreneur and technology professional,
Vanessa grew up in a rural factory town in southern Illinois. During
her childhood, there were times when both of her parents were unemployed. While attending a university, she financially assisted her younger

brothers, who were still living at home. Like most of the Black women interviewed, Vanessa grew up without class privilege and had to negotiate the stigma that comes with poverty. Describing why she never felt that she belonged in predominantly White middle-class professional environments, Vanessa recalled her experiences before she became an entrepreneur:

> I grew up with very humble beginnings, you know, welfare, those sorts of things. And being first generation and being in a wealthy, upper-echelon atmosphere . . . and I was never able to ask my parents for advice, right? But I always made it work. I was always honing [skills] and seeing what my counterparts were doing and how you maneuver in these worlds. . . . I think that I did become the token because I was like the outlier. I was like, for lack of a better term, "the black girl" that they enjoyed being around and they invited to the parties. And so I lived in two spaces. Inside my workplace, there was no diversity, and working on the client side of development with staff, . . . they were all very White. And it got like, "Where do I ever see anyone who looks like me in those spaces?"

Like other Black women in this study, Vanessa was the sole Black person at her firm. In contrast to the Asian American women, Asian Indian women, and most of the White women interviewed, she explicitly identified structural racism as something that she had to constantly negotiate. She described how she is treated as "exceptional" due to the structural racism that keeps people who share her background out of these jobs. She described the cultural climate that she endured:

> Prior to joining my firm, they had no people of color that weren't cleaning the bathrooms or serving in that kind of capacity. And I was met with a lot of the common stuff that people of color go through, like "You're so articulate. You're so competent." . . . You're met with all of these stereotypes [White people being surprised]. . . . This was the first time that a lot of colleagues were coming to work with someone like me. . . . A lot of stereotypes that they may have seen on TV or movies—they're like, "Oh, my God! You're not like the rest of them!" I didn't let it affect me initially because I'm just like, "You know what? I'm here." And I came from a place of gratitude! I was just happy to be in the building! . . . I mean, in my

first year working in the firm, I made more than my parents' combined household income, even when they were both working. So it was just one of those things where I was just grateful. And when you're moving in a space of gratitude—I mean, I laugh at it now, thinking I was so grateful to have this toxic work environment because it paid me [*laughs*].

Vanessa, like other Black professionals, recognized that the meritocracy is a myth that does not align with or reflect her experiences as a Black women in the tech industry. Describing the first phase of her career as a Black woman, Vanessa explained why, as a racial and class outsider, she remained grateful and had been passive in the face of daily insults:

These frameworks are not set up for people [who look like me] to succeed—you're like, "Oh my God, I made it through the bubble!" . . . So I never pushed back when someone was speaking down to me or doing those things. I just dusted it off and moved forward. When I was just the "yes" person, I worked myself to the bone. . . . I allowed bad behavior. Like—I should have done a better job. . . . [My name] was such a big deal for everyone—and you just get so annoyed with that, you just start doing things to make other people feel comfortable. And another thing—I didn't speak a lot about my background in terms of where I came from, and so having that *imposter syndrome*—being thrust into something and not talking about *anything* in the past. And so I was a friend to a lot of people at work, but they weren't friends to me because I never allowed anybody to penetrate that system of mine. And so, because I didn't trust people to have my best interest in mind all the time, um—and, again, it wasn't anything that—I was very well liked, and I got along with everyone. It was just that I wanted to be this cookie-cutter person that they could eat with and have a glass of wine with—and not rock the boat by sharing too much because I don't wanna get into anything deeper than it needs to be.

As a Black woman whose family had spent periods receiving welfare in order to survive, Vanessa was very conscious that her class background distanced and distinguished her from her White coworkers, who were uniformly from middle-class and upper-middle-class backgrounds.

Vanessa did not present herself as a victim; rather, she emphasized her agency. She could not control the behavior of her coworkers, but she could control her emotional response to the situation. Like the other Black women in this study, Vanessa described the adjustments she has had to make as the sole person of her racial and class background in her firm. In contrast, regardless of the forms of discrimination that the Asian or White women encountered, none of them described having to adjust to being the only person of their racial or ethnic or caste background at their company, although they might be the sole woman on their team.

In Vanessa's analysis of how she negotiated her cultural, racial, and ethnic isolation as the sole Black woman at her firm, she recalled staying in a place of gratitude and essentially carefully controlling her emotional response while she worked. In a study of Black professionals and how they negotiate White-dominated occupational environments, Wingfield identified a form of "emotional labor" that they have to perform as racial and gender tokens. "Yet, while black professionals understood that the feeling rules of their jobs mandate displays of congeniality and likability, they also argue that this feeling rule is difficult to sustain given the racism they encounter in their work environment."[28] Black women do not conform to the idealized image of the racialized and gendered technology worker, and this places them outside of the norms. Thus, the burden that Black women negotiate differs from that of White and Asian women, who belong to groups that are dominant in Silicon Valley. As a racial, gender, and class token, Vanessa had to negotiate multiple degrees of alienation and outsiderness. Her management of the stigma of being a Black woman has best been described by Wingfield: "Tokenism operates such that black professionals are scrutinized not only for what they do, but how they feel. This establishes an emotional culture that is built on racial inequality— feeling rules that are applied generally are harder for blacks to follow, and the rules that are selectively applied are done in a way that leaves black professionals with fewer options to express emotions."[29]

As Vanessa responded to a question about how she managed without Black peers, she described turning to a group of friends outside of her workplace:

> You just grin and bear it or you go home and cry. I mean, I did have girlfriends that I could talk to that are in similar situations at other companies. So we would talk about it, but against—we're all kind of peers, so we don't have the real advice [that mentors could provide]. . . . Even

if someone is treating you bad or harassing you, . . . everyone's going to think it's the race card that you're trying to play. So you have to be careful in terms of walking on eggshells. And so it was hard! I mean, there was no one to talk to. . . . After a while, I started to think it was more possible to have a mentor or a sponsor that looked like me because I never met anyone—I was never exposed to them. But then I realized Sheryl Sandberg isn't the only one doing something. I think she's great, but there are others. And so I started to dig and find and uncover these women because the media isn't putting them at the forefront. And so that's something that I didn't want any other women to go through.

Wingfield's research on Black professionals has advanced the theoretical literature on tokenism in sociology, as well as the emotional climate that they negotiate in predominantly White corporate environments. Wingfield has examined a dimension of inequality that had been previously neglected, and that is the emotional labor that Black professionals are required to perform. By utilizing an intersectional analytical framework, Wingfield theorized and illuminated the specific racialized restrictions on emotional display that Black professionals negotiate. The type of emotional labor that Black technologists perform, distinguish their experiences from those of White women in this study, who performed gendered labor in workplaces where they were members of the racially dominant group.

Research on the occupational experiences of Black professionals demonstrates the "emotional and etiquette labor" demanded of them in predominantly White workplaces.[30] Wingfield and Renée Alston introduced the concept of "racial tasks" when theorizing about the ideological, interactional, and physical labor that minorities are expected to perform. This labor maintains the ethnic hierarchies that place Asians and Whites on top. Wingfield and Alton argue, "Sociologists who study work and race generally lack a theoretical apparatus designed to connect the organizational structure of the workplace to the cultural and social practices within that serve to reproduce racial inequality. We attempt to address here by emphasizing the ways that the job requirements and implicit responsibilities associated with work at different levels of the organizational hierarchy are imbued with racialized meanings."[31] Black women feel the need to engage in forms of emotional labor and etiquette in a context in which there are no coethnics and typically no mentors of their background. Thus, the burden that Black women negotiate as members of the 1 percent differs from that of White and Asian women, who belong to the dominant racial and ethnic groups in the Silicon Valley technology sector.

Vanessa recalled her growing awareness of the emotional costs of the social isolation and cultural marginalization that characterized her work life as the sole Black woman in her office:

> As I matured, I started to see that there's a lot of structures in place that don't allow anyone who looks like me to move forward. And I think that I was lucky and blessed at the same time because I wanted to learn more and I was used being the only person in the space in order to advance my career in a very diplomatic way. But at the same time, it was a very difficult because I felt like I didn't relate to anyone beyond the surface. . . . And then I stared to think, "Wow, we need to bring in more people that look like me. What are some things I can put in place to work on that?" . . . I just worked really hard, I guess hoping that the meritocracy would take over. And I didn't say anything because I was like, "I don't wanna rock the boat"—you know, like any woman would, but then when you layer it with being the only person of color, then you really don't wanna rock that boat. So it's like, "Let me just be quiet, because you're making a great salary, and just deal with the stuff that comes."

The "surface acting" that Vanessa performs supports earlier research on the calculations and racialized performance expectations that Black professionals endure.[32] It reveals a consciousness and awareness of the racialized power structure and her position as a Black woman in this system. She recognized the structural obstacles that had prevented other educated Black people from entering the industry. As a result, she explained why, during the early phase of her career, she did not actively confront racist practices or behavior that she observed.

Nicole: White Coworkers and Workplace Sabotage

Nicole, a forty-eight-year-old technology consultant and the mother of two children, is a generation older than Maya, Yvette, and Vanessa. A native of San Francisco, Nicole has worked in the biotechnology industry for more than two decades. Ten years ago, Nicole transitioned from being an employee to working as an independent contractor. She now works remotely and travels to meet clients. Like the other Black female technology workers interviewed, Nicole recalled a number of challenges that she had experienced as a Black woman, including anti-Black racism and workplace sabotage. Describing a recurring challenge that she has had at every job and in every location where she has worked during the past two decades, Nicole recalled,

> I notice this same pattern. . . . There's always this small clique of White people who have an issue with me. . . . Every job I have ever had, I've been called into a supervisor's office because of a complaint of a coworker. And that coworker's complaint would be, "She's not working" or "How come she's leaving and everyone else is here all late?" And usually it's because I come in [to work], I'm efficient, I do my stuff, I go home, I meet my deadlines. But their perceptions were that I was flaky and not doing my work. . . . None of these [people] have ever attempted to talk to me or ask me about myself. It's never happened.

When Nicole was in her midthirties and her children were ages ten and twelve, she was informed by her clients and later her White female supervisor, a vice president, that her White colleagues were attempting to sabotage her relationships with clients. Her supervisor told her that her coworkers were saying negative things to clients about her in an effort to undermine their professional trust in her and sabotage her client base. The clients had reported this back to her supervisor. Finally, the supervisor took her aside:

> My VP just told me flat out one day, "I'm going to tell you what the problem is. This is the problem: you come here, you do your job, you do it efficiently, and you go home. That's the problem." And I looked at her, "What?" "[Your coworkers] like to go and do their cliquey stuff . . . and go hang out at the pub after work," my supervisor said. Because I didn't play their social game, they did their little attempts to undermine me and ostracize me.

Instead of offering Nicole professional support, her supervisor placed responsibility on her for the problem and asked her to culturally conform

to a workplace culture in which her European Americans colleagues routinely drink after work. Nicole's disinterest in socializing after work and
going to bars to drink alcohol after work, and instead organizing her day
around returning home to spend time with her young children, alienated
her from her colleagues. It also placed her in a vulnerable position. Her
outstanding job performance and strong relationships with White clients
ultimately protected her from losing her job. In contrast to Maya, Nicole
is a parent who did not attempt to culturally conform but instead rejected
social codes that would interfere with her efforts to balance her home life
as a working parent and to spend quality time with her children.

Nicole's experiences represent a pattern that has been described by
Black and non-Black women in blogs, memoirs, and journalist reports,
in which women in tech are pressured into attending after-work off-site
social events involving alcohol consumption.[33] It is not clear how many,
if any, of her male colleagues were parents, but regardless of whether
her colleagues were unmarried or child-free, they did not respect her
decision not to participate in off-site drinking. Despite her competence
in her job, Nicole struggled to maintain a work-life balance and a clear
boundary between her personal life and professional life.[34]

Tokens and Impression Management: Producing Social Unity

In *Men and Women of the Corporation*, Rosabeth Moss Kanter argues
that "tokens get attention" and that they "have higher visibility" due to
their status as tokens. Tokens have a limited number of options as they
respond to performance pressures. Maya is employed at a technology
company where the demographics are characteristic of what Kanter classifies as a "tilted" group.[35] Kanter classifies organizations into four types
based on "different proportional representations of kinds of people."[36]
These types include (1) uniform, (2) skewed, (3) tilted, and (4) balanced.
The Black women in this study worked in organizations where the numbers were skewed, with Whites and Asians making up roughly 70–90
percent of technical and nontechnical workers at many of the largest
technology firms including Dropbox, Facebook, Google, and Twitter as
representative. Kanter defines tilted groups as situations in which the
dominant group is just a "majority," making up roughly 65 percent, and

the tokens represent between 30 and 35 percent, becoming a "minority."[37] The number of Black women is so small that they do not even constitute a token in Kanter's framework. The ethnic composition of start-ups varies. In this study, Asian and White technology workers identified either no Blacks in their company or a small number that barely registers.

Presentation of Self: Minimizing Racial Visibility

Maya has adopted a strategy that minimizes her racialization and hypervisibility as a Black woman.[38] I interpret Maya's strategies as evidence of her cultural literacy and the complex emotional labor that she has to perform.

Maya's presentation of self at her job resembles that of the middle-class Black professionals interviewed by Karyn Lacy. In *Blue-Chip Blacks*, Lacy provides a trenchant analysis of the ways that middle-class Blacks negotiate their "public identities" and create social unity.[39] Although Lacy is describing the process of house-hunting and is not examining technology workers specifically, she identifies a cultural practice that bears directly on the experiences of Black professionals in workplaces where Whites or other non-Blacks dominate. Lacy argues, "Middle-class blacks engage in inclusionary boundary-work to establish social unity—to show that middle-class blacks are much like the white middle class. These identity construction processes are mutually reinforcing in that they each help to affirm respondents' position as legitimate members of the American middle class."[40] Maya does not perceive herself as a victim and never employed the term "racism" when discussing all of the barriers that she had to overcome to secure her current position. Here we will examine the form of agency that Maya employs as she negotiates racial stereotypes commonly held about Black people and her hypervisibility as a racial and gender token. As Maya described how she manages her appearance and asserts an aesthetic style that is dominant among Anglo-Americans, we see an example of what Lacy conceptualizes as social unity:

> But because I've been in a mostly dominant White world, I know how to communicate what I'm saying. I don't—I personally don't look like a Black person. I have hair extensions, highlights. It's not my naturally curly hair. I don't wear a fro—*ever*. I have very smart, casual clothes that I wear

every day. I don't come in jeans and T-shirts. I don't wear like big, chunky jewelry. I look very clean, very professional. I try to wear makeup most of the time. But I fit into the mold, with the exception of my skin color. I don't speak typically African American. I carry myself with "executive presence" because I've trained myself to do it that way—be that way.

What is striking about Maya's aesthetic presentation is that it differs from the White and Asian engineers who typically wear no makeup and dress very casually in jeans and T-shirts. What we see here is that Maya is distinguishing herself from the norm by adopting an overly professional style that is more common in elite law firms. She has adopted what she perceives as an "executive" uniform that is more common among management.

Lacy's research on Black residents in the suburbs of Washington, DC, demonstrates the value of cultural capital as distinct from economic capital: "Middle-class Blacks have obviously secured a privileged position in the occupational structure. But cultural capital differs from such economic capital in that cultural capital indicates a 'proficiency in and familiarity with dominant cultural codes and practices—for example, linguistic styles, aesthetic preferences, styles of interaction.' These signifiers of middle-class status are institutionalized and taken for granted as normative, hence the underlying assumption that groups that cannot activate cultural capital fall victim to systematic inequality."[41]

Maya's careful cultivation of a middle-class, mainstream, and feminine style associated with an Anglo-American managerial style reflects the cultural literacy that she possesses as a Black professional. At the time Maya was interviewed, it was still legal for firms to discriminate on the basis of "ethnic" hairstyles like braids and dreads. The rejection of hairstyles, clothing, or jewelry that would racially or "ethnically" mark her in a way that symbolizes a Black aesthetic is a form of communication that attempts to mark a boundary between her and other types of Black people. Maya is not trying to be White; rather, she understands that Black hairstyles are a form of speech—they are read.[42] One of her goals is to minimize her hypervisibility and to control how she is evaluated by non-Black colleagues by conforming to an idealized image of tech workers. She minimizes the degree to which she symbolizes "Blackness" in her hairstyle and clothing style. In contrast to the White and

Asian women interviewed, Maya also rejects a casual dress style. Clarifying her decision, she argued,

> And this may not be the right way. This may be terrible. There's already enough in the world that I have to fight against. Right? . . . Not having a master's degree, not being White or a man. There's already enough. . . . I don't need to openly be like, "I'm African American." . . . If there's something that I can personally do to not be outside the norm . . . when someone hears me or someone sees me speak. I already know that I look young. There's already enough. I don't need to add to that. I can change my hair. I can change my makeup. I can change my clothes, to have an outward appearance of fitting in, which is one less thing that I have to combat to move forward.

Not all Black women adopt this strategy. Another Black technology worker in this study, whom we met in earlier chapters, had worked for the same company as Maya. She wears her hair locked in dreads and does not chemically straighten her hair. Black women adopt a range of strategies to manager their hypervisibility. Another Black woman, who works for the same company as Maya and who self-identifies as queer, brings a different set of expectations, educational credentials, experiences, and anxieties.

The Black women who had earned degrees in computer science or engineering and had social referrals, social capital, and credentials that Maya lacked adopt a different style code. Regardless of how much cultural work that Maya does to "not be outside the norm," she remains part of the statistically invisible ethnic group. Maya argued that it would be much harder for a Black woman who wears her hair natural to "connect with [her] interviewer. . . . First impressions are everything because they make immediate assumptions about you."

As a token in a technology firm where technically skilled Black women make up less than 2 percent of most firms, Maya is a hypervisible racial and gender token. She manages her status as a token by carefully curating her image and presentation of self. Like all women, Maya has adopted an aesthetic style. In her case, she has to manage the anti-Blackness that can affect how Black workers are evaluated when compared to their White and Asian peers. Maya alters the texture, length, and style of her hair to aesthetically match that of the Anglo and Asian managerial staff. Maya's hair-care and clothing regimen demonstrates her efforts to blend in with her non-Black peers. She has "socialized" her natural hair and made it less visible by using hair extensions to lengthen and straighten it. This enables her to adopt a "brown-skinned White girl" aesthetic.

Maya's experience and perspective represents one strategy employed, but not all Black women adopt this method of minimizing their visibility. The experiences and perspectives of the Black women working in the Valley vary by the forms of educational, social, and cultural capital that they possess when they enter the industry.

A Culture of Silence

In an essay about "sexism in tech," Katy Levinson describes her experience of routinely and repeatedly being sexually harassed while working in the tech industry. She identifies a "culture of avoidance." This culture of avoidance creates a situation of "constrained agency" in which Black women and their Asian, White, and Latinx peers may feel unable to report or explicitly confront the racial abuse and microaggressions that they experience. For Black women, this is even more intense because they typically have no coethnics, no other Black men or women, in leadership positions from whom they can seek support specifically on anti-Black racism. Levinson writes,

> This culture of avoidance is very prevalent in tech. In the last three years, I was asked not to use the words "sexism" or "racism" when speaking on a diversity panel because it might make the audience uncomfortable. The person who asked this had significant financial stake in the institution I worked for. . . . Silicon Valley at least seems to understand that culture is important, but a lot of times when we talk about cultural power imbalances we default to a minimum standard of avoiding liability instead of actually handling problems. In fact, I'm not sure I have ever seen a sexual harassment seminar or mandatory-video-to-watch which strove to be anything more than plausible deniability.[43]

In Silicon Valley, the routine use of nondisparagement agreement clauses (NDAs), also called nondisclosure agreements, is embedded in employment contracts. NDAs have created a "blanket of silence." These NDA clauses are used by employers to force employees to give up their freedom of speech. NDA clauses prevent employees from discussing the reasons for their departure or their compensation (pay). It allows gender inequalities and structural racism to be sustained while the company maintains a progressive corporate image. Reporting for the *New York Times* about a "shift in culture" in Silicon Valley, as more women began to come forward, Kate Benner writes, "Employment lawyers say non-disparagement agreements have helped enable a culture of secrecy. . . . Nondisparagement clauses have played a significant role in keeping . . . accusations secret. Harassers move on and harass again. Women have no way of knowing their history. Nor do future employers or business partners. Nondisparagement clauses are not limited to legal settlement. They are increasingly found in standard employment contracts in many industries. . . . Their use has become particularly widespread in tech employment contracts, from venture investment firms and start-ups to the biggest companies in Silicon Valley, including Google."[44] Due to NDAs that are signed upon hiring, it has been very difficult for women in the industry to share their experiences without fear of retaliation. In June 2017, female technology workers began speaking out about their experiences of sexual harassment. In another *New York Times* article, about the culture of sexual harassment in the technology start-up industry, Benner interviewed more than two dozen women:

> The disclosures came after the tech news site The Information reported that female entrepreneurs had been preyed upon by a venture capitalist, Justin Caldbeck of Binary Capital. The news accounts underscore how sexual harassment in the tech start-up ecosystem goes beyond one firm and is pervasive and ingrained. Now their speaking out suggests a cultural shift in Silicon Valley, where such predatory behavior had often been murmured about but rarely exposed. . . . Most venture capitalists and entrepreneurs are men, with female entrepreneurs receiving $1.5 billion in funding last year versus $58.2 billion for men, according to the data firm Pitch-Book. Many of the investors hold outsize power, since entrepreneurs need their money to turn ideas and innovations into a business. And because the venture industry operates with few disclosure requirements, people have kept silent about investors who cross the lines with entrepreneurs.[45]

Binary Capital collapsed as investors withdrew their funds and Caldbeck left the firm. This incident reflects a larger problem, which is that men control the money. They determine which ideas are funded, and this has led to an underrepresentation of women receiving the same level of financial support.

Conclusion

In this chapter, Black women have described the barriers they negotiated as they entered the industry. The occupational trajectory of Maya illuminates the efforts required to break through glass walls into a two-tier system in which contractors work under precarious conditions. Nicole, who attended one of the feeder schools into Silicon Valley technology jobs, demonstrates that the Black women who belong to powerful alumni networks in the Bay Area and have transferrable skills do not need to have technical skills to secure positions. However, they are often sorted into "equity work" in positions as diversity consultants.[46] The quantity and quality of the social capital that Black women possess play a significant role in their access to technology jobs. In the cases of Maya, Camille, and Nicole, they had social connections to people in the technology ecosystem. Social closure, that is, the distance one has from people employed in tech, shapes the opportunities that are available.

Half of the Black women in this study pointed to friendships with Asian or White women who provided social referrals that helped them secure access to part-time contract and occasionally full-time jobs in the industry. They adopted a range of strategies to manage their hypervisibility and respond to microaggressions as well as racial abuse as tokens. Because Black women were more likely to be first-generation technology workers, they typically lack the organic forms of social and cultural capital to access technology networks that the Asian and White women possess.

Black women do not have uniform experiences in the technology industry. The occupational experiences of the Black women we met in this chapter represent both patterns and variation. Their career pathways have departed from and, in a few cases, overlapped with those of their Asian and White peers. As gender tokens, they have shared some of the same struggles that non-Black women have reported, for example, when negotiating with male supervisors who hold the power. However, as racial tokens in an industry dominated by Asians and Whites, most do not share a racial, ethnic, class, or regional background with most of their colleagues and supervisors. This racializes the emotional labor that they have to perform in ways that are different from the Asian women in the study, who symbolically represent "model minorities."

In addition to being gender tokens in their workplaces, Black women have to negotiate racial and cultural isolation as first-generation technology workers. Highly educated and experienced Black women still typically lack the geek capital and social currency that is provided by having family members, friends, or social acquaintances employed in the industry. Black women are less likely to be embedded in a network of Black tech workers or coethnics in the industry from whom they can receive emotional support in their firm.

Among the Black technology workers in this chapter, Vanessa possesses more social capital than Maya. Camille was able to gain information and guidance from a friend of her husband's, which enabled her to secure a job at CBS with one interview rather than the fifteen interviews that Maya had to endure. In an industry in which Whites and Asians represent the racially dominant groups, Blacks must work hard to cultivate relationships with members of the dominant groups and accumulate the social capital needed as racial and ethnic outsiders. In other words, in an industry in which they do not share the racial, ethnic, or other social characteristics of most of the technical workers, they must compensate for their network distance, that is, their lack of social ties to the decision-makers in the industry.

4

First-Generation Geek Girls

The empirical literature on women employed in the "new economy" and in particularly in the IT sector has assumed that earning a degree in computer science or engineering is the first step on a linear pathway into a career as an engineer or computer scientist. However, the occupational trajectories of the women in this chapter demonstrates that women follow a number of different routes into technology careers in Silicon Valley. The professional challenges that women negotiate vary significantly, based, in part, on the bonding and bridging capital that they possess—that is, the forms of social capital that they possess that link them to technology networks.

In this chapter, I introduce the concept of *first- and second-generation* technology workers to theorize the ways that family resources are leveraged by women entering the industry. First-generation technology workers do not have parents, older siblings, or extended family members who have earned degrees in engineering or computer science and have been employed in the technology industry. The Black first-generation technology workers in this study were concentrated among women who grew up in working-class or lower-middle-class families, based on their description of their parents' income, occupation, and level of education and their own social capital. As children, and later as adults, first-generation technology workers were "socially closed off" from the technology ecosystem and had to negotiate what sociologists call "network distance."[1] If they did not attend a prestigious university whose alumni base was linked to Silicon Valley and well networked, they described having to work much harder to enter the industry. In their narratives of their occupational trajectories, they described attending numerous job fairs hosted by other schools and enduring multiple interviews over many months to secure a full-time, permanent position at a technology firm.

In Silicon Valley, social referrals are routinely used by prospective job applicants who have friends, spouses, siblings, or parents in the industry. They are thus more likely to have privileged access to knowledge about job openings, social referral to positions at established firms as well as start-ups, and easy access to recruiters. Asian American and Anglo-American first-generation technology workers in this study were more likely than their Black peers to have social access to coethnics in the industry, even if their parents were not in the industry.

Pathways into Technical Careers

The women who participated in this study followed six pathways into the technology industry: (1) social referrals, (2) recruiters, (3) internships, (4) online platforms, (5) international migration on student, work, or family reunification visas, and (6) accelerated engineering academies, also called "coding boot camps." This chapter examines the occupational pathways of seven technology workers in Silicon Valley, including one European American, one Chinese American, and five Black and Black Latinx women. Race, class background, family resources, alumni networks, and social networks all shaped the ways that these women negotiated their entry into the commercial computing industry in Silicon Valley. Some had to leave the United States to secure training because they lacked mentors or networks in the United States. In the following sections, I detail the pathways employed by technology workers to acquire the educational credentials and the technical skills needed to secure jobs in US-based technology firms.

The Value of Social Referrals

One-fifth of the women in this study drifted into the technology sector. They did not choose engineering or computer science as fields of study; instead, they enrolled in art, drama, or the humanities. In this section, I introduce Jade and Geneva, two women who entered the technology field after working in a different field. Social referrals from friends and others in their orbit played a role. The quantity and quality of their social relationships to people in the technology industry constitute a form of geek capital that linked them to other technology workers (friends, lovers, boyfriends, former classmates). These relationships provided them with access to information about jobs at start-ups and established technology firms and introductions to gatekeepers. Half of the women in this study secured their first jobs through internships or social referrals. While these women possessed the educational credentials and basic technical skills, it was their proximity to company founders and cofounders that facilitated their getting information about new positions and interviews at start-ups or small firms that were not yet publicly traded.

Jade: A Chinese American Graphic Designer

Jade, a thirty-seven-year-old Chinese American, is a senior product designer. A native of California, Jade earned her undergraduate degree in communications from the University of Southern California, followed by a graduate degree in graphic design from the Parsons School of Design in New York City. Her career trajectory represents one pattern found among first-generation technology workers who studied art or design. Jade drifted into the technology industry through her proximity to friends who were embedded in the industry. She possessed social relationships that enabled her to transition into a technology career. Her boyfriend was a "built-in" mentor and a crucial form of geek capital. Describing her educational trajectory after she earned her undergraduate degree and secured a job in New York, Jade recalled her first years in the advertising industry before she secured a job at a start-up. Like some of the Black women in this study, she taught herself to code.

> I went to graphic design school at Parsons, New York. And again, we had Drawing 101 and Color Theory and Typography. . . . I would say my graphic design degree . . . did not prepare me for a career in design, in that the fundamentals were really important. But when I was in New York, working at a design agency, it was very evident that our clients needed websites designed and mobile apps and annual reports that were interactive. . . . It was a very small agency, and my boss was very old-school New York, strictly graphic design. So he started to rely on me and another designer as the young people to figure it out. So I would ask

friends, take online courses. . . . In terms of doing . . . information architecture, I felt like I had to learn on the fly. I felt like making it up as I
went along.

In 2010, when Jade was in her first job, a new commercial real estate
technology start-up called WeWork, headquartered in New York City,
began to provide flexible shared workspace for start-ups. The technology
industry was in a growth stage. This was the moment that Jade entered
the technology start-up industry.

I stayed at that agency until I felt like I wasn't learning very much from my
superiors anymore, and that was also around the time when, I don't know,
I guess tech start-up started cropping up. And I had a [girl] friend—do you
know WeWork, the coworking spaces? So I had a friend who was in business development, . . . director there. And he goes, "Yeah, I work with all
these start-ups. And they're all coming to our offices." And I went to visit
the first WeWork headquarters in New York and was like, "This is amazing.
Like, who works here?" So that exposed me to the world of start-ups. . . . I
was curious about it and felt that that was where things were going for me
to stay relevant in the industry. That was something that I should strive
towards. So that was when I joined my first tech start-up company.

The dramatic changes in client needs and the rapid shift from a print-
based to a digital culture prompted Jade to teach herself basic coding
languages and to build webpages. Once again, she turned to her boyfriend, an engineer, to help her upgrade her skills and develop digital
literacy.

When I was still in school, we had a class about a physical portfolio. So
that's what we learned. But right after I graduated, that same year things
started shifting. So I knew I needed something on the web. And that was the
first webpage that I coded myself in HTML and CSS. And luckily, . . . my
boyfriend at the time did computer science. He's an engineer. So he really took me through the baby steps and helped me a lot in buying the
server space and getting my own URL. So he was actually pretty instru-
mental in [developing my technical skills]. . . . I remember just going on
really simple websites and going to View Source. And there you could

see the code behind it and learning from that—like copying and pasting some things, then going into Dreamweaver and seeing it render into the visuals. I think we spent, uh, two or three weeks every evening, just kind of him walking me through it, me creating the assets that are needed for the websites.[2]

In addition to the mentoring that Jade received from her boyfriend, whom she met in high school and began dating during her senior year of college, a female friend and former classmate at Parsons School of Design provided her with a key contact. Her friend introduced her to a White male friend "who had his own start-up," which led to Jade employment at a tech start-up in New York.

> It was a good friend of mine at Parsons. She was the first person that I met there. She had an undergrad friend who was also in New York at the time who had his own start-up. His name was Matt. . . . It was like three degrees of friendship where I met this college friend. A friend of mine worked with Matt in the past. And Matt was the WeWork guy. . . . So Matt was sort of the hub of all these networks because he rents spaces to start-ups. So he knew the cofounder—I guess they rented a space from him in the past. So the cofounders of [the start-up], they're friends with Matt or they're coworkers, acquaintances. So, um, Matt and I started talking about how stagnant I felt at this agency. And he's like—this is—I remember this conversation at a bar—and he's like, "Okay, you don't sound happy at your job. Why are you still doing this? This is your life. Your work is the majority of your everyday, and you're living through it. So you need to find something, and let me ask around to see if anybody I know is looking for a designer." And so he put in touch with Cheryl, who is the founder of this company. And I interviewed with them and got the job.

An introduction from a friend and former classmate provided Jade with information about a job and access to the decision-maker, who interviewed Jade in a shared coworking space in the same building as a friend worked. We see that a social contact, rather than experience in this industry, provided Jade with an introduction to a female founder and a job offer. When we compare this to the experience of Maya, whom we met in chapter 3, we see the critical role that social referrals play early in one's career. Describing the interview process, Jade recalled, "I went to their office. . . . I showed them my—I had both the web portfolio and both my print list. So I walked them through all my work at the agency. And they told me about the responsibilities and what they needed for . . . a vision of what she wanted the web design to look like, and . . . we clicked well. It all felt very friendly. They were all nice, and, um, yeah, it wasn't a long process at all." Jade's pathway into Silicon Valley was facilitated by the social capital that she possessed.[3] Nan Lin defines "social capital" as "an investment and use of embedded resources for expected returns. . . . Social capital is conceptualized as (1) quantity and/or quality of resources that an actor (be it an individual or group or community) can access or use through (2) its location in a social network. The second conceptualization emphasizes locations in a network and network characteristics."[4] When we compare Jade's experiences to those of the Black women we met in chapter 3, we see the benefits of her social relationships—specifically her proximity to the founders or employees of start-ups in New York—and we see the costs of social closure for women whose friends are not embedded in the tech ecosystem. Jade is part of what she described as a "mini-migration from the East Coast." The founders of the start-up who hired her applied to a California-based accelerator program and were accepted. Jade then moved with the founders to Silicon Valley with the cofounders of the company,

Geneva: A Tenured Professor Becomes a Diversity Consultant

Geneva, who identifies as Black and Native American, is the head of global diversity for a technology firm. She is a forty-seven-year-old former university professor with degrees from Harvard and Stanford. Her career trajectory represents a second pathway found among women who had drifted into the technology industry after earning degrees in the arts or humanities. The transferrable skills she cultivated as an academic and the Stanford and Harvard alumni networks in which she was embedded smoothed her pathway into the Silicon Valley technology industry. The highest paid woman in this study, Geneva reported earnings of $250,000 per year. As a Stanford alumna, she did not experience the social closure and other obstacles described by the other Black women in this study.

Geneva entered the technology industry as a second career after teaching for more than a decade in the university system. A native of San Francisco, she was also embedded in two elite alumni networks, Stanford and Harvard, which provided her with a pathway into Silicon Valley that is common for women who have not earned degrees in computer science or engineering. Her alumni networks also shielded her from the forms of racism and workplace discrimination described by her Black peers. Before applying for positions at top technology firms such as Facebook and Google, she spent years developing her networks as a consultant in Silicon Valley. She ultimately secured a position at Google, which led to her current position at another major technology firm.

For almost a decade, Geneva taught at several universities in the Midwest and on the East Coast. Geneva left the academy because she "was desperately unhappy." With transferrable skills and more than a decade of experience in academia, she returned to her home of San Francisco and secured a job working for a research and consulting firm. After several years, Geneva launched her own consulting business. Describing her reasons for changing careers, she recalled her emotional state: "And I'd never been happy as an academic. It was always a series compromises, and when I got to the University of Massachusetts, I realized that I wasn't willing to compromise anymore. And so I didn't want to go back on the academic job market—you know exactly how that is. And so I just decided that I was really unhappy, and . . . whatever I did next— like even if I hated my job, if I got paid more, it would be better than hating my job and being paid very little." Geneva worked with a lot of clients, and they produced large-scale studies. After working in human resources and developing networks, Geneva started a consulting firm with a partner. Recalling how she successfully transferred her academic skills into a career in the corporate consulting world, Geneva noted, "If you've been an academic, you know how to teach, you know how to talk to audiences both large and small, you know how to build curriculums. So it was a way that I could use some of the skills that I'd gained as an academic in the corporate world. So that was my first role."

From there, Geneva applied for jobs at Facebook and Google. "I got a job at Google, and I actually applied on the website." Summarizing her transition from academia to securing her previous job at Google, she recalled,

That's how I got an expertise in HR and ended up working on diversity issues, so that when I applied for the role at Google, I had the experience to do it. . . . I had started a consulting practice with a partner. And then she left after nineteen months and decided she wanted to be an executive coach, and I didn't. And so that's how I got the role at Google. . . . And I was at Google for almost five years, and then a headhunter called me— well, a number of head hunters—and that's how I got the job at [name of company].

Geneva's transition from a moderately paid academic to a six-figure corporate salary demonstrates the ways that her status as a Stanford alumna provided her with access to technology networks—a form of geek capital and cultural capital that the Black women in this study, like Maya, Yvette, and Nicole, lacked. As a Stanford and Harvard alumna who was embedded in alumni networks of two of the most prestigious universities on the East and West Coasts of the United States, Geneva had a relatively smooth career transition. Her educational and social capital, combined with her academic skill set, enabled her to enter the technology industry without earning a degree in computer science or engineering.

The technology industry has been a rewarding experience and a place of refuge for Geneva. With no big data available on women who change careers, Geneva's career trajectory may represent a small fraction of the women employed in technology, but her experiences provide evidence of the value of social capital and belonging to an alumni network that provides access to information and social referrals to jobs. Her transition from an academic job to a technology consultant further highlights the role of social and cultural capital in career pathways. With a large amount of cultural, symbolic, and regional capital, Geneva successfully changed careers in midlife and entered the human resources sector of the technology industry, where women are more concentrated. Her occupational trajectory also calls attention to the absence of rigorous qualitative or quantitative data on women who leave their careers and do not follow a linear path from a degree in computer science or engineering but nevertheless earn some of the highest salaries in Silicon Valley. The career transitions of Black women in elite labor markets deserve more analysis from sociologists interested in gender and the new economy.

In the next section, we meet Simone, an engineer who also used social referrals to secure her current position. In Simone's case, we see the value of having a Black coethnic, who can serve as a mentor. Friends can become forms of geek capital. Like Jade and Geneva, she had access to a friend—through her husband's networks—who provided her with a social referral from a Black engineer in New York's technology sector.

Simone: A Ward of the State Becomes a Software Engineer

Simone is a twenty-eight-year-old Black software engineer. Simone has a heart-shaped face, wears no makeup, and wears her shoulder-length hair locked in dreads that are dyed blue toward the bottom. She has seven ear piercings and wears a mix of gold geometric studs, which is similar to how Beyoncé wears her earrings. When I met her, her nails are painted a neutral gray with brown undertones. She wore a round-neck black fitted blouse, and an arm-sleeve tattoo was visible. The yin and yang tattoos done by an artist based in Brooklyn, New York, remind her of balance. These symbols represent her values, and she has felt a need to signal these values as she described having to learn to embrace her body in all-White occupational spaces where she reported being routinely harassed.

A native of Virginia, Simone was a ward of the state as a child and grew up in a foster home in Virginia. She earned her bachelor's degree at the Rochester Institute of Technology (RIT). The financial support that she received from a state program in technology for high school students enabled her to enter RIT. She began her academic career as an international business student. After graduating, she became more committed to a career in technology.

> When I looked at my transcript at the end of it all, I had As and Bs in all of my tech courses. . . . I quickly realized these project-based courses that were oriented around tech were points where my GPA rose and points where I was most excited and most invested. I probably should have been in . . . the computing college at RIT. . . . I can't go back and change time. What I did do is to continue teaching myself code in grad school. . . . I integrated my tech world with change management, because I felt like those went hand in hand because technology changes all the time. I sort of just focused on management in grad school.

After Simone had earned her graduate degree, she began working as a data analyst for a nonprofit organization. She described her first year after graduate school: "I had to set up a data website for our data specialists. It was a network of seventy-something schools in New York City. Each school had a data specialist, so we had to cater to them in many ways. Not only did I have to do that, I also had to do other things that were highly related to coding, and a lot of it was database work mainly. It restarted the fire under me to remain in tech." Simone identified gaps in her experience and knowledge and created a plan to learn specific skills. Simone recalled how she gained her technical competence:

> I taught myself web development along the way. I created my own websites, my own portfolio, and I realized the base knowledge that I really need in order to fulfill the greater need of mine. I needed software engineering experience. So . . . my first job out of college . . . was actually a technology consultant or project manager . . . for this organization that served people who used to be in jail, prison, juvenile detention, or ex-cons and things like that. . . . The founders had a huge falling out, and the organization imploded at the end. My job ended after one month.

Like Maya, whom we met in chapter 3, Simone taught herself how to build websites. Simone met a South Asian software engineer who was recruiting for Google at a job fair. He placed her on the interview list, and she was called for a series of video interviews with Google. Describing her career trajectory and how she ended up withdrawing from the interview process with Google and accepting another position, she recalled asking him a series of questions:

> I went to this tech fair. I went around to different booths, . . . and then I ran into the Google tent, and there was this Indian man, Sanjay. . . . I wasn't really about to ask him for a reference or a job. I was just kind of wondering . . . what it is like being a software engineer: What tools do you use? What languages are you learning? What do I need to do to know so I can go out here and learn it so I can get these interviews? He saw that, and he was like, "I can put you in for an interview?" . . . He gave me his email, his Google email, his Gmail, and I sent my résumé and stuff. Then I got that interview with them.

Describing the interview process and why she accepted a job with the local CBS station instead of waiting for Google's decision, Simone recalled,

> It was tough. Google was tough. . . . Most of it—the first interview was a very screenish, . . . HR interview. The second was actually with a Google employee. The third interview was also with a Google employee with the team that I was most likely to be placed with, which was the YouTube team down in California. . . . They gave me a centralistic test, but like I said, I had three, so I got through it. I stumbled through it. . . . Then they were—these areas were like two, three weeks apart, but by the time the third interview came around, CBS local offered me the job. This is my first engineering job, so do I wait for Google, or do I just take this job? So I took the job at CBS local, and I had to email Google. I expressed interest with them, but I was like, "I'm taking this job offer." . . . They sent me [an email] back saying, "Well, we decided that you need a little more experience, anyway." . . . And I was like, "Okay, why interview me three times and waste my time?"

Simone lacked the cash reserves or savings to survive financially, that is, to remain unemployed while waiting for a decision from Google. Unlike women who had fathers, husbands, or siblings employed in the industry, she had no one who could provide economic support so that she could survive financially while she endured an interview process that could take several months, so she accepted the CBS job offer.

Women from poor and working-class backgrounds who cannot rely on their parents for support are not able to compete with middle-class young adults who can afford to remain unemployed for extended periods of time. Simone's experience highlights the lifelong effects of class privilege and the disadvantages that women like her have when competing with their middle-class peers in an interview process that can take several months without producing a job offer. She recalled, "I had to turn Google down in the process because they were just taking too long." Rather than waiting for an unknown period of time, taking the risk of not getting offered a position from Google, Simone accepted the position at the CBS affiliate.

Simone's husband, now a professional chef, began his academic career as a computer science major. He developed a close friendship with another Black engineering student. So Simone possessed a form of social capital that was not common among the Black women in this study. Her husband provided a crucial introduction to his friend, a Haitian American, who became a mentor. This Haitian American male friend told Simone about an available position, providing her with a social referral. He also coached her through her first interview. This interview was her first big break. "He reached out to me because I was already talking to him for a year. I was like, 'How do you do this? How do you do that?' We were talking back and forth. . . . He was like, 'Well, we're looking for a junior software engineer at my company,' which was CBS local, the news network local division. . . . So I just jumped into that shift once they gave me an interview." She described her relationship with her husband's friend: "He was one of the few people in my network, in my very small [Black] tech network at that time, who actually reached back and helped me. . . . He was like, . . . 'It's going to be a hard interview process, but I'm going to give you this chance.' So I got that door, and I just ran with it." Simone was coached on what to expect. Her husband's friend warned her about a specific White man and how to prepare for him. In her words,

> He basically warned me about the personalities that I'd be interacting with, and there was one personality [a White man] that would be generally tough, who was hardcore about computer science. . . . He said, "Just brush up on your computer science principles real quick and try to do your best with him. He's typically a hard ass." . . . Everybody else is just more personality questions . . . "[The White male interviewer] is going to ask you trick questions and stuff like that and try to trip you up and make you nervous because he's one of the many programmers I have come across that has a God complex almost." Especially as a White male programmer. . . . I did practice trick questions.

Simone expressed frustration that trick questions were consistently used when they were not relevant for the job. She explained, "I interviewed a bunch of times since then with different companies, different people, and they were very much asking things that they would consider a nice trip-up question for you. But it's not something they actually use at their own job or had probably thought of in a while. . . . It's very annoying when they do that because it doesn't actually test my knowledge in terms of what I actually know." In descriptions of the interview process, there was a pattern in which Black women described being asked questions that were not relevant to the actual job.

In relation to the other Black women interviewed in this study, Simone is an outlier because she is the only Black woman who received a referral from a Black engineer. She did not have to overcome social closure because she met a Black engineer who provided her with a social referral. Like Maya, she needed a referral from somebody already employed at a technology firm. Her pathway as a first-generation Black engineer further demonstrates the need for a social referral from a tech insider who can provide information about specific job openings. We also see the value of a coethnic who can provide specific information about how the interview process could unfold in ways that could sabotage an applicant and prevent her from performing her best.

Internships and University Job Fairs

Two related pathways to a technology job are university job fairs and summer internships. As students, some women had access to internships, which functioned as entry-level jobs that provided undergraduate and graduate students with technical training, work experiences, and industry mentors who could provide future social referrals. These internships served as a bridge to entry-level jobs at technology firms. The engineers and other technically trained women in this study identified summer internships as stepping stones that provided them with technical training and social referrals to secure their full-time positions. Internships were described by students who majored in computer science and engineering as bridges to full-time positions. These were skills-building opportunities that allowed them to establish relationships with technology workers while developing technical skills that they had not learned in the classroom in formal courses. In other words, paid internships provided them with opportunities to acquire and apply their classroom-based knowledge to real projects in the summers, while enrolled full-time as students.

In this section, we will meet three women (one White, two Black) who developed their technical experience through internships that led to social referrals. Their experiences as interns provided them with job skills and social relationships that enabled them to secure full-time jobs in the technology sector. For Natasha, Jasmine, and Monique, their experiences as interns at technology firms led to rewarding jobs. In Jasmine's case, an internship at a Google office led to a rewarding job in Silicon Valley. In the case of Monique, a Black Caribbean engineer, an internship in Costa Rica provided technical skills and experience that facilitated her securing a job at a start-up in New York City. We will also meet Natasha, a White woman from a rural background who attended an elite women's college on the East Coast. Although she was from a poor family, a scholarship provided her with access to an upper-middle-class network and an internship. Although by her own accounts, she was neither an exceptional student nor technically skilled, her Whiteness and a computer science degree enabled her to secure a competitive position in Silicon Valley immediately after graduation. I first turn to Natasha, an unmarried White woman who is a first-generation engineer employed in her first job.

Natasha: A Russian American from Rural Poverty

The twenty-four-year-old daughter of an Anglo-American mother and a Russian father, Natasha has been employed as a software engineer for six months. She met a recruiter at a university job, which led to her current position. She is currently seeking another position. Natasha grew up in White fundamentalist Christian community in rural Alaska. She earned a degree in computer science from an elite all-women's college in Massachusetts. Among the White women engineers (n = 30), she is the only one who grew up in rural poverty and did not grow up in the continental United States. She is one of the few non-Black women in this study from a poor and rural background, and her career trajectory is an example of the role that Whiteness and the symbolic value of a degree from an elite educational institution can play in a pathway to full-time employment in Silicon Valley. Although Natasha grew up without class privilege, her friendships with White middle-class peers and her access to knowledge enabled her to move up and become integrated into a

White upper-middle-class network. Describing her childhood interest in computing, she recalled, "I didn't grow up with anyone who was a software engineer. I had literally never read a line of code, didn't know what that meant. I thought computers were boring until a friend told me that our computer science classes were actually interesting. I would say that since then, the department kind of lit a fire under me. And I thought, 'This is really cool. I want to put a lot of effort into doing this.' I ended up taking a lot of computer science classes each semester."

As the daughter of a divorced mother who survived on welfare and parents who were not college educated, Natasha is an outlier among the White engineers. Nevertheless, her childhood friendship with a White middle-class girl and her own Whiteness and education at an elite East Coast school provided her with forms of cultural and symbolic capital that allowed her to "pass" as middle class. While the Black women in this study represented the most class diversity, with some growing up poor and others lower middle class or upper middle class, the White women who were engineers were almost uniformly from middle and upper-middle-class backgrounds. Among the technically skilled Asian American and Asian Indian workers, all had grown up in two-parent homes with university-educated parents. And through their familial and social networks, they acquired knowledge and direction from their parents, siblings, and extended family about their future academic choices. This was a form of capital that was taken for granted.

Natasha expressed a heightened awareness of the way her admission on a full scholarship into Wellesley had given her access to the experiences of women who had grown up with more class privilege. Her pathway into a technology career began with a childhood friendship with a White middle-class girl, who provided her with information that prompted her to apply for admission to an elite all-women's college in Massachusetts that she had never heard of. Due to her class background, she received a full scholarship and earned a degree without any debt. Describing her career trajectory, she recalled,

> I went to a liberal arts college in Boston that wasn't mainly focused on tech but had a computer science department. . . . And I started taking computer courses halfway through college—end of sophomore year. I'll start there because that's the first step I made in trying to get a job in tech.

I still felt like that there as a big disconnect between trying to get a job in the industry and trying to . . . succeed academically because we were a small school, and there wasn't a huge focus on tech like there is, for example, at MIT—the pipeline wasn't really there.

Natasha described the events in her career trajectory that led to her pathway toward a job in the technology industry. Natasha did not have the same extensive internship experiences as others did, so she began regularly attending job fairs at several universities in the Boston area, with the hope of meeting recruiters.

I went to a lot of events at other schools in Boston. I went to a lot of Hackathons sponsored in Cambridge, like at Harvard, MIT. . . . I got a sophomore internship. I was feeling really discouraged. . . . I know a lot of people in undergrad, in order to get their first full-time job, they usually have like two or three summers of internship. And then their last internship they convert into a full-time offer. I talked to this one person at a career fair who I didn't even remember talking to, and she emailed me back: "Hey, I remember you at the career fair. Would you like to interview?"

Natasha was thus able to access the social, symbolic, and network resources available to White women. Although her parents were not middle class, the status of her degree transferred symbolic capital to her. Describing the opportunities that came to her with little effort, she recalled,

I had one internship. . . . And it was definitely an internship geared towards people who are still trying to learn how to code—like not fully functional members of a software development team. And I end up getting offers to interview at large companies . . . with like basically . . . no experience. Some of the interviews were like really, really crazy. I'm going to talk about Amazon's interview because you probably won't believe me. I was not actively seeking out these jobs. . . . Honestly, I was definitely like severely underqualified for like competing with full-time jobs at these large companies, with people who had several more years of experience than I did. But I was offered to interview at some of these companies, and I took the offer.

When asked why she had been successful in securing a job as a software engineer, despite her limited technical skills, Natasha identified her gender, while not mentioning her race. She identified her gender as a crucial form of capital for companies trying to recruit more women as software engineers so that they could increase their diversity numbers among new hires. Natasha concluded that, in her view, most women applicants do not have a computer science degree, so her degree was an asset—a form of geek capital—when compared to the graduates of coding boot camps, even though she did not perceive her technical skills as superior. In her words,

> 'Cause I had a CS degree. I didn't actually really realize how important or what a big deal having a CS degree was, until I started going into the industry. . . . I'm on my second job now. And going back into the job market, I realized that I could basically get an interview with almost any company because I have a CS [. . .] Having a [computer science] degree and being female—there's not a lot of [us]. So they'll just ask you to interview probably. At the large companies, they have the resources. . . . In the Bay, [there] are a lot of women who code. A lot more of them are junior. And a lot more of them don't have CS degrees. We have a lot of boot camps and stuff. [The male recruiter at my firm] is desperately trying to hire women who are senior engineers—'cause all of them are at large companies basically.

In Natasha's analysis, the shortage of experienced women engineers has created many opportunities for women who possess her specific educational credentials. Although Natasha's computer science degree has not provided her with the technical skills that some of the Black women in this study possessed, she successfully secured a position as an entry-level software engineer. The small number of women engineers in Silicon Valley, combined with the gender gap in degree attainment in computer science and engineering degrees, enhanced the value of her degree.

Natasha also identified the coding boot camp phenomenon that emerged in 2012 in the San Francisco Bay Area. The emergence of so many coding boot camps increased the value of having a computer science degree for women. Natasha noted,

> So many people are learning to code right now [in the Bay Area] and going to coding boot camps for like three months and then trying to

find a job. If you have four years where you just decided to practice coding, you have such a huge advantage over people who have been coding part-time on their own for a year and then doing a full-time three-month gig. I was just not aware of that dynamic prior to coming to the Bay Area. But there are definitely enough start-ups out there. If you like do a boot camp, you'll find a [job] at a startup. . . . You'll find someone who needs someone to code, whatever your level.

Unlike the Black women from working-class or poor backgrounds in this study (see Maya and Camille in chapter 3), Natasha had a close childhood friend from a White upper-middle-class family. Her friend shared knowledge with her about elite all-women's colleges and encouraged her to apply for early admission to Wellesley. As an undergraduate, she secured internships that led to interviews with Amazon and other top technology firms. Her computer science major functioned as a form of cultural and symbolic capital that signaled a technical competence that she acknowledged she lacked. As a White woman, she also possessed racial capital in the form of Whiteness and symbolic capital—a degree from an elite school, which further integrated her socially into an upper-class network. Her racial status, that is, her Whiteness, and her educational credentials intersected with her perceived class status to give her access to an internship that was a stepping stone to a lucrative job in San Francisco.

Natasha's career trajectory and successful job search reveal how a symbolic system operates in Silicon Valley in which the value of a computer science degree for White women is enhanced due to the small number of young women who have computer science degrees and the dearth of experienced women engineers in a male-dominated profession. Natasha's lack of technical experience was not a liability in her job search because many technology firms are trying to increase the number of women engineers and improve their statistics on gender disparities in their workforce. They are willing to invest resources in training entry-level engineers, yet these same opportunities are not being offered to Black and Latina women, as reflected in the low numbers of these groups in technical positions.

In Natasha's analysis, the proliferation of accelerated engineering academies, or coding boot camps, has enhanced the value of her computer science degree. Her Whiteness, gender, and computer science degree from an elite school in Boston constituted forms of symbolic and cultural capital that gave her a competitive edge while not disrupting the racial and ethnic caste system in Silicon Valley, in which Asians and Whites continue to dominate. The forms of symbolic capital that Natasha possessed as a White women allowed her to secure interviews and offers for entry-level software engineering jobs at the top Silicon Valley technology firms.

I now turn to two two Black women, who also developed their technical experience through internships that led to social referrals. Their experiences as interns provided them with job skills and social relationships that enabled them to secure full-time jobs in the technology sector. In the case of Jasmine and Monique, their experiences as interns at top firms led to rewarding jobs.

Jasmine: A Black Pansexual Security Engineer from Kentucky

Jasmine is a twenty-nine-year-old Black engineer, employed as a dev-ops security engineer in San Francisco. She earned her degree in security engineering. A native of Kentucky, she grew up as the middle child in a family of five children. Jasmine identifies as pansexual and queer. All of her siblings have earned university degrees, and some have earned graduate degrees. However, in striking contrast to 90 percent of the Asian Indians and half of the White women in this study, no one in her family is employed in the technology sector. Describing what her job entails as a technically skilled security op, she explained how she works on infrastructure: "So usually when you're running an app like Tumbler or Twitter, you have to have a server that, you know, that runs that app—that takes the requests from users when they click on a tweet button. A server has to run that. So basically, what my job is to provide infrastructure that the app runs on and make sure that infrastructure is stable enough to keep the app running."

Since moving to the Bay Area, Jasmine has come out to her mother and her four siblings. She has not yet shared her sexual identity with her father: "My dad doesn't know because he is a very, very old southern man. . . . I think my dad wouldn't be able to handle it. . . . My mother's handling it by being in denial." She described her parents as religiously conservative Jehovah Witnesses, so as a child, she struggled to understand her attraction to women as well as men.

In the San Francisco Bay Area technology industry, identifying as LGBTQ is not stigmatized in the ways that it may be in other professions or regions of the United States. In Silicon Valley, gender fluidity and sexual expression is a celebrated form of diversity. Members of the LGBTQ community constitute a large and powerful political constituency there. However, Black and Latinx LGBTQ members continue to be invisible and excluded form most management and leadership positions, except in "diversity and inclusion." In 2014, the visibility of the LGBTQ community increased in the Silicon Valley technology industry when Tim Cook, the CEO of Apple, became the first CEO of a Fortune 500 company to come out publicly as gay. On October 30, 2014, in an interview with *Bloomberg Business*, Cook revealed, "For years, I've been open with many people about my sexual orientation. Plenty of colleagues at Apple know I'm gay, and it doesn't seem to make a different in the way they treat me."[5] Cook's decision to come out publicly as the first openly gay CEO in the Valley reflected a larger change in cultural attitudes in the United States.

In some Silicon Valley circles, while heteronormativity remains dominant, identifying as LGBTQ for the Asian and White techies in this study nevertheless functioned as a form of symbolic capital at their technology firms. Gays and lesbians who are members of the dominant ethnic groups can represent diversity and inclusion while not disrupting the ethnic and racial order that places Blacks and Latinx technology workers at the bottom of the power hierarchy. When asked what it meant to be queer, Jasmine replied, "I think queer for me is . . . a kind of the identifier without saying specifically what's your sexuality. . . . But if I had to get down to specifics . . . I stated 'pansexual' [on the survey] because I've been attracted to a lot of people, and it's not just male or female. Some of them have been trans[sexual]."

At almost six feet tall and full-bodied, Jasmine performs in drag in her leisure time and does not make efforts to adopt markers of conventional femininity. Why is her sexual expression important? In the Bay Area, being queer or pansexual is no longer a status or identity that is always associated with the job discrimination that Blacks and Latinx continue to endure. Thus, as a woman who self-identifies as queer and pansexual, Jasmine has access to a large professional community of support in the tech industry.

When Jasmine was asked how she got interested in a career in technology, she recalled her passion for computing in childhood and how she benefited from a state program in Kentucky:

> I got into tech because I was very, very curious and liked to work with my hands. So—but the thing that got me into it is because I saw computers, and I wanted to know how they worked . . . and taking stuff apart. In middle school, there was a program called the Student Technology Leadership Program (STLP). It's an organization in Kentucky. So I got involved in that when I was in middle school, and it taught me kind of the basics as computers were becoming kind of a big thing or the internet. And things were starting to become interconnected, and people started becoming more dependent on computers because they had UIs [user interfaces] at the time that were actually usable. So I started using computers, and I also at the same time started teaching about how to use computers. When I was young, I was teaching older teachers how to use a computer and how to use a mouse and how to interface with the desktop. And this was when I was twelve, thirteen years old.

Jasmine's paid work experience as a teenager distinguished her from all of the other technology workers in this study. Jasmine's career trajectory differed from that of the other women of working-class origins of all backgrounds because she began working and being paid for her technical labor as a teenager. Describing her first paid employment when she was fifteen years old, she recalled,

> I worked for them for two summers. . . . It was for Louisville Gas and Electric. It was a utility company in town, and I had gotten an internship with them. . . . They were basically phasing in new models to replace old models of machines, and they needed somebody to just basically go through and image the new machines and configure them for the users and transfer their data before, you know, in migrating to new machines. So basically, I did that for two summers. . . . I got that job through the Student Technology Leadership Program (STLP) in high school. And I was

able to talk with them and go through interviews. I forget which specific program STLP was connected with in order to get me that job, but I got it. It was not only my first tech job, but it was my first taste of a tech [firm] paying higher wages. . . . When I got my first paycheck from tech, and my dad was looking at my pay stub, he was like, "You are getting paid more than I did on my first construction job."

Jasmine is the only Black technology worker among the women technology workers in this study (n = 65) who identified as queer and pansexual. Jasmine's experiences as a young girl growing up in a working-class family differ from the other first-generation technology workers in this study due to the young age in which she entered the paid labor force. None of the other technically skilled women had worked as a technically skilled paid employee as a teenager. Her wages helped support her family. Instead of "playing" with technology as a toy or a game, as some of her middle-class peers who did not have to work for wages as adolescents did, she entered the paid workforce and developed on-the-job technical skills before entering college.

I did a really great job for the first summer, and so they let me back the second summer before I left for college. And yeah, it was a really good job where I learned a lot about different technologies and networking. . . . I also learned about Oracle and all the minutiae in trying to install and troubleshoot Oracle machines. Because Oracle is a devil. . . . Try to install their software suites. It's always like a ten-step process that could break in any sort of way. Or you have to specifically have some special type of configuration. But it's helpful to have that experience specifically in those technologies because when I went to future jobs, they were like, "Oh, can you install this Oracle suite?" And I was like, "Okay, where's the documentation?" They're like, "Oh, it's this ten-step process." And it's like I'm already familiar with it and the ways that it can break. . . . It made me prepare for when I went to college and I was looking for jobs on campus. That's how I became a lab technician on campus, because I had that background experience.

Jasmine was self-taught before she entered college. This pattern of informal learning was pronounced among half of the Black women in this study and represents a pattern that distinguished them from the Asian American and Asian Indian women in this study. Jasmine was self-directed, self-motivated, and self-employed. Describing her period working as an intern at Google's Boston office, where she spent two years, she recalled,

> [The interns] learn everything that they need to know about Google and infrastructure and enterprise at that big of a scale, and then at the end, they pick the best and the brightest of the group to either stay or they can pick whether to apply internally or that can leave and go someplace else— which is exactly what happened. I was a part of the very, very first class of that program. There were only two women. Both of us were Black and female out of thirty [interns]. . . . We did have two other men of color. One was Hispanic. One was Black. . . . There were more people of Asian and Indian descent in tech than anything else. They're considered in the White demographic because there's more of them [in the technology industry].

After interning for two years, Jasmine decided to leave before her Google residency ended. When asked why she left, she explained, "I ended up leaving early for two reasons: first, . . . a job was offered to me, and second, I just got tired of working at Google. I just got tired of being in the program, and because I had found a different job, I was just like, 'Okay, I'm ready to go.' . . . Basically because . . . I had a really, really bad manager, and that led me to having no support." Describing her job-search process, Jasmine pointed to her internship at Google and the social referrals it provided as a significant stepping stone to securing a permanent full-time on-site position at a different firm. That internship on her résumé provided her with a form of symbolic capital that opened doors. Summarizing her job search, Jasmine recalled,

> I eventually wanted to be a system administrator. That's what I wanted, so I started looking for jobs that either put me in a position to make that move or would kind of be a close stepping stone. And I eventually—I interviewed at a whole lot of places. I interviewed at Twitter. . . . I basically hit the ground running when it came to inter-views. But I eventually ended up at another company, and I think I

either applied to them or reached out to them, but once they read my résumé, [they offered me a job]. It was basically probably the first company that courted me, like I was an ex-Google employee.

The value of an internship at Google cannot be overstated. It was like a social referral. When Jasmine was asked how she learned about jobs, she replied, "For most of the jobs, I've either been [socially] referred, or I've applied for the job. And when it comes to vouching, you know, references and who I'm connected with, usually somebody's who's trying to hire me knows somebody [I know]." The role of social contacts and connections can be more important than one's actual technical skills because Black women need to be "authorized" by non-Blacks in the industry. Although Jasmine's experiences as an intern had been very challenging, because she was grieving the loss of two family members during her first year, the value of being a former Google intern verified her "geek cred" and made her desirable.

Monique: A Black Latina Graphic Designer

The twenty-six-year-old daughter of a Puerto Rican father and a Haitian mother, Monique identifies as a Black Latina. Employed as a user interface designer for two years, Monique earned bachelor's degree in graphic design. The daughter of a bilingual parents, including a Spanish speaking father who worked as an accountant, she grew up in upstate New York in a two-parent family, who had high expectations for her. As an interface designer, Monique is responsible for how an app looks, which includes the visual architecture of the app. Her job is to design the menu that is used to navigate an app, including the buttons, typeface, colors, and location of icons. In other words, Monique is responsible for the functionality of the app and the user's interaction with the navigation tools.

Monique attended a large public high school in a neighborhood in upstate New York that she described as "crime-ridden." Yet she took advantage of the educational opportunities that were available to her. In high school, she developed a passion for visual communication and graphic design, which she majored in when she attended college. She described the public school that she attended:

My high school was pretty large, around three thousand kids. I graduated with around eight hundred. So the way it was broken up into different academies, I entered the communications academy. . . . My sophomore year, every quarter, they would take a different type of communications. One quarter was more writing focused; one was video-production focused. And then the visual communications one happened to be the last quarter of my sophomore year. That's where I had a really awesome teacher, Mr. Gabeheart, and that's where I learned Photoshop and Illustrator and all that. The next year, I kind of decided to continue [visual communication] as an elective. . . . I worked for the *NFA Word*; it was our school magazine. My title was photo editor.

After earning a degree in graphic design from the Rochester Institute of Technology, Monique needed to gain experience before entering the US job market. Although her father was an accountant, as a Black man who did not work in the tech industry, he did not have the networks to get her a job at a New York–based tech firm. She did not have mentors in the industry, so she searched online and applied for internships outside the United States in order to get work experience. She left the United States in order to build up her résumé. She reflected on her transition after graduation: "I went to Costa Rica, . . . an internship for a nonprofit org. I did that for about three months. . . . And then I moved to [New York City], and I started working for this start-up company in financial technology. My title there—I started as an intern for a month or two, and then I was a junior graphic designer. That was when I first kind of started doing what I'm doing now, like user interface design."

Because Monique did not have mentors and did not have parents employed in the industry and did not have experience as an intern, she had to leave the country to get the experience to compete on the job market. Her fluency in Spanish was also a skill that helped her to navigate in a bilingual environment. Describing the first two years of her career development, she recalled,

When they first hired me, I was doing a lot of different things. I would do user interface design but then also marketing stuff, branding stuff, and kind of that. I was there for two years. My last year there, there was the creative director, and then it was myself and one other graphic designer.

And then as the company started growing, they started separating. So he was more on the marketing side, and I was more on the product side. I was in charge of doing all the interface for the application. I was the liaison between our team and our tech team—we had an outsource development team in India. So I was the liaison between that. I ended up not being as happy there, so I left and came to the job that I have now, . . . which has been great and I absolutely love so far. Now I'm officially a user interface designer. . . . Over this past year, I learned a ton about UX and a lot more—because with UX, you know, we need to know a lot about psychology and sociology.

Monique's experience, once again, represents a nonlinear path into a technically skilled position. Lacking the friendships, family capital, and social capital that some of her Asian, White, Latinx, and Anglo-American peers possessed, she leveraged her fluency in Spanish and left the United States to gain the experience that she needed to compete on the job market. An internship in Costa Rica gave her the professional experience that she needed in order to secure her next job in New York City, where she was hired at a start-up. Monique's experience shows how an exclusive focus on science and math education can be a barrier and operate against the recruitment of Black women who want to combine their interest in arts and technology into a career.

Although Monique did not have the class privileges and educational advantages of her middle-class peers, her experiences represent how Black Latina women can mobilize their resources to position themselves so that they can gain the additional work experience they feel they needed. As a first-generation Black technology worker, Monique was able to leverage her language skills to gain work experience in Central America, which enabled her to establish the foundation for a technology career in the United States. She developed transferrable skills that enabled her to move both horizontally and vertically into a higher-wage and more rewarding job in a more supportive environment.

Carla: A Black Technical Trainer

Carla, a forty-six-year-old, cisgender, Black Caribbean software engineer, is a technical trainer for a San Francisco firm. The daughter of a college professor and a teacher, she grew up in a solidly upper-middle-class household on the East Coast. Her parents sent her to an elite private boarding school in preparation for college. She earned a degree in computer science from the University of Massachusetts at Amherst and later earned a master's degree in technology. She described her early exposure to computing: "I had been coding since I was in high school. My dad bought me a Commodore Pet. . . . I was the one who was the computer geek in the computer lab [at my boarding school]." In contrast to the other Black women in our study, she had an upper-middle-class childhood of privilege, which enabled her to try out a number of other fields before deciding on computer science.

Carla's class privilege gave her the confidence to experiment with different jobs before changing course and switching to the tech industry. She knew that her parents could provide her with the financial support needed to take risks as she considered a range of career options. Like some of the White tech workers interviewed, Carla first majored in several other subjects before committing to a computer science course of study. She began as a dance major and described the realization that led her to change her career goals: "Every summer I would go to New York City in between breaks in college. . . . I would live the life of a starving actor or actress. I rented a room, would do auditions. I'll never forget. I was working at a restaurant called Honeysuckle as a waitress. And there was another waitress. . . . She was thirty. And I thought, 'Oh my God, she's so super old, and she's a waitress still trying to make it.' That's when I came back, and I was like, 'I need to find a different degree.'" She then switched to oceanography before settling on computer science. After securing a position in the technology industry as a consultant, she switched her job:

> I decided I wanted to do less consulting, and I kind of wanted a more stable nine-to-five. So I became a software developer. . . . And I wanted to actually code and create something, a system. . . . So I went to [this company] and became a software developer. I did that for three years. . . . But it was very isolating. While at [this company], I saw this job opportunity as a technical trainer, where you teach developers how to code using our tools. . . . Within six months, I excelled and became the top trainer. They said I had a gift for being able to take very technical information and break it down in a way that was consumable by the masses.

When her company was bought in a hostile takeover by Oracle, she found herself unemployed. Carla then took what she described as "some really mundane job: "[It] paid me a lot of money but I did nothing. After a year, I quit. I went to grad school full-time while having my own company full-time because I did consulting. . . . I was back in the whole development realm. So we did data mapping, data management, converting systems over. I did that full-time while I was in grad school for two years."

Carla's class status and friendship network provided her with the social capital and the opportunity to be promiscuous in her job experiences, distinguishing her from all of the other Black women in this study, except for perhaps Geneva. In Carla's case, a network of technology professionals helped her pave the way to her current position as a technical trainer. Her upper-middle-class network also shielded her from some of the overt forms of racial discrimination routinely reported by Black tech workers who grew up in lower-income and poorer communities and in racially and socially segregated urban neighborhoods in the Bay Area without a critical mass of Black technology professionals.

Conclusion

An analysis of the career trajectories of seven women from diverse ethnic, class, and regional backgrounds shows the role that social networks, alumni networks, and racial capital play in the technology job market. For Natasha, her childhood friendship with an upper-middle-class White girl provided her with information and the encouragement to apply to an elite private college, where she received financial support and became immersed in an exclusive network. Once she earned her degree, she leveraged her gender and racial status as a White woman to enter the technology industry.

All of the Black women in this study were first-generation technology workers, and more than half (nine out of fourteen) were from impoverished or working-class backgrounds. In striking contrast, only 20 percent of the Asian Americans in this study and 10 percent of the India-born women in this study were first-generation engineers—that is, they were the daughters, siblings, cousins, and spouses of engineers.

5

Second-Generation Geek Girls

Ellen Pao is the US-born daughter of Chinese immigrants, including a mother who was "one of the first women to earn a PhD in computer science from the University of Pennsylvania." Pao comes from a distinguished and highly educated pedigree. Her mother was a trailblazer in a male-dominated industry, who successfully combined marriage and motherhood and spent "much of her career at Bell Labs, where she became a star, joining one of the most hardcore, respected research teams there."

> My dad was a born professor. He loved to teach, to do research, to be part of intellectual discussions. After Princeton, he spent most of his career at NYU's Courant Institute, with stints at Brown, MIT, and the Los Alamos National Laboratory.... Together, my parents encouraged our interest in math and science from a very early age. I can recall the exact moment I fell in love with learning how things work: at age four, after playing with a toy electric train with dying batteries. Seeing and understanding how something could go from working to not working and back again seemed to me like magic.[1]

Ellen Pao's trajectory represents a pattern of class advantages, including access to elite educational institutions, found among the US-born Chinese daughters of immigrants and India-born women from middle-class and upper-caste backgrounds in this study. Pao, like her Asian Indian peers, had been socialized by her parents to perceive engineering and technology careers as gender neutral and class appropriate. In her memoir, Pao says that she did not perceive her gender as a liability until she began to experience workplace sabotage. In contrast to many of the first- and second-generation White women engineers in this study, Pao did not describe engineering as a "masculine" profession.

In addition to Pao's hard work, she benefited from the resources that flowed from parents who were able to buy a home in an area with excellent schools. "When my father started teaching at NYU, we settled in Maplewood, New Jersey, for the good schools, the space, and the privacy."[2] While Pao describes forms of discrimination that she encountered as a child, these forms of discrimination were mediated by her parents' economic capital, which gave her exclusive access to educational experiences restricted to only the most privileged precollege teenagers, including attending classes at NYU as a thirteen-year-old. "As I became more proficient, my mom brought home a battered copy of *The C Programming Language* book, the now iconic coding bible written by her coworkers, and gave me access to the servers at her office. At age thirteen, I was taking the train into the city to take computer classes at NYU. It was thrilling and inspiring and sparked a love for technology that still drives me today."[3]

As these recollections by Pao show, her highly educated and well-positioned parents transferred class advantages to her that provided access to forms of educational, symbolic, and social capital that mirrored those reported by the India-born women in this study. Pao's educational credentials, her ethnicity, and the class status of her parents gave her access to exclusive schools, which distinguished her from her peers of working-class backgrounds.

I begin this section with the educational trajectory of Ellen Pao because her experiences represent a pattern of intersecting advantages (class, educational, family capital) found among second-generation engineers. Because she was the daughter of two engineers, her childhood socialization created a matrix of opportunities found among the US-born Asians and Anglo-Americans and the India-born engineers who were the second generation and in some cases third generation of engineers in their families. I provide an intersectional analysis of second-generation technology workers who are Asian American, Anglo-American, and Indian women who come from middle-class and upper-caste backgrounds to illuminate and theorize how non-meritocratic factors operate and their role in career outcomes. The university-educated and technically skilled Black women in this study described having very different experiences from their Asian and White peers. Although they were native English speakers and had relevant job experience, they described struggles that distinguished them from the women who entered the US industry as foreign nationals. Black women who had years of experiences described struggling to get hired after presenting evidence of their skills, while White women with no experience described being offered jobs by top technology firms.

I now turn to three Asian American and European American engineers, who represent one pattern found among the second-generation US-born engineers. In the following section, we meet Tyler, Joelle, and Britney—all three are the daughters of male engineers and the second generation in their families to become engineers. For 40 percent of the White American women in this study, their fathers who were engineers played a decisive role in supporting their daughters' early interest in technology. They also, like many of the Asian Indian engineers in this study, identified their parents, usually their father, as playing a significant role in directing them into computing careers as children.

Tyler: Transgender Daughter of White Immigrants from South Africa and New Zealand

Tyler is the thirty-three-year-old White daughter of a South African engineer. She identifies as female at work and as a nonbinary transgender outside of work. Employed as an engineering manager at a Silicon Valley technology firm, she earned her degree at MIT in 2007. Describing her career trajectory, she began with her childhood in North Carolina, growing up as the daughter of a White South African father with roots in Latvia and a mother from New Zealand:

> I kind of came to [computer science and engineering] because my dad suggested it at one point in high school, "Take this computer, take this programming class. I think you'll like it." He didn't really do programming, but he was an electrical engineer, and I actually had to like—it was actually at the same time as orchestra, so I like quit doing music to take this programming class, and it was pretty great. And so I didn't have a lot of intentionality with how that then progressed. I also took like an after-school program, Science Olympiad, where I was building like Rube Goldberg machines with friends, and for me there's just like this collaborative aspect that I hadn't found in my personal life other than through

sports. . . . There [was] a lot of discouragement around sports and arts and a lot of encouragement around, you know, more masculine professions like more employability in the standard sense in the US.

Among the daughters of White male engineers, Tyler is exceptional in that she did not grow up with the class privilege or financial stability of the other second-generation Asian and White engineers in this study. She was also keenly aware of the precarity of her class privilege. Her analysis of power aligned her more closely with the racially conscious Black women than with the White women in this study. Her family had experienced downward mobility and was not solidly middle class. As a result, her parents were not able to provide her with the economic stability that her White middle-class peers took for granted.

Tyler's family history is that of a mixed-status family with regard to education and class position. Her father, who is of eastern European origin, experienced downward mobility to the United States for a job. Her mother did not have a college education and worked in gender-segregated, low-wage, low-status, and feminized secretarial positions. In contrast to the other White daughters of engineers, Tyler is very conscious of the economic stability that she now possesses, which distinguished her from her parents.

> I mean, my whole family has had a lot of employment trouble throughout my life, and I haven't. And I do feel a certain kind of privilege. I'm now thirty-two years old in tech in San Francisco. . . . I can see this. Like, it wasn't always clear to me that employability was like a good path, but I feel a certain privilege from that. I think that's what [my parents] were shooting for in their understanding of, like, you know, a math, science, engineering degree kind of thing.

Although Tyler described her class background as "middle class," her parents did not possess the wealth—the economic or social resources—that the middle- and upper-middle-class daughters of Indian and Chinese immigrants described. She described her parents: "My mom didn't graduate college, but also some of this may have just been being foreign. . . . My dad had a degree, but it's a foreign degree. . . . No one would think they're immigrants—you know, we're White—but I think navigating all that, my mom just had a lot of trouble in holding jobs." In describing her family's immigration trajectory, Tyler identified a series of migrations beginning in Latvia to South Africa and then from South Africa to Australia, ending in North Carolina.

In Tyler's description of how her father's health condition led to a downward spiral, we see the fragility of class status even for White European immigrants from South Africa who have professional degrees and class privilege at the time of migration:

> My dad . . . got diagnosed with a disease that was like meant to be fatal in the short term, but he actually lived for like twenty years with it before he got a liver transplant. He's still alive. But once he had his transplant actually, he got fired. I think the insurance was too much. I don't know. I don't exactly know all my parents' situations. They went bankrupt during the—they had a house, and they foreclosed on it like ten years ago or when the recession happened. So yeah, it's kind of been—it's hard for me to know exactly. It's hard for me to describe.

Describing why she chose MIT for college, she noted, "I went to MIT for people who care about credentials." Tyler provided a nuanced analysis of the symbolic value of her degree and of gender politics. While she recognized that femininity can be a liability for cisgender women in the industry, it was not an issue for her. Tyler's experiences represent a pattern found among queer or gender-fluid women who identified socially and culturally with men and had established good mentoring relationships.

> I definitely didn't feel so isolated, I think for me, and this is why I think I'm a terrible woman. For me, navigating the male-dominated world is like way more familiar than—I didn't really learn how to have female friendships, or like relationships, until like five years ago. So to me, [male-dominated teams] was a more comfortable space. I didn't really fit in, but I didn't really fit in anywhere. And so I think I also have been really—I think I'm very mentorable. . . . I think it was a lot easier for older guys to see in me like someone they wanted to mentor, like see themselves like more so than someone who is just really feminine. . . . In that sense, I've actually, I think, had some successes that I found that kind of encouragement and support. In some places, you know, . . . there's definitely been

times I have not had that. I've left jobs like numerous times with terrible managers. I wanted to change my major in college, but didn't like—I couldn't figure out what else to do. I mean, like, that happens, but I've been pretty lucky.

What Tyler described here complicates and nuances the sociological literature on gender discrimination and inequality in the workplace. We see the importance of an intersectional analysis, one that does not flatten the experiences of gender-fluid White women nor erase important distinctions in their class background, immigration status of parents, and occupational culture of their firms. In this study, White and Asian American who also identified as gender-fluid or gender-queer, as reported in earlier research, expressed more satisfaction and belonging in the workplace.[4]

The economic challenges that Tyler's family faced limited their ability to help her financially and highlight the limits of analyses of career paths that homogenize White women or the daughters of highly skilled immigrants. As the daughter of White immigrants who had grown up in South Africa and then migrated to Australia, a former British colony and one of the Commonwealth countries, Tyler did possess the comparable racial advantages of the daughters of highly educated immigrants from Asia, Europe, and Latin America. However, her mother's lack of educational credentials and possible mental health issues, which Tyler alluded to, placed her in a very different economic and emotional climate from that of her middle-class peers who immigrated on student visas or family reunification visas. They had larger support networks that Tyler's father lacked, and as White nationals of South Africa, they would not be perceived as "African Americans" in the same way as immigrants from Nigeria or other Black-majority African nations.

Joelle: The Daughter and Sister of Engineers

Joelle is a twenty-six-year-old White software engineer who has been employed at a top technology firm in San Francisco for five months. A second-generation engineer in her first job, Joelle is the daughter of a mechanical engineer and a geologist. Joelle secured her current position after completing an internship at the company that now employs her. Her sister interned at this same company but now works as an engineer for Google. Internships like these, in which students are trained for full-time employment, are essential for securing an entry-level position after college graduation.

Joelle's father and sister played a central role in her pathway into technology. When she was a child, her father encouraged and actively supported her interest in robotics. Her older sister referred Joelle for her current position after having secured an internship years earlier at this same company. The role of Joelle's sister in helping her secure an internship is an example of an opportunity-hoarding mechanism that Richard Reeves calls "informal allocation of internships."[5]

Like the other engineers interviewed for this study, Joelle's parents provided her with experiences that exposed her to the field of electrical engineering. As a very young child, Joelle began working on electrical engineering projects with her father. When she was six years old, she and her father began working on soldering projects, where they made computer circuit boards. Later, as a high school student, Joelle joined a robotics club. She described how her robotics club solidified her interest in pursuing engineering as a career: "And I was also one of the original members on our robotics teams that formed during our junior year. These robots would be five feet tall and like 120 pounds. They're big robots. There was a big component of mechanical engineering—just kind of figure out where the electricity needs to go and lay everything out. From what I saw there, I thought that electrical engineering would be the most interesting."

Joelle's father volunteered to serve as a mentor to the robotics club after he learned that his daughter had joined the club. For Tyler, as for other White women interviewed, her parents played a key role in supporting her informal education in childhood, through play and coursework:

> My dad, when he found out I was on the robotics team, he started mentoring. It was good. Everybody learned how to . . . do whatever they needed to do to make the robot happen. . . . Mentors helped the team by breaking down the new problem. Each year you got a new problem. Shooting basketballs into targets might be one of them or balancing on some sort of balance board. . . . They have a couple of different ways that you do offense and defense. So they would help break down what was just

announced to us. Everybody would say all the ideas they had for making theirs the best strategy. They would kind of guide us through it.

Joelle had a family member who mentored her as a child, or what Judith McIlwee and J. Gregg Robinson term a "built-in" mentor.[6] As the daughter and sister of engineers, she had access to an ongoing source of information, support, and social referrals that was a pattern among the second-generation engineers in this study. Like other second-generation Asian and White technology workers interviewed, Joelle described an educational and social universe where Blacks and Latinx were completely absent. In other words, her childhood and educational environment was racially and culturally homogeneous. When she described her workplace, another pattern emerged that was similar across both generations—the stark absence of Black and Latinx coworkers on her team or in her workplace. The demographics of her current workplace mirror the dismal demographic data reported by Silicon Valley technology firms during the period 2014–19.

Joelle's father played a key role in cultivating her interest in engineering. Both Joelle and her older sister are engineers. The daughters of engineers in this study learned to model themselves after their fathers, which may have insulated them from feeling isolated if they found themselves in male-dominated classrooms when they pursued their undergraduate and graduate degrees in engineering. Like the Asian Indian women in this study, Joelle did not perceive engineering as a "masculine" profession. This pattern also emerged in the narratives of the career pathways of Anglo-Americans and Chinese Americans.

Britney: The Daughter of an Engineer and a Chip Designer

Britney is a native of California, an engineer and the twenty-six-year-old daughter of Chinese immigrants in the technology industry. She represents another pattern among the US-born Asian American women in this study, as her career pathway illuminates the ways that family resources, class privilege, residential status, and access to elite alumni networks can facilitate a smooth and linear path to a career as a software engineer. Britney grew up in an upper-middle-class and exclusive residential neighborhood in the heart of Silicon Valley. After she completed graduate school and earned a degree from Stanford, she returned home to live with her parents. She is now saving money so that she can buy a home in one of the most expensive residential markets in the United States.

Small in stature, Britney exudes confidence and speaks in an authoritative tone. During her interview, Britney wore the standard tech uniform: a dark T-shirt, no makeup, and no jewelry. As a child, she attended distinguished and high-ranking public schools. Britney benefited from class privilege and guidance from her father, who has worked in the tech industry his entire life. Her well-resourced high school in Silicon Valley provided her with access to computer science courses. Residential segregation by race and class in Silicon Valley also gave her access to educational resources that are not available to Black, Latinx, and White students living in segregated and poorer school districts.

Britney recalled having no interest in computer science when she entered high schools. Describing her educational trajectory, she identified her engineer father as responsible for her decisions to enroll in specific courses: "He's always been on top of the tech industry. . . . He was also the one who pushed me to do the computer science AP test—the class and then the AP test—because he thought that would be a good fit for me. I was originally not interested in that at all." Despite her disinterest and reluctance to study computer science, her father pushed her and her younger sister into technology careers. He bought the family a home computer and, later, a personal laptop for Britney to do her school work. On her fourteenth birthday, Britney's father bought her a video-game system. She admitted to rarely playing and recalled that they were mostly used by her friends. Though gaming seems designed as a leisure activity, Britney's father viewed it as a strategic resource to build her technical competence.

Britney attended an elite public high school that offered an elective course in computer programming, which was designed and led by one of the school's English teachers. It was a course that Britney described as the teacher's passion project—one that was unusual for high schools of this era. This is an example of the benefits she accumulated by growing up in an upper-middle-class residential neighborhood in Silicon Valley. Britney was a reluctant student of computer science. As she recalled,

I didn't want to take this computer science class. My dad made me. . . . [I learned that] computer science is much more creative [than I had initially thought]. You're developing something. You're using this language to write out what you're trying to do. There are multiple right ways to do the same thing. One is more elegant. One is more straightforward. . . . And so [my father] felt that it was artistic enough to interest me and that, yes, later one that would turn into a good career if I continued with that. So he convinced me to take [an] AP class [in computer science].

In Britney's narrative of her occupational pathway, she clearly identified how her father, a built-in mentor, directed her career and gave her privileged access to a wealthy and well-resourced public high school with a computer science curriculum. Britney was a reluctant computer science major and had no particular passion for the subject. Rather than being passionate about and interested in computer science, she was a dutiful daughter who obeyed her father and pursued the path that her parents chose for her, which led to a graduate degree at Stanford after an undergraduate degree at a University of California campus. Britney's experiences follow a pattern among Asian Americans and Asian nationals that has been documented in the literature on degree attainment in STEM fields.[7] Asians and Asian Americans, regardless of their interest or passion in a subject, are more likely than non-Asians to enter computer science or engineering because of parental expectations.

Later, as an undergraduate, Britney chose computer science as her major. The program offered a general overview of computer science as a field, with limited technical training. After graduation, Britney entered Stanford University, where she pursued a master's degree in computer science. The move from a public university to Stanford highlights the superior and exceptional resources available at private elite universities. Describing her transition from undergraduate to graduate school, Britney recalled,

I was always a computer science major, so I went from undergrad and started looking for jobs. And I had internships over the summer. My current job, . . . someone from this company reached out to me. . . . I think they just found my email address off one of our Stanford websites. Like, I was a Stanford alum. . . . Basically, his strategy was to contact the TAs of certain classes that were related to what his company does. . . . Then I did a phone screen. And [then] I did a couple of on-site interviews.

Here we see the value of attending one of the top-ranked US universities from which Silicon Valley recruits entry-level engineers. The resources and internships that flowed to Britney as a Stanford alumna are evident. Britney, like the India-born women in this study, followed a linear path established by her father. In contrast to the Black women in this study, her pursuit of a degree in computer science was neither self-driven nor a result of her passion for the field. It was a pragmatic decision initiated by her parents. Britney followed her father's pathway. As the resident of an upper-middle-class community full of technology workers, Britney acknowledged that she had privileged access to excellent educational, social, and cultural resources that the working-class Black women who grew up in poor and racially segregated communities did not have.

Conclusion

In this chapter, I have employed an intersectional analysis to show the variation in the experiences of second-generation Chinese American and European American women. While the daughters of engineers often benefit from their childhood proximity to parents who can serve as "built-in mentors," as we see in the case of Britney, for Tyler, the mental and physical health of her parents mediated the forms of capital (and advantages) that they possessed. Due to the struggles of Tyler's parents, they did not have the economic stability that is assumed in middle-class families. Tyler's experiences provide a cautionary tale and suggest that intergenerational transfer of class privilege is not guaranteed and is not always a smooth process. Tyler's experiences also show how Whites who are marked as "foreign" are not always advantaged, particularly if they do not have a visible and vibrant diasporic niche to support them. Women like Ellen Pao who have parents who can offer them economic support, access to the best education, and childhood mentorship are prepared for a career in technology.

In chapter 6, I shift my focus to the occupational pathways of foreign nationals. I examine the central role that transnational migration plays in providing opportunities for middle-class women from Colombia, Mexico, and India, who have portable forms of capital that they bring with them and that provides them with the economic resources and educational credentials that are then interpreted as "meritorious" by recruiters and technology firms. The women engineers we will meet in chapter 6 arrived as foreign nationals on student visas or spousal visas and benefited from a matrix of privileges including several forms of "family" capital that established a clear legal pathway for them to secure permanent residency.

6

Transnational Geek Girls

Mobile, Middle Class, and Upper Caste

This chapter focuses on immigration as a pathway to a Silicon Valley career for middle-class women from South Asia and Latin America. This pathway involved immigration to the United States to attend graduate school on international student visas or H-1B visas (temporary non-migrant visas). In this chapter, I focus on the pathway that India-born women and women from Latin America identified as they narrated their occupational trajectories. I introduce two White, middle-class immigrants from Colombia and Mexico and Indian Americans who immigrated to the United States as adults and followed a pathway into the technology industry established by their parents or older siblings.

Mercedes and Bianca are middle-class, married heterosexuals who both earned graduate degrees in engineering from Carnegie Mellon, a feeder school into Silicon Valley technology firms. They possessed the family and financial resources to pursue those graduate degrees. Among the five Latinx women in this study, the women engineers who expressed the highest degree of satisfaction with their jobs were Mercedes and Bianca, who are White, highly educated, middle-class, and heterosexual women who earned degrees in their native countries of Colombia and Mexico before pursuing graduate study in the United States. Their experiences raise the question of how class background, Whiteness, elite educational credentials, and family resources shape the career trajectories of White Latinx women who possess class privilege.

Mercedes: A White, Middle-Class Mexican

A twenty-seven-year-old, White, Mexican software engineer, Mercedes immigrated to the United States to pursue graduate study at Carnegie Mellon. Mercedes grew up near Cancun, Mexico, in a middle-class family of professionals. After earning a bachelor's degree in computer science from a top-ranked university in Mexico, she applied to a computer science graduate program at Carnegie Mellon. Mercedes immigrated to the United States on a student visa to pursue her graduate degree. After earning her master's, she was contacted by a recruiter from several top technology firms and accepted a job offer at one of the most prestigious and powerful technology firms in San Francisco. "They found me through LinkedIn, which I found to be bizarre because I would never expect LinkedIn to actually work! Like, they told me to keep my profile updated. . . . They sent me their recruiter, who was super nice to me, and I was like, 'Okay, sounds like a good company.' . . . But to be quite honest, they reached out to me and most engineers at Carnegie Mellon." After being interviewed by Google, Adobe, VMware, and other big companies, Mercedes accepted a position as an entry-level engineer at her current firm, where she has worked for three years. After a few months, she was moved to a team that was responsible for building the "whole infrastructure to make sure everything was working in all languages." Explaining her role, which does not involve translation, she clarified her job:

> I speak Spanish, but it's more like coding. People think that I do translation work, but we actually have a third party that does translation for us. What I did was more like the coding background of how to do things through Zendesk. So I did that for two years. . . . And when I started, we only had like two apps, and we were able to launch a third app. And we moved from—the things that are displayed, we call them "strings"—so we moved from having maybe two hundred strings to eighteen thousand strings. So the whole architecture behind the strings had to change because we couldn't handle any more. So my role was doing that as well.

Although Mercedes is a cisgender, middle-class Mexican, her educational credentials from Carnegie Mellon, her class status, and her Whiteness enabled her to easily negotiate entry to the industry when compared to her first-generation US Black female peers. However, as the only woman on a team of male engineers, Mercedes reported some of the same experiences with sexism that Black and White women reported. Explaining why she left her team, Mercedes described a situation that began as a microaggression but developed into overtly abusive be-havior: "The reason I actually switched teams was because I was getting tired of my manager. . . . He would storm out to me and start screaming at me for something that wasn't even my fault. . . . And I was like, 'Calm down. . . . It wasn't even my fault.' I didn't agree with him talking to me like that in front of everyone." Here we see that despite her educa-tional credentials and talent, Mercedes's experiences resemble those of the White women surveyed who also described microaggressions and poor treatment. What distinguishes Mercedes's experiences from those of her Black peers is that as a full-time worker with a degree from Carn-egie Mellon, it was easier for her to find a new team to join so she could remain at the same technology firm. This is where her Whiteness, class privilege, and educational credentials operated as forms of cultural and symbolic capital. When compared to Maya, we see the value of a degree from a top engineering school. Mercedes was immediately hired with-out any extensive work experience and without having to endure a long series of fifteen interviews.

Bianca: A Latina Engineer from Colombia

Bianca is a married, thirty-five-year-old engineer and a native of Colombia who immigrated to the United States with her fiancé to attend Carnegie Mellon. She earned her undergraduate degree in Colombia with a major in systems engineering. Both she and her fiancé were accepted into a graduate program in engineering at Carnegie Mel-lon, which, as mentioned, is one of the top feeder schools into Silicon Valley. Employed as a program manager at a technology firm, Bianca has been in her current job for two years. Her husband, who belongs to the same graduate cohort at Carnegie Mellon, is also employed as an engineer.

Like Mercedes, Bianca grew up in a middle-class family of profes-sionals. Her parents had the economic resources to buy her a personal computer when she was fifteen years old. She went to college at sixteen years old, and before finishing college, she went to Chile to complete an internship with a mentor whom she described as "a very impressive or very inspiring mentor, who later became a very important person in the Bay Area." Like other middle- and upper-middle-class immigrants in this study, she brought her class privileges in Columbia to the United States. She was able to convert her class background into educational capital in the United States. Bianca possessed forms of capital and followed a career trajectory that mirrors the forms of marital and class capital that second-generation engineers born in both India and the United States possessed.

Bianca is aware that the demographics in the industry do not reflect a good picture for Blacks and darker-skinned Latinx, both US-born and immigrant, yet she defended the tech industry. Drawing on her personal experiences as a Columbian elite with a degree from one of the top-five engineering schools in the United States, her defense of the industry represents a pattern found among middle-class immigrants in this study from China, Mexico, Columbia, and India.

> And again, I wanted to bring a different perspective [into your study] because I know the numbers are not good, but I know we can do something, and it's not that bad. At least, it's not for me. And I'm telling you from fifteen years of experience, it's not that bad. And maybe it's because in Latin America, the experience is different. We don't have that much race problems or these community problems. . . . I think it would be good for you to show that there's also a good side, that it's not always so negative, that some of the women in technology are actually having good experiences and good opportunities and having all these events and spaces to share and to grow networks. So—it's not that bad, at least from my perspective.

As a first-generation Latinx engineer, Bianca had a career trajectory that closely resembles the second-generation Anglo-American and immigrant Indian women in this study, who possessed high degrees of network capital, racial or caste privilege, and family capital and, if married, shared their spouse's ethnicity, class status, and national origins (see chapter 6). Bianca volunteered to participate in this study after learning about it from a Facebook posting among her "Latina in Technology" network because she wanted to provide a positive view of her experiences in the technology industry. Bianca did not identify her gender or ethnicity as a disadvantage for her working on a male-dominated team or as a barrier to entering the tech industry. And she described being thrilled with her job as an engineer.

Bianca's narrative of her experiences in a male-dominated industry differed from virtually all of the White, Asian Indian, Indian American, and Chinese American women in this study, who identified negotiating gender discrimination on male teams. From Bianca's perspective, being the only female member working on a male team was not a disadvantage. Instead, she focused on how diverse her team is, although she did not identify a single female or Black team member. Describing the things that she really enjoys about her work life, she argued,

> This is a technology entertainment company. So they really respect who you are. You don't feel like you have to be a certain way just to please your colleagues. You can be yourself. If you want to have your hair pink, you can have it. If you want to use a dark jacket, you can wear it. . . . But on the other side, the video-gaming industry is also known for the hard work, right? We have very tough deadlines. So there are times where we have to work long hours, but that's not all the year. . . . But that's actually really good because I feel like I'm learning new things. I work with very interesting and very knowledgeable people. And, yeah, I love it.

Bianca placed emphasis on the pleasures and rewards that she experiences as a woman in the technology industry. Her focus on the diversity in hair color, hairstyle, and self-expression can also be interpreted as a race-evasive and power-evasive discourse that does not address the systematic racism that some Black and White women described. Bianca did not identify any Black or US-born Latinx coworkers or teammates and does not appear to have any social interactions with Black or Latinx technology workers on a daily basis at work. Like Mercedes, she works on all-male teams and is the only Latina on her team.

What distinguished Bianca, a White Latina, from the Black Latinx women who grew up in the United States is that her accent that marks her as nonnative English speaker, and she does not identify with brown or Black communities. In Bianca's analysis, her lack of fluency in English has not been a barrier to employment. As an immigrant who earned a graduate degree from Carnegie Mellon, Bianca possessed several forms of capital including geek capital, class privilege, social capital, and extensive job experience. Bianca had a decade of work experience in Colombia before migrating to the United States to pursue a graduate degree.

Her knowledge of the technology industry informed her plan as she prepared for her first job interview in the United States.

> I already knew the type of jobs that I wanted as an entry job here in the US. So there was this company with a very interesting program that kind of matched what I was doing back in Columbia. So from a background perspective, I was a little more advanced than the other candidates because I had already spent nine years working in similar areas. . . . I wasn't able to speak that fluent in English. I remember the first career fair that I attended, I actually memorized my script. Like, I stood up in front of my recruiter and just spoke what I had memorized the night before. It was a very stressful situation because I knew I had to get the internship. . . . I know I was competing with a lot of really good people, but I couldn't speak English. I was very nervous. I don't know how I did, to be honest. I don't know if I said what I was supposed to say. But they got interested in me, and then they took me to their offices in New York. They interviewed me, and they saw that I had good knowledge, that I was kind of a different candidate, mostly because of my age. Right? I was not in my early twenties; I was already in my thirties. So I got the internship—three months in New York. And after that, I got the offer in San Francisco.

From Bianca's standpoint as a highly educated, middle-class immigrant from Colombia, Silicon Valley has been a rewarding place for her and her husband to work. Like the women engineers interviewed by McIlwee and Robinson in Southern California in the 1980s, Bianca was neither a gender rebel nor a feminist.[1] Instead, like the Asian Indian and White women in this study who have achieved their occupational dreams, she has adapted to a highly segregated workplace where Asian and White men dominate on technical teams.

Indians' Investments in Their Daughters

Indian women employed in the Silicon Valley technology sector belong to a "transnational class" of knowledge workers. A growing body of literature in the fields of South Asian studies, labor studies, and migration studies has examined the transnational migration, skills, and cultural ideologies of a "new Indian middle class," which has been described as a highly educated, skilled, and mobile transnational professional class that is part of a "flexible" labor system.[2] Studies of transnational Indian IT workers describe them as an "overwhelmingly urban and upper caste, mostly from families in which the fathers worked at government jobs. . . . IT professionals comprise a small elite class segment."[3]

Scholars studying the new Indian middle-class and the Asian Indian diaspora in the United States have found that women with engineering degrees are highly valued as potential wives among the upper castes for a number or reasons.[4] In India, highly educated women are seen to enhance the status of families and belong to what has been called the emerging "IT caste" of the new Indian middle class.[5] In the South Asian diaspora in the United States, marriages continue to be arranged or semiarranged in ways that valorize computer science and engineering as lucrative professions that facilitate the reproduction of transnational mobility, as well as caste and class inequalities and social stratification. A rich body of interdisciplinary literature has examined the ways that caste, class, gender, and migration structure the educational experiences and opportunities of Indian women and men employed in the IT industry.[6]

In a study of highly educated Indian women in the Seattle area who had earned engineering degrees, Amy Bhatt found that they had become "high tech housewives."[7] Bhatt argues that an engineering degree is a form of cultural and symbolic capital that supported rather than undermined traditional gender norms that prioritize homemaking and domestic duties for women. She identifies a paradox for educated Indian women who pursue engineering degrees. Evaluating the economic and symbolic value of an engineering degree among Indian women, Bhatt argues that they may have more agency and choices because of caste preferences and that a preference for sons has produced a gender imbalance in India and a shortage of "appropriate" brides— what is called a "marriage squeeze." She writes, "Potentially, going into computer science and engineering creates agency for women to marry men of their choosing and to migrate abroad. . . . As a form of symbolic capital, women's education can be understood as an important metric of appropriate womanhood that allows Indian families to reproduce cultural norms while aspiring to modern notions of class and status. . . . As a result, women must walk a fine line between demonstrating their education and ability to work while also foregrounding their desire to conform to traditional gender roles."⁸ Bhatt details the complexities of a transnational family migration system that "can benefit men's careers and open opportunities for good matches," but "the story is often more complicated for women."⁹ The emotional, psychological, and social costs to highly educated Indian women w migrate to the United States on family-sponsored visas are challenges for highly educated women who have children before entering the US labor force. Bhatt also underscores the significance of paid labor for housewives: "Among transmigrants, working is symbolically meaningful for women, particularly because many have had to work hard to obtain their credentials abroad or in India, where they are often compelled to push against patriarchal norms that devalue women's education. When they are forced out of the labor market, their education is rendered meaningless in the face of an economic system that equates skills with wages."¹⁰

The India-born engineers who participated in this study share some of the characteristics that Bhatt found among the educated women she interviewed in Seattle. They are university-educated women from urban, middle-class, and upper-caste family backgrounds that included economic and social privileges.

In an analysis of women IT workers employed in India and the United States, Smitha Radhadkrishnan discusses the ways that Indian women who enter the IT industry represent a new symbol of a modern and global version of Indian femininity. Their caste background shapes educational achievement. Radhadkrishnan argues, "The unique symbolic position of professional IT women allows them to legitimate the success of the elite class of knowledge professionals. . . . Unlike women in the United States, young Indian women from urban families, especially upper-caste ones, encourage their daughters to study science and math. Although these subjects remain dominated by men at the college, the availability of IT jobs, combined with the widely accepted perception that these jobs are some of the only 'good' professional jobs for women, has attracted more and more women to engineering and computer science degrees."¹¹ The narratives of the immigrant Indian women who participated in this study confirm the findings of scholars who study Indian IT workers employed in India and North America. These women followed caste and class prescriptions that reflected a "gendered self."

Yet their choice of engineering affirmed both their caste and class status while also empowering them as "gendered." Working in the IT industry was an expression of their place as "modern" Indian women and elevated them in the marriage market.

Devah: Caste, Class, and Transnational Networks

Devah is a forty-something immigrant Indian woman who was born in Chennai and immigrated to the United States on a student visa to pursue a graduate degree. She explained that international migration is the norm for Indians from her middle-class and upper-caste background and that immigration was not a difficult journey. Although she did encounter barriers as an international student arriving on a scholarship for her graduate study, she had access to widespread Indian networks that provided her with information and support.

> I think of my class and caste status in India because there are many, many Indians in my class, which is middle and upper-middle class, who immigrate to the US. It's a fairly well laid out path. And so it's not like I had to figure everything out from scratch. You kind of have your cousins or your aunts and uncles or your neighbors or your friends. Somebody has already done it, if not several people. It's just very very common, I would say, in a particular class. . . . The reason that sense of fear of the unknown in terms of "What's America going to be like?" was not there.

Among the Indian women in this study, traveling to the United States to pursue graduate study, as Devah did, was an expression of caste and class privilege. It was also part of a family project of middle-class kinship groups migrating to Canada, Europe, and the United States to find better employment opportunities. Devah explained that because international migration is very common practice—almost universal among the Brahmins in this study—there is familiarity with the process, and migrants know that they will have to navigate cultural isolation, at least temporarily.

> You know how to navigate them. . . . You know you will not have access to too many Indians or you may not have Indian food maybe where you

are. But those are all anticipated, so you're kind of prepared for that. So I would say as an Indian immigrant coming here in the '90s, I was definitely not fearful in any way. It was not a difficult process for me because you know you must take control. So you do all those things, and then I think the hardest part of it was really the application fees and all that, the money part of it. . . . So, even though in spite of your class privilege, you spend a whole lot of dollars on top of the application. That really was the hardest part, I think. And my parents were supportive too. Because, again, not as many women come usually as men. . . . My parents did not put any barriers for me. . . . Parents can be a barrier but not the American system per se.

Devah explained that once she obtained a scholarship, her parents did not need to spend as much of their savings to send her to the United States. Winning a scholarship increased her chances of securing a US visa. She also pointed out that Indian students organize and support each other, as there has been a significant increase in the number of graduate students migrating since the 1990s.

It's very, very common for 70 percent of the graduating engineering class to come to America; it's extremely common. . . . So they're all applying together. . . . They have this system where within the same class, when x number of people are applying, they all don't apply to the same school so they're not competing against each other. . . . They've figured out the system, and they play the system very well. This all translates to when you come to the US, there is so much social support for each of them, you know, apart from support during the application process. Later, they go looking for a job, when, you know, you're working with your buddy that you knew back in India.

The Asian Indian women who participated in this study were engineers who identified their caste as Brahmin and were from urban middle-class backgrounds. Although some of the women interviewed stated that they did not support the caste system, several acknowledged that, in addition to their hard work, their caste background had generated educational and labor-market advantages. These advantages demonstrate the portability of caste privilege that allowed them to immigrate to the United States, secure high-paying jobs, and eventually gain permanent residency and/or US citizenship. Some married Indian nationals on employment visas (H-1B) or Indian naturalized citizens after arriving in the United States.

The term "middle class" is elastic and complicated and can accommodate a wide range of backgrounds. However, as Radhadkrishnan reminds us, "Claims to middle-classness also overlook entrenched caste divisions that have historically segregated India's educational system, as well as public life more generally. Class and caste have a complex relationship, and this relationship varies greatly among different regions of the country. In general, however, the highest castes, though not always wealthy, are associated with a culture that places a high value on education, while lower castes are more alienated from the still extremely segregated system of education in India."[12] India, the world's largest democracy, has an educational system that reflects its caste system with regard to access to the top spots at desirable schools. In this study, the majority of the Indian women identified as Brahmin, the highest caste, and they were able to secure spots at the top Indian Institutes of Technology, which are feeder schools into Silicon Valley.

Indians constitute a highly visible majority among non-Anglo groups in the Silicon Valley technology sector. Indian women software engineers represent a highly educated and elite group of workers who have benefited from access to a number of resources, due to their privileged caste background, middle- and upper-middle-class status in India, and kinship networks that include engineers, computer scientists, and mathematicians, who provide them with guidance and support. The India-born women who participated in this study were mainly second-generation technology workers, having followed their parents, cousins, and extended family into the industry and into the United States technology sector. Their kinship networks, economic capital, and social networks allowed them access public and private engineering and computer science colleges in India. Educational access to computer science and engineering, combined with US immigration policies that privilege educated foreign nationals with English-speaking skills, opened the door to entry for transnational migration to the United States and other Western nations. While the women worked hard, they also benefited from a class-based opportunity structure that was only available to a small, elite group of upper- and middle-class students, whose parents had the resources to finance their graduate degrees.

In addition to a student and employment visa regime that provides the opportunity to migrate to the United States and establish a path to permanent residency, these women benefited from the employment discrimination against non-Asian ethnic minorities in the United States, who find themselves, like Dalits, rejected for jobs by informal processes as well as structural discrimination.[13] When compared to highly educated Black and Latinx women in this study, the India-born women were embedded in a global technocracy, with family members, former classmates, and friends in the industry. They possessed social capital, marital capital, and financial capital that enabled them to take advantage of the opportunities offered by US technology firms, including employers that have shown a preference for hiring Asian workers.[14] The majority of women graduating from Indian engineering colleges stay and work in IT companies in India, either as software engineers or in the outsourcing IT service companies.

After having obtained an undergraduate degree in one of STEM fields, particularly in engineering and computer science, many of the Indian women in this study applied for graduate study to consolidate their engineering education, which enabled them to get sponsored by employers on an H-1B work visa. Companies spend between $11,000 and $14,000 to sponsor workers on these visas. Some scholars have argued that Indian workers employed on temporary work visas are vulnerable to labor exploitation and are paid lower wages. However, others have argued that the majority of Indian workers do not perceive working on these visas as a high risk because the majority of H-1B visas are eventually converted into permanent resident status.

In a study of Indian women in computing professions, Roli Varma found that among middle-class Indians, engineering is considered a gender-neutral profession, rather than being gender-typed as masculine as it is in the United States. Varma and Deepak Kapur found that roughly 40 percent of the Indian students studying computer science and related fields were women.[15] Women in India do face informal barriers to acquiring an education as a coder due to patriarchal gender roles. For example, middle-class daughters are expected to be home early, due in part to restrictive respectability rules.

In the following section, we will meet Ashima, Kamala, Tehmina, and Naheed, four Asian Indian engineers from urban, middle-class, and high-caste backgrounds who are employed as engineers in Silicon Valley. Their occupational trajectories confirm what earlier research on the South Asian IT diaspora has found. Two of these women immigrated to United States on international student visas, and a third immigrated on a family visa as a spouse. In striking contrast to the half of the US-born White engineers in this study who attended accelerated engineering boot camps (see chapter 7), the immigrant Indian women followed a linear educational pathway, often at their parents' direction and with the economic, emotional, and cultural support of their extended family. Their families' economic resources and investment in them distinguished them from the first-generation US-born Black and White women in this study, from working-class and middle-class backgrounds, who did not have family members embedded in the technology industry. None of the Black women and few of the White women belonged to a family system that provided equivalent levels of knowledge and support or were as embedded in the industry as their immigrant Indian peers were.

Ashima: Caste, Capital, and Family Support

Ashima, a thirty-eight-year-old, married heterosexual and a mother, is a civil engineer and chip designer who immigrated to the United States fifteen years ago to earn a graduate degree in engineering. A native of Kerala, she had worked as a trainee engineer for eighteen months, before applying for an international student visa. Like the other Brahmins who participated in this study, she followed a path that was established by her cousins and extended kinship network. In other words, she possessed family capital and networks that provided her with the economic and social support to successfully migrate and purchase the educational credentials needed for Indian nationals to enter the industry.

> My parents always encouraged us to study, and they said it's probably the way you can make the most of your life, because once you know what you want to do, then making money is a different thing. But if you have a specific field that you like, then they always encouraged us with that.

There were not many engineers in my family, as such. I just have a couple of cousins. Actually, there are more doctors in my family. I didn't really want to take advice from them that way. But I had a few seniors in my undergrad who had migrated for their masters degree, so I kind of got in touch with them and asked them, "How do you go about this? What colleges to apply to?"

Ashima's parents also provided guidance and support to develop her love of her subject and not to get distracted by focusing on "making money," which is a common motivation for Indian engineering students coming to the United States. The acceptable occupations were doctor or engineer. She completed the required exams to fulfill university application requirements. Ashima elaborated on the kinds of networks that facilitated her educational and career goals. In contrast to the Black women and Latinas who participated in this study, she had the guidance, family mentors, and the geek capital of her spouse, family, and friends. Like many of the married Asian Indian women, in addition to economic, cultural, and caste capital, she also possessed marital capital—that is, the emotional, financial, and cultural knowledge of a spouse that facilitates entry into the technology industry.

Ashima described the college she attended in the United States: "The college I went to [in the United States], . . . it's not one of the top colleges, but it had a good program for the field I was looking for. And I did pretty well there, so that was a good choice for me." Ashima began her engineering career in Silicon Valley at a small start-up that focused on chip design. She had good memories of working at a small start-up, where she received support and community, in contrast to the large company where she is currently employed. It is much easier to obtain employment sponsorship, an H-1B visa, from one of the established global tech companies than from a small start-up. Smaller start-ups do not have human resources departments or the expertise in completing the immigration paperwork. Ashima accepted her optional practical training (OPT) at a small start-up. She pursued civil engineering as a profession rather than software engineering, which distinguished her from most of the other India-born women in this study. Like the Black women in the study, she expressed passion for her career, rather than following an occupational pathway chosen for her by her parents. "One benefit of working in small companies is that you get to learn much more, because you're not in a specific group where you do this one thing. So you have to learn more. You have to adapt yourself, figure it out. It's not like there's somebody who will come and help you with everything."

Ashima relied on colleagues and friend in the United States. She met her husband on the job, married him, and is now a wife and mother. She feels supported by her husband in discussing her career choices because she argued that he is not threatened by her success. She explained that it helps because he is in the same industry: "Yeah, it did [help] to an extent, because he knows what the industry is like. But he's more in software and I am in hardware, so he doesn't exactly know the specific field I'm working. But he can generally give me advice about a lot of things, and he's one of those people who wants women to go again and come ahead and do things. So he always says, 'If you make more money than me, I'll be happier.'"

Ashima's motivation to enter engineering as a career was ascribed to siblings and cousins in the near and extended family. It was often narrated in terms of parental guidance, sibling support, and/or competition between closely related family members. The choice between becoming a doctor or an engineer is repeated as a joke in educated Asian Indian contexts, as a way to challenge parents and their power over their children's future careers. It is obviously also a middle-class choice, although this is changing to some degree in India. This particular discourse reflects the class and caste backgrounds of these Indians because there are clearly many other career choices that people who have ambition but not class privilege pursue outside of becoming a doctor or an engineer. Ashima was not at the top of the class and could not get admitted into one of the Indian Institutes of Technology, so her family's economic support played a central role in her getting a university spot. She recalled, "I was very adamant about getting into IT, so I took a lot of tuition to get into it. But . . . I couldn't make the cut. So I ended up going to a private institution that my parents supported and paid for. College was just fun."

There was fierce competition among Indian engineering students to gain admission to US universities. In Ashima's view, the Mandal reservation system has inspired the outmigration of upper-caste groups in India. The Mandal reservation system for scheduled caste groups is a form of affirmative action, which unlike the weak programs in the United States, sets aside a certain percentage of positions in universities and government jobs to redress the caste oppression and lack of opportunity that the lower castes have suffered in India. It was one way to correct some of the discrimination that the lower castes face in access to education and jobs. Resistance to this form of caste justice has been a seen as a primary motivation for international migration among middle-class and upper-caste Indians.

In Ashima's case, her parents' financial resources, or economic capital, provided her with access to the fees that allowed her to sit for exams at the Indian Institutes of Technology. Ashima's experiences illuminate the changes introduced by the reservation system, in which upper-caste Indians can no longer take for granted that their caste status will allow them to dominate all of the spaces in the universities. Ashima detailed the ways that upper-caste Indians get around the reservation system by buying their way into different tiers of engineering colleges. The most competitive and the top tier are the Indian Institutes of Technology, public universities that are viewed to be the equivalent of Ivy League schools and "Public Ivies" (e.g., UC–Berkeley, UCLA) in the United States. Established in the 1950s (rather than the eighteenth and nineteenth centuries, like US Ivy League schools, which are named for the ivy that grows on the buildings), these schools enabled India to cultivate a class of well-educated and mobile engineers.

Kamala: Following the Migration Pathway of Siblings

Kamala is a thirty-eight-year-old male-to-female transgender engineer who married a cisgender woman in a same-sex marriage in 2018. Kamala earned a master of science degree in electrical and computer engineering at a US university. Kamala is a transwoman who identifies as a Tamil of the Brahmin caste. Kamala undertook sex-reassignment surgery after attaining permanent residential status. Like their elder sister, Kamala also immigrated from India to the United States as a graduate student. Before transitioning, they obtained permanent residency and became a citizen after many years. Kamala worked in research and development before acquiring an H-1B visa, as a software engineer. Describing their pathway into the industry, Kamala recalled,

I came to the tech industry by accident, actually. I have two sisters. My other sister, she was the first engineer in our extended family. . . . She was the first woman engineer. . . . I have a lot of common behavior with her. . . . In the 1980s, when I grew up, there were three choices, mostly to make a good living. . . . You had to either go through the computer world, the medical world, or through the economics world. My sister was already in the US. She got married, and she came here and she did her master's here. . . . I just followed her. She came in 1994.

In Kamala's case, before transitioning, they followed the international migration path of a family member into the Silicon Valley technology industry. Although Kamala followed in their sister's footsteps, often a common pattern of family chain migration, they did not pursue a family-sponsorship immigration route. It took Kamala more than a decade to transition from a student visa to permanent resident status. Kamala explained that an older sister and mother were the inspiration for their engineering career. Kamala elaborated on the importance of education that her mother ingrained in them growing up as a male child: "I grew up in a very typical Tamil Brahmin family. It's a very typical middle-class Tamil Brahmin family, where the emphasis was on education, and it is what gets you celebrated—without education, there is nothing! The economic and social progress [i.e., mobility] are purely a thing by schooling and good marks. So the emphasis was on schooling a lot. I think my mom has played a very important part."

Kamala's case also represents a pattern in which middle-class Brahmins invest in and support their children's education as engineers. Kamala's elder sisters were the first migrants and established the pathway for Kamala to follow. Although Kamala was assigned and identified as male at birth, their situation is nuanced in that they established a career as a social male and then transitioned to a transwoman. In Kamala's analysis, their transition to becoming a transwoman did not prevent them from moving up into management. The India-born women who were assigned as female at birth and were socially recognized as cisgender girls, among the upper castes and middle class, described receiving strong support from their families in their pursuit of advanced degrees in engineering and computer science as the first step toward a well-paying career.

Tehmina: A Designer Who Followed Her Father's Footsteps

A thirty-eight-year-old Indian engineer, Tehmina is a Brahmin from an upper-middle-class Tamil family. The cisgender daughter of an Indian engineer, she earned a bachelor's degree in computer science at a private Indian technical college. Tehmina immigrated to the United States on an international student visa to pursue a graduate degree in engineering. She earned a master's degree in electrical engineering and computer science from a state university in the Midwest. Her career trajectory reflects a pattern found among other Indian women who pursued graduate degrees in the United States. When asked why she decided to study computer science and engineering, she recalled, "I wanted to be like my father. He was an electronics engineer. I like technical aspects, and I like programming. I like the logical aspect of breaking down and solving problems. I have been doing it for ten years. And I'm good at it."

Tehmina modeled her career after that of her father, also a trained electrical engineer and businessman, who had worked for the government of Oman. Like most of the other upper-class Indian women who participated in this study, Tehmina followed an established transnational educational pathway that fulfilled her parents' goals for her. She has been employed as a software engineer for a decade. When asked why she decided to come to the United States to pursue a graduate degree, she replied, "I just followed the crowd." In her narrative of her career, Tehmina argued that a degree in engineering enhanced the prestige of her family and that her parents viewed this as helping their daughter to secure a higher-status spouse. Parents view their investment in their daughter's education as one component of preparing them for the marriage market. The educational achievements of highly educated daughters are interpreted as a form of cultural and symbolic capital for their natal family and their husband.

Social referrals played a central role in Tehmina's entrance into the industry. Half of the White women interviewed for this study and most of the Asian Americans had worked for companies that used social referrals as a recruitment mechanism. Tehmina explained how she got her first job at Intel: "I got my first job straight out of graduate school, as one of my fellow students was working for Intel and she forwarded my résumé to her manager. Her manager thought I had relevant experience, and it worked out." After launching her career in Oregon, Tehmina later moved to Silicon Valley. She described the culture in Silicon Valley as more competitive and isolating.

Tehmina's trajectory resembles that of Britney, the Chinese American who grew up in Silicon Valley (see chapter 5). Both followed in their father's footsteps, and both received support from their families. The middle-class Asian Americans in this study who attended elite schools like Stanford share some similarities in their trajectories with Indian nationals with regard to their access to financial, family, and social resources.

Naheed: Entering the Industry on a Family Visa

A forty-four-year-old Brahmin, Naheed is also from the state of Tamil Nadu in South India. Naheed's experiences as a twenty-year veteran in the industry conform to another pattern among the Indian women in this study. She represents those highly educated Asian Indian women who had developed technical skills as interns prior to marriage and immigration to the United States. She was overqualified for her first job in the United States. She earned her undergraduate degree in physics, followed by a graduate degree in engineering. After being sent to the United States on a six-month internship by her employer in India, Naheed soon became engaged to an Indian student enrolled in a graduate program on the East Coast. Her fiancé was on an international student visa. She subsequently quit her job in India and returned to the United States as a spouse on a family-reunification visa.

Now as the director of engineering, Naheed has overcome the barriers that she encountered early in her career. She acquired her basic training as an engineer and began to develop her technical expertise in Bangalore prior to immigrating to the United States. Describing her family background and the expectations that determined her career aspirations, Naheed pointed to her childhood as a member of a Brahmin family: "I was the only girl among a group of cousins. And I was never treated like a girl because my cousins were very well accomplished. They went to IITs. You have to either get into IIT, become a doctor, or get into a REC [regional engineering college]. You have to get into those;

otherwise, your life is ruined. That mentality was always there. My cousins are all in the technology industry. . . . My grandfather was a professor; my aunt and uncle were mathematics professors. My mom was a gold medalist in mathematics."

After Naheed's marriage and entry to the United States on a spousal visa, she remained unemployed for nineteen months, since the spousal visa did not permit her to work. Being bored at home, Naheed was concerned that she would not be employable if she did not keep her skills updated. Her husband was working full-time, so she only saw him in the evenings and on the weekends. As a recently arrived immigrant with no close friends and a husband she saw only on weekends, Naheed struggled to adjust to the social isolation and periods of unemployment. Feeling bored and socially isolated due to her nationality, her accent, and lack of South Asian friends in a midwestern city in the United States, she described the support that she received from a White American couple: "Initially I was shy, but once I worked with the American couple, both the lady and her husband were very kind and taught me how to be in America. I had an Indian accent; they said they did not understand my accent on [the] phone. They taught me how to answer the phone. They told me if you smile, then "hello" comes across differently. . . . This gave me confidence. I learned from the American family, and even today I am in touch with them."

Naheed found a job through a previous coworker who provided her with a social referral. At that time, all the South Asians in her city of residence shopped at a single store for the ingredients that they needed to prepare traditional Indian dishes. During a chance meeting at this Asian grocery store, she received a social referral from a former work colleague with whom she had worked in Bangalore. "There was only one Indian store where I went to do grocery shopping, and I ran into a lady. This lady was smiling at me, and she remembered my name and she said [her name]: 'I worked with you in [name of company] in Bangalore.' . . . She asked me what I was doing. . . . I was looking for work. She referred my résumé. . . . I was able to interview, and they offered me a job, and they sponsored my H-1B visa." Here we see the critical role that social capital plays and the value of ethnic-based networks in providing social referrals and information about job openings as well as introductions.

Asian Indian women also recounted the struggles in their pathways as immigrants, as they searched for employment that included sponsorship by a technology firm. Indian technology workers endure a number of exploitative labor practices that benefit their employers. On an H-1B visa, workers are legally tied to their employer. In order to accept another position, their current employer must be willing to officially transfer their visa to another employer that will sponsor them. This is extremely difficult for employees to arrange. Furthermore, termination of employment results in termination of their visa and loss of legal status. The women interviewed for this study reported that they could not complain about their labor conditions because they did not have the flexibility to change jobs.

Naheed and other Indian women in this study understood that they had privileges that provided them with long-term benefits including citizenship or permanent residency, access to six-figure salaries, and the ability to work in environments where they are allowed to conduct their work in languages other than English. They noted that despite the hardships they endured, they achieved the financial stability, permanent residency, and a lucrative career in one of the most desirable labor markets and housing markets in the United States. Compared to US-born Black and Latinx women in this study, the Indian women possessed many advantages due to their high-caste backgrounds and class status and their transnational family support system. This allowed them to convert their caste capital and class status in India into a lucrative career and achieve their goals of permanent residency in the most desirable regional technology hub in the United States.

An analysis of the experiences of Joelle, Britney, Ashima, Kamala, Tehmina, and Naheed demonstrates the significant role that family resources and economic capital play in the career pathways of second-generation cisgender and transgender women in Silicon Valley. Compared to some of the first-generation women we met in chapter 4, the second-generation technology workers benefited from caste and/or class privilege and the educational advantages that flow from having family members employed in the industry. Their family background enabled them to leverage their caste and class privileges into successful careers in Silicon Valley.

Conclusion

Highly mobile Latinx and immigrant Indian technology workers negotiate a different set of challenges than their US-born Asian American and Black peers do. In striking contrast to Blacks, immigrant Indian technology professionals successfully converted their caste capital into the economic and educational resources needed to enter the US technology industry on student visas, spousal or family visas, or temporary work visas. While immigrant Indian women face unique forms of discrimination, they entered an industry where they typically share the national origins, caste, and class background of founders, CEOs, CTOs, and CFOs of many of the most powerful firms in Silicon Valley.[16]

The occupational trajectories of the second-generation India-born women engineers in this chapter represent a pattern across age, in which they possessed the family resources, parental support, economic capital, and educational credentials to pursue their version of the American dream and achieve their professional goals. None of the India-born women who were second-generation technology workers offered a sustained critique of either anti-Black discrimination or employment discrimination against other underrepresented domestic minorities.

A comparative analysis of the narratives and career trajectories of engineers across race, gender, and class suggests a lack of solidarity across divides of class, racial, ethnic, and national origins. Among the non-Black women, only a few of the queer, US-born, White and multiracial women directly challenged the racial, ethnic, and gender inequalities in the industry. The issue of racial and ethnic exclusion of non-Asians in Silicon Valley technology firms was not identified as a priority among women who were employed full-time in high-status and high-paying jobs or who had the family resources that enabled them to temporarily leave the labor market to invest their energies in child care and homemaking. Only a small minority of the women in this study reported being involved in multiracial coalitions fighting for changes that would benefit all women.

Second-generation technology workers benefited from a range or privileges that facilitated their entry into the industry. In the case of women who immigrated from India, their transnational migration on student or family visas was financed and facilitated by their immersion in middle-class and upper-caste family networks in India. In this sense, as a highly select and privileged group in India, they are structurally and socially isolated from Blacks and other non-Asian domestic minorities, who remain underrepresented and excluded from the Silicon Valley technology sector. The success of members of the racially dominant groups in Silicon Valley may operate against the coalition building needed to change a system in which first-generation Black, Latinx, and working-class White women remain underrepresented among women in the industry.

7

All-Women Coding Boot Camps

An Alternative Route to Engineering Careers

In 2011, Shereef Bishay, an Egyptian entrepreneur and engineer who had worked at Microsoft, founded Dev Bootcamp, an immersive, nineteen-week accelerated engineering curriculum based in San Francisco. When Dev Bootcamp began offering classes in 2012, it represented the first coding boot camp of its type and launched a new model of postsecondary education. In 2013, Dev Bootcamp was bought by Kaplan Group.[1] In an interview with *Quartz*, Tarlin Ray explained why Dev Bootcamp was unable to sustain its model:

> There has been tremendous growth in this market since 2012, but the overall size of the market is still relatively tiny in comparison to other industries. . . . With an influx of more boot camps each year, often concentrated in similar geographic locations it becomes challenging to break through the clutter. We do think the market will evolve towards specialization, in which bootcamps can figure out how they can better support specific skills development. . . . As with any new industry with a rapid influx of new players mimicking the original, it takes time for customers to differentiate quality programs from those looking to take their money.[2]

The first coding boot camps opened their doors in the San Francisco Bay Area in 2012. Six year later, in 2018, there were 108 coding boot camps operating in forty-four US states and four provinces in Canada. With forty-two in-person coding boot programs, California has the largest concentration of for-profit, accelerated engineering academies, followed by New York (twenty-nine), Texas (twenty), Washington (thirteen), Illinois (ten) and North Carolina (ten).[3] These alternative learning communities teach programming languages used in web design and software development and provide a coding-specific curriculum with a focus on full-stack web development or front-end web development.[4]

This chapter examines the pathways of university-educated White women who moved from a nontechnical career to a full-time position as a software engineer in Silicon Valley. I call these women *code-switchers*: women who switched careers and learned to code after working in nontechnical jobs. We meet White women between the ages of twenty-eight and thirty-three who used coding boot camps to job-hop from nontechnical to technically skilled careers. They were able to secure what they considered to be lucrative, creative, and rewarding career as software developers.

All-women coding boot camps offer an alternative to four-year traditional colleges in providing a skills-based education that responds directly to industry demands. All-women coding boot camps are gendered educational spaces that offer a female-friendly, gender-segregated, and emotionally supportive learning community for university women who want to enter or reenter technology labor market. These engineering academies also provide women with forms of gendered geek capital, which, as mentioned earlier, is a set of technical skills in the ability to code, social relationships, and symbolic capital needed to be perceived as "culturally fit" for a technology job in Silicon Valley.

The Coding Boot Camp Phenomenon: The Birth of a New Market

Writing for the *New York Times*, Steve Lohr profiled women from different backgrounds who had entered the technology industry after attending a coding camp: Savannah Worth majored in English and graduated last year from Colorado College. Jobs that might use her skills, she says, "seem limited to writing marketing materials or blog posts for websites. . . . In college, she had dismissed computer programming as all math and numbers, and not a creative pursuit." After going to an open house in Denver at Galvanize, she reconsidered it. She signed up for a twenty-four-week web programming class. After completing this course, IBM hired her as a software developer in San Francisco. "Savannah now helps corporate clients design and build web and mobile applications that run in remote cloud data centers, and she earns a six-figure salary."[5]

On March 10, 2015, President Obama pledged $100 million to launch an initiative called TechHire to support access to training to expand local tech sectors.[6] The Department of Labor provided funding to support thirty-nine public-private partnerships in twenty communities to help address a skills gap by providing accelerated nontraditional training to a range of groups including veterans, people with disabilities, and youth. At least $125 million of the funding would provide an estimated eighteen thousand young people between the ages of seventeen and twenty-nine with technical training. The White House issued a press release: "As part of that agenda, TechHire is a bold multi-sector effort and call to action to empower Americans with the skills they need, through universities and community colleges but also nontraditional approaches like 'coding bootcamps,' and high-quality online courses that can rapidly train workers for a well-paying job, often in just a few months. Employers across the United States are in critical need of talent with these skills. Many of these programs do not require a four-year degree."[7]

One year after President Obama launched this TechHire educational initiative, the Pew Research Center published a report that found there were 17.3 million workers over the age of twenty-five employed in STEM-field occupations. The second-largest cluster of STEM workers were in computing occupations. This report also confirmed that engineering is a male-dominated field. The authors of the report, Cary Funk and Kim Parker, summarized the dismal findings related to the gender composition of engineering: "Engineering occupations have the lowest share of women at 14%. Computer occupations follow, with women comprising a quarter of workers (25%) in these fields. . . . Since 1990 women have made large gains in some STEM occupations, but in others growth has been far slower or has even reversed. In fact, the share of women has decreased in one of the highest-paying and fastest-growing STEM clusters—computer occupations. In 2016, 25% of workers in these occupations were women, down from 32% in 1990." One of the conclusions made by Funk and Parker is that "women's representation among the college-educated STEM workforce depends, in part, on women completing college training in STEM fields."[8]

Coding boot camps that offer an accelerated and immersive engineering curriculum provide a fast track to a technically skilled career for women. These accelerated and immersive curriculums represent a fast-growing market that is filling a gap that traditional four-year universities have left. By providing a less expensive alternative to a four-year university degree and access to mentors in the technology industry, these new alternative learning environments challenge orthodoxies that presume that women who have earned four-year degrees in the arts, humanities, or social sciences cannot secure jobs as software engineers. A growing number of women in the San Francisco Bay Area are following a nontraditional pathway into computing careers by enrolling in these accelerated engineering academies, after having worked in another field and changing careers.

Based on industry reports, the coding boot camp market has grown ten times since the first coding boot camps launched in 2012. Two new trends in the coding boot camp market have been identified. The first trend is the emergence of online boot camps, which experienced a 173 percent growth between 2017 and 2018. According to one report, these online coding boot camps are longer in duration (15.4 weeks) and more expensive when compared to the in-person boot camps. A second trend is that coding boot camps are shifting their resources toward corporate training, with twenty-four boot camps reporting that that have partnered with corporations to teach programming to their employees.[9]

Educators, industry analysts, and technology reporters have debated the quality, value, and effectiveness of the instruction provided by in-person and online coding boot camps.[10] Supporters of coding boot camps have argued that traditional four-year universities have not provided the number of skilled workers needed in the computing and IT industry. They have also argued that coding boot camps offer a viable pathway to a middle-class income for the poor, working class, veterans, women, and others reentering the technology labor market.[11] Coding boot camps only represent a small part of the postsecondary educational market and do not represent an alternative to a four-year university degree in computer science or engineering.

There has been no rigorous independent research that focuses on all-women boot camps and very little that focuses on the coding boot camp phenomenon generally. The limited research that exists has relied on self-reports and survey data provided by the industry.[12] Technology journalists and bloggers have recently begun to provide comparative analyses of the value and merit of a credential from an accelerated engineering program in coding and a four-year degree from an accredited university. There are ongoing debates about the educational outcomes of this emerging unregulated market. Reporting for *Wired* magazine, Clive Thompson suggests that coding jobs represent the blue-collar jobs of an earlier century—jobs that provide middle-class incomes and economic stability:

> The Valley employs only 8 percent of the nation's coders. . . . What if the next big blue-collar job category is already here—and it's programming? What if we regarded code not as a high-stakes, sexy affair, but the equivalent of skilled work at a Chrysler plant? Among other things it would change training for programming jobs—and who gets encouraged to pursue them. . . . You could learn how to do it at a community college; mid-career folks would attend intense months-long programs like Dev Bootcamp. There would be less focus on the wunderkinds and more on the proletariat.[13]

In the San Francisco Bay Area, the boot camp phenomenon has exploded since 2012 and has produced six years of cohorts that are now employed by major technology firms. These graduates serve as evangelicals for this new postgraduate model of engineering education. Critics of coding boot camps have questioned the intellectual rigor of the curriculum, but in a study of coding boot camps in the United Kingdom, Graham Wilson argues, "It is certainly a model to which education does not appear to have any direct response. . . . Initial concerns over the boot camp model have faded somewhat with the model gaining a reputation for quick success. From a boot camp perspective, the traditional degree route is an outdated model and out-of-step with the pace of technological development."[14]

From the perspective of women seeking to enter the technology industry as software developers, all-female coding boot camps provide a community of women who are also pursuing technical skills as well as a professional network of mentors. While these women may not explicitly use feminist language or directly challenge corporate hiring practices, these academies do challenge the "pipeline myth" by undermining the argument that continues to be made by some technology firms that women are severely underrepresented in their companies because there is not an adequate pool of technically trained women in the pipeline. Demonstrating technical competence is not enough for female applicants; they are also expected to demonstrate their ability to conform to what can be a toxic masculine occupational culture in many, although not all, technology firms and start-ups.

Drawing on the work of gender scholars and Pierre Bourdieu's concepts of capital, I argue that coding boot camp credentials provide newly minted female engineers with weak ties and several forms of geek capital.[15] In addition to technical skills, the final two weeks of the coding boot camp involve practicing "whiteboarding," which involves writing and thinking through problems on a board while the interviewer watches. Women explained that this is not something that they would necessarily do on the job, but it is a way of evaluating a candidate's logic and problem-solving skills. Thus, learning how to whiteboard is a form of capital that a technically skilled job applicant would not necessarily be proficient in or be able to do with confidence unless they practiced. Women described whiteboarding to me as a "male practice at places like MIT" but one that bears little resemblance to their daily work.

Sociological research on gender inequality in STEM fields has focused on academic computer science degrees—that is, enrollment in engineering and computer science majors—and has documented an ongoing problem.[16] Yet this research has not illuminated the alternative routes into careers in engineers and computer science. Academic computer science has demonstrated the ways that female students are disempowered and driven out of computer science and engineering by the classroom culture.[17] All-women boot camps shield women from classroom dynamics in coed classrooms, in which femininity, gender, or sexual expression can be experienced as a liability or a cultural barrier to technical learning. By providing women with basic technical skills—the coding languages currently in use—all-women engineering academies may also facilitate social change by disrupting the symbolic link between masculinity and technology. In other words, by producing cohorts of technically skilled women who are eligible for jobs in software engineering, these coding boot camps are challenging, if not changing, the perceptions of what "talent" looks like.

The Hackbright Academy: An All-Women Coding Boot

The Hackbright Academy was founded in San Francisco in 2012 to "change the ratio in engineering and technology by providing the industry with strong, smart, and talented women."[18] Its rapid growth between 2012 and 2018 produced a cohort of more than one thousand alumna who have successfully secured jobs as engineers in the San Francisco Bay Area. Hackbright offers adult learners who identify as cisgender and transgender women an intensive twelve-week curriculum in three locations: the East Bay (Oakland), the South Bay (San Jose), and its founding location in San Francisco.

In 2018, the average cost of coding boot camps ranged between $11,400 and $21,000.[19] In the summer of 2018, the cost for a twelve-week (full time) or twenty-four-week (part-time) curriculum at Hackbright Academy was $17,000. Hackbright provides an intensive short-term curriculum that includes a ten-day foundational prep course that is free and remote. The first ten weeks focus on learning coding skills, and in the last two weeks, students practice interview skills such as whiteboarding, a problem-solving exercise on a whiteboard. The average starting salary for Hackbright graduates who become software engineers is $89,000.[20]

In the summer of 2018, the Hackbright Academy wrote a blog post titled "12 Outstanding Web Apps Built by Female Engineers." Among the women featured were Israelis, Russians, Indian Americans, East Asians, and Whites. Although some of the women had previous experience in engineering, the majority had worked in nontechnical careers. One engineer profiled was Juliette Gil, whose prior work experience was described this way:

> She spent many years as a Concierge for a four-star, luxury hotel in midtown Manhattan. Over time, she noticed that some of the more impact ways to make things easier came from the application of technology to real life problems. However, oftentimes a perfect solution to a problem would require a very customized solution, unavailable off-the-shelf. This sparked her interest in building customized software and shortly after, she left the Big Apple to live remotely and focus full-time on her self-studied career switch into technology and to attend Hackbright.[21]

Juliette, like half of the women profiled in the class of 2018, had not earned a degree in computer science or engineering and had no previous experience. Other women in her cohort had worked as architects, acupuncturist, high school teachers, administrative staff, and small business owners. In 2018, women constituted 34 percent of the boot camp students. A 2018 Coding Bootcamp Market Survey identified 108 coding boot camps, including 95 in-person coding boot camps and 13 online boot camps; 64 percent of the boot campers were White and 76 percent had earned bachelor's degrees and/or graduate degrees. Graduates of coding boot camps who were employed in California had the highest starting salaries, over $100,000, while the average national salary was $64,528.[22]

All-women coding boot camps such as Hackbright provide a fast track into careers as software engineers for women who have not earned academic degrees in computer science or engineering. In addition to providing women coding instruction in a supportive environment with other women, Hackbright Academy provides its students with a network of mentors, access to employers, and training in whiteboarding, which helps women market themselves to employers who want to hire more women as engineers. These engineering academies enable women to quickly gain access to an employment network. They work in ways not unlike job fairs at traditional universities. While a "leaky pipeline" of women departing the technology industry has been identified, less analytical attention has been given to women who enter the computing industry as software engineers after having worked in nontechnical jobs.

In the narratives of White female software engineers, they often identified coding boot camps as their pathways to secure a full-time position as a software engineer. The women who had enrolled in these boot camps had earned their degrees in the arts, humanities, or social sciences and had no previous formal training in computer science or engineering. In the next section, I introduce four White women between the ages of twenty-six and thirty-three who are employed as software engineers. They represent a nontraditional pathway into an engineering career for the White women in this study. Three of the four women in this chapter belong to the first two cohorts of boot campers to complete a ten- to twelve-week curriculum during the birth of this industry (2012–14). Among the White female engineers in this study, roughly 25 percent reported attending a coding boot camp. With one exception, all had chosen all-women coding boot camps.[23]

Isabella: The Path from Marketing to Engineering

A twenty-eight-year-old software engineer, Isabella works as a front-end developer at a major technology firm in San Francisco. The daughter of a mechanical engineer and the wife of a male software engineer, Isabella is a second-generation engineer who was embedded in the technology ecosystem through genealogy and marriage. Isabella earned a bachelor's degree in psychology and worked at several San Francisco–based start-ups in nontechnical positions before securing her current position as an engineer. In her previous job, Isabella worked in a marketing role at a small software service company.

When Isabella began working as the liaison between the engineers and management, she recalled, "That was the first time . . . that I was actually interfacing and talking to other software engineers and realized like, 'Hey, this is a job, and I have a little window to what this is.'" Describing her previous job with a "catering concierge service" that organized meal deliveries for tech start-ups and venture capitalists, she recalled, "I just felt so underutilized, and I didn't feel like I was leveraging my strengths in my job. . . . And it was the first time in my life that I just left a job without anything lined up because I was like, 'I have to do something else and figure out what that's going to be.'" She described her improvisational career trajectory:

> So way back, I worked in the nonprofit sector and worked for a series of companies that didn't have a lot of funding. And then my next move was like, "Okay, I want to try and actually make some money while actually doing things that I love." So I ended up at this company kind of hoping like, "Can I actually make a living, um, intersecting technology with food?"— something that I'm very passionate about. And I found the opportunity through a friend. So that's kind of how I landed in that particular start-up.

After being burned out, Isabella quit her job and took time off. She recognized that she did not possess the technical skills to be hired as an engineer. So she developed a plan to reach her new career goals and transition to a job as a software engineer. "So, I took a little bit of time to just like get myself back into a space where I felt more like myself. And then I dived into trying to teach myself to code on my own, and I started by just reaching out to people that I knew and asked if they knew any engineers that they could put me in touch with. And so my first step that was like, 'Okay, . . . I don't have the tech skills yet, but maybe I can find people that will have the tech skills.'"

For some women, it took time for them to understand that they had the emotional makeup to become an engineer. Isabella's male partner is an engineer, and she was already embedded in a network of engineers at her job. This gave her an opportunity to reflect on and compare herself to these men: "I have worked with plenty of engineers who are great engineers but they are really lacking in a lot of other skill areas like communication, being courteous, being a good team member—that builds people up. And I sort of had this idea in my mind as like, 'If I can just get the missing technical skills, that will be the missing piece to unlock the type of agency that I want in my life, not only for financially but just like the power and the influence to like make real decisions at work and have my voice be heard.'" Isabella invested all of her energies into building a network and learning what path to take to acquire more technical skills:

> I'm aware that a lot of opportunities in my life have happened through personal connections, or people just directing me towards something, so I wanted to sort of build a professional network. I also just wanted like practical advice on what do I learn? . . . I asked a lot of people questions about what their pathways into the field were, and that . . . led me to a lot of people who had gone through these accelerated coding boot camps in the Bay Area. And once that sort of avenue had been revealed to me, . . . "Could I go to one of these ten- or twelve-week programs and come out on the other end like with the skills that I need?" It took me a few months of sort of networking and studying online to kind of like reach that point where I was like, "I think a program like this is what I want to do."

She decided to enroll in the twelve-week course at Hackbright Academy. In her analysis of the people with whom she networked during this period, she compared the boot camp to the traditional computer science degree: "Yeah, I think it was probably like two-thirds of the people who went to a boot camp and were pretty new to the industry, and the other section were people who had traditional computer science degrees. And I think I talked to one person I think who was self-taught."

Isabella was embedded in a social network that provided her with crucial information as she considered her future career options. As the partner of an engineer, she had social capital that gave her access to women engineers employed in the technology sector. Isabella's social capital provided her with knowledge that enabled her to make a comparative analysis of the options available to her. As a financially secure, middle-class, White professional, Isabella had the economic resources to pay for a course that cost $12,000 for twelve weeks.

Isabella represents a pattern among four-fifths of the White women who enrolled in boot camps. They possessed several forms of capital, including educational, economic, social, marital, and symbolic (Whiteness), to enter the coding boot camp market as they prepared to change their careers. In other words, they were already integrated into the technology ecosystem, when compared to the Black women and White women of working-class background. I employ the term *marital capital* to refer to their access to spouses, domestic partners, or lovers who were embedded and employed in the technology sector. These social ties to romantic partners and family members gave them access to informal training, information about jobs, and introductions that led to job offers. In addition to their tenacity, hard work, and previous education, their family capital provided economic resources, sponsorship, mentoring, training, and emotional support that enabled them to transition into a technically skilled job in Silicon Valley.

Anastasia: The Wife of an Engineer Transitions in Ten Weeks

Formerly an administrative assistant at a university, Anastasia is a thirty-three-year-old White software engineer, whose husband is a White male programmer. The daughter of two artists and a sister employed in the industry, Anastasia earned a master's degree in education. Anastasia has been employed in her current position at a top San Francisco–based technology firm as a software engineer for three years. After working for five years in an unfulfilling administrative job, she decided to change careers. When she enrolled in Hackbright Academy's ten-week course during its first year in operation, the tuition and fees were $12,000. She described how she transitioned from a staff member at a university in what she described as a "dead-end job" and had no clear plan:

> Well, I was kind of flailing around trying to figure out what I wanted to do with my life. . . . I got my master's in education. And I got my teaching [certificate]. And right at the end of that, I realized that the classroom wasn't the right place for me. And I spent five years from that point trying out a lot of different stuff and trying to figure out what I was going to do because I had wanted to be a teacher since I was like in the sixth grade. It was the first time in my life that I didn't know what I wanted to do. . . . And even before that time, [my husband] had been telling me that I would like programming. But I had this idea in my head of what an engineer looked like, and it wasn't me.

Anastasia was thus initially reluctant to change careers because she held gendered beliefs and stereotypes about what an engineer looked like, but she was inspired by an article that she read about a sixteen-year-old girl who fell in love with coding:

> [Coding] just seemed very robotic to me. And then I had been reading all of these articles about getting more young girls interested in STEM and all of this stuff. And then I read this one article about a sixteen-year-old girl who said, "Oh, I didn't think I'd be interested in programming, but then I started taking computer science at my high school. And it's so much fun. And I really love it. And I never thought that I would like it." . . . If this sixteen-year-old girl—which is fundamentally who I am at heart—if she thinks that it's fun, and it can be relatable for her, then I might as well give it a try and see if I like it. And I actually didn't want to tell my husband. . . . I started coding in secret. And I went on Code Academy. That was the very first place I went.

Anastasia started taking courses in secret. After taking several free online courses including courses on Code Academy, she moved on to online lessons at Coursera. "I took the HTML and CSS course on Code Academy. . . . And then I started learning Python. And I took a class on Coursera, which was much more in-depth. It was like you watch videos that explained certain concepts. And then you have like a weekly project where you build a game in Python. And so, every week, it got a little bit harder, until the end, where our final project for the class was basically building a version of Asteroids, the old arcade game, where you fly around and pew-pew, pew-pew."

In Anastasia's narrative of how she ended up enrolling in Hackbright, she identified a childhood friend who lived in Oregon and asked if she could move in with Anastasia while she attended a coding boot camp. This friend enrolled in a different coding boot camp and is now an engineer. Anastasia described the forms of economic, emotional, and technical support that she received from her husband:

> I finally came out to my husband that I wanted to be an engineer. And I was like, "I want to do this as my job. I want to go to Hackbright. It costs $12,000." That's how much it was at the time. And he didn't even bat an eyelash. He was like, "Let's do it." He was super supportive. And honestly, there's no way I could have afforded to do it. I could have gotten a loan to pay for the tuition, but to pay for living expenses at the same time and having enough time to like adequately job search afterwards—like I know a lot of people in my class didn't have a significant other to lean on the way that I did. So I know that I was really lucky. But also I had his emotional support, and he helped me when I was confused about things or when I got stuck. But, basically, I applied to Hackbright, and I continued to learn on my own. And then I got an interview at Hackbright.

Anastasia belonged to the second cohort that attended Hackbright in 2012, so she was one of the first women to enroll when this industry was being launched. When she was a student, the curriculum was ten weeks and did not include two weeks of learning how to whiteboard. A recurring theme across interviews with most of these women was the role that a friend or a male partner played in providing forms of support. Like the other White women in this study who enrolled in coding boot camps, Anastasia was thirty something, middle-class, had a bachelor's degree, and had geek capital—a husband, partner, or friend who was an engineer. The forms of social and economic capital that Anastasia possessed were crucial to her ability to devote all of her energies full-time to developing coding skills and networking.

In Anastasia's explanation of why she really wanted to enroll in an all-women coding boot camp, she described her insecurities:

> But when I got my acceptance letter, I immediately panicked. And I was with my husband at the time. . . . I was like, "I tricked them into thinking that I'm smart enough to do this, but I'm not. And I shouldn't have said this because that made it sound like I know things, but I don't. And I'm going to get there, and I'm not going to be able to do it. Everyone else is going to be smarter than me." And I knew about imposter syndrome, and I knew that it was imposter syndrome. But I also said to him—I was like, "But if everyone thinks that everyone else is smarter than them, isn't it like statistically impossible for none of those people to be right?" Some of them have to be right.

In 2012, when Anastasia enrolled in Hackbright, it was among twelve boot camps in San Francisco. Except for a few blogs and testimonials by the first cohorts, there was very little information about coding boot camps. Anastasia benefited from living in the Bay Area, which was ground zero for the birth of this movement.

> And then I kind of had found out that there were other similar programs. But knowing that Hackbright was all women was like crucial to me. And I think it's just like—I don't know what it is. I mean, there's been research that shows that the more females there are in a class, the more everybody learns. . . . I just had this instinct like I needed to be in a group of women. And I knew that there wasn't anything else out there like it. And so I started reading up about it and reading people's blog posts and stuff talking about their experiences there. And so yeah, so it's a ten-week program. The first five weeks are going over the fundamentals of computer science. And then the second five weeks is a personal project that they sort of help mentor you through.

During the past six years, Hackbright has expanded and now offers twelve-week and twenty-four-week courses in three locations in the Bay Area. The support that Anastasia received from the three mentors assigned to her at Hackbright led her to a successful hire within weeks of completing the Hackbright curriculum. Anastasia recalled the final weeks of the program, in which technology firms were invited to meet graduates and demonstrated their projects: "And so it's like thirty speed interviews basically. . . . Like Google and Facebook are always there. And then Yahoo will sometimes be there. Pinterest will sometimes be there. . . . You also have your ten-person start-up or two-person start-up, or 'You would be our first engineer' kind of thing. So it runs the gamut. . . . A few people got probably eight or ten interviews, which is a lot. A few people only got one or two. But I think most people got like three to six [interviews]." With an introduction provided by one of her mentors, a Hackbright graduate, Anastasia was hired on a three-month temporary contract, which was converted into a full-time position at the end of the contract.

Anastasia's occupational trajectory conforms to the survey research conducted by Course Report, in which 88 percent of the students reported having secured a full-time job within 30 to 120 days after completing the curriculum. The coding boot camp provided Anastasia with access to mentors and embedded her in a network of female engineers. Immediately upon completing her coding boot camp curriculum, she contacted a female engineer and learned about a position. She recalled,

> So the contracting job didn't actually really exist. I had a mentor who was an engineer at [name of company] who also had gone through Hackbright. And I contacted her and mentioned that I was interested in getting an interview at [company] and could she help. And she said, "Yeah, why don't you come down? I'll give you a tour of the office. You can meet the recruiter." So I did that. I saw the office. I met the recruiter. I asked her a lot of questions. It sounded like a great place to be. And the recruiter said, "I'm going to try and find something for you." I was originally going to be interviewing to be an intern.

Anastasia needed a job immediately and pushed the recruiter about the possibility of working earlier. Her timing proved to be good. "'Hey, I really want to work sooner than later. Is there anything we can do? . . . Even if I'm not part of the regular internship program, if I can just start early and work on a project?' And there happened to be a team that needed some extra work done. And I fit the bill. And so I ended up getting an offer to contract on their team. . . . I'm still on that same team now."

The mentor who had been assigned to Anastasia and who was a former graduate of Hackbright is an example of what Mark Granovetter calls a "weak tie" who produced a job for her that "didn't exist." Granovetter, a sociologist who has studied labor markets, labor processes, and the job search, has found that being embedded in networks is an advantage on the job market.[24] Weak ties reflect having access to a large network that facilitates job searches. A history of structural racism, including de jure and de facto residential segregation by race and class, privileges White and Asian women, who are more likely to be embedded in networks, at the group and institutional levels, that give them access to jobs. In Anastasia's experience, we see that her weak ties to a former graduate of Hackbright gave her crucial introductions to a manager at a top technology firm. That introduction led to a contract that became a full-time job.

One critical resource provided by Hackbright is social referrals. Hackbright assigns all students a former graduate of Hackbright or a technology entrepreneur or engineer who has agreed to be a mentor and is employed in the industry. Upon students complete the program, mentors provide them with the opportunity on "Career Day" to show off their work to corporate partners and link them to a network of female alumnae who have been hired within the past five years by a technology firm. A major strength of Hackbright is the community of female mentors it provides to women who have not earned traditional computer science degrees and have no previous work experience as interns or employees of technology firms.

Anastasia identified three mentors whom she acquired at coding boot camp: career, technical, and personal. Her technical mentor is a sixty-two-year-old White man, while her career mentor is the woman who helped her get her current position. Mentors were identified by women in tech as someone that they have lacked. Anastasia described the mentors whom she acquired through the coding boot camp:

> They pair you up with three mentors. They try to get at least one of those to be a Hackbright alum, but that does not always happen. And they try to get someone who is an engineer and someone who is not an engineer to get different perspectives. A lot of times, it will be a CEO of a small company or a VP or whatever. So one of my mentors was a Hackbright alum, and she worked at Survey Monkey. . . . My other two mentors were male. And the night that I met the three of them, because we have this mentor mixer, I sat there chatting with them. And we talked. . . . And then the two guys left. And I turned to the woman. . . . I was like, "So have you ever cried at work?"

I just wanted to know all the lady things, right? And she laughed. . . . And I just asked her all of these questions and immediately just felt so much more comfortable. And I think a lot of it was because she was a woman, but a lot of it also was that she was from Hackbright. She had been through the same thing. . . . All three of my mentors were White. And then the other was a really nice guy who I got a lot of help from during Hackbright. . . . It's very important to me to have career mentors who are also engineers. . . . One person who I sort of view as a mentor is a White male.

We see from Anastasia's narrative that the male and female mentors who were assigned to her at Hackbright were career resources and that without them, it may have been more challenging for her to have secured a job. The White female mentor assigned to her was the person who arranged for her to get interviewed at her current employer. She is now a senior software engineer and has been working full-time for her firm for more than two years.

Celeste: Best Practices and Whiteboarding

The daughter of a software engineer, Celeste is a twenty-six-year-old, White, second-generation engineer. Celeste earned her bachelor's in international relations at UC-San Diego. Like Anastasia, Celeste is also a White, cisgender, and heterosexual woman married to a male engineer. She enrolled at the Hackbright Academy because she wanted to change careers. Two weeks before my interview with her, she had completed the Hackbright curriculum. With enthusiasm, she described the forms of support she has received:

There's a great alumni network and really great career counselor, and we also had a career day at the end of my session where we each presented projects that we developed to twenty-five different companies on this one day. And so we met some recruiters and engineers that way also. So I'm kind of trying to first exploit all of my connections that way. And so that's kind of one piece of it, and then because the interview process is technical and you have to, as you probably know, work out problems and do coding challenges and things like that during the interview process, I am also working on studying and reviewing and kind of preparing technically too.

There are two different components to the education received at Hackbright. There are ten weeks of education followed by two weeks of "good practices" for interviews. During the final two weeks, students receive training and feedback on how to perform in interviews, including being required to solve problems on a whiteboard. Whiteboarding is a practice that is actually unlike what one would do at work, but it is something that originated out of engineering school. Celeste recalled her final two weeks of the program:

> The education team kind of introduced us to whiteboarding and good practices for how they work and how you should approach it and everything. And then during our additional two weeks—the career counselor herself isn't a very technical person, but she set us up a bunch of speakers and kind of workshop event type things for us, during which two of us, we kind of learned about whiteboarding from other people in the industry. And then there were two incidents where we actually went to two different tech companies that are partners of Hackbright and we did whiteboarding practice with some engineers.

As coding boot camp pioneers, alumnae of Hackbright who are currently employed in the industry take an active role in setting up on-site visits and demonstrations for the graduating cohort. So Hackbright alumni play a central role as mentors in the industry, helping their Hackbright sisters by providing them with access to decision-makers in their companies and setting up demonstrations and site visits. The role of mentors is central to the job-search process. Alumnae of Hackbright are the social glue: they provide the access and open the door to the industry for their "geek sisters." White men and women were identified as providing this type of support. Celeste described her experience:

> Yeah, so I was set up with three mentors. . . . Pretty much everyone had three. . . . They try to set you up with an alumna if possible; but there aren't enough alumni who are around, so I didn't have a Hackbright alumna. But I did have one woman, which was good, and then two men. . . . I've tried to stay in regular touch with them since we were first introduced in July and kind of at the beginning just kind of got to know them, met up for coffee or dinner, asked them about what they do and how they ended

up doing what they're doing, and kind of just getting to know each other and stuff. And then more recent, the project that I developed as part of Hackbright was an individual project. . . . We were also encouraged to use our mentors as support. So a couple of times I met up with two of my mentors, and they looked up specific coding problems with me or helped me work out certain things that I was trying to do with my project.

In Celeste's narrative, her mentors, which included two men and one woman, worked closely with her as tutors, guiding her and preparing her for the interview process. They reviewed her work and helped her with coding problems and with whiteboarding. The mentor with whom she had the strongest connection was a White man:

Yeah, he's just been super supportive. And I can tell he's happy to meet with me and happy to help me, and that's really nice. And one of them, I think—so two of my mentors have had done this before through Hackbright, so they kind of knew what was going on, like what our program was about and what was expected of them of everything. . . . A lot of them [the mentors] do end up being men, just because there are so many men in the industry, but it's awesome to see them there and supportive of getting more women in tech. It's really cool. So it's one of the guys that I was describing—like, I feel like he's super supportive and always happy to meet for me and "I'm totally here for you, and anything you need help with, if you want to complain about Hackbright and you want to complain about stupid little coding things or just talk about things in general."

When asked to describe the mentor who provided the most consistent support, Celeste did not identify the White woman assigned to her but the White man: "Yeah, the one that I like the most, he is—I think he's twenty-five, White male. I don't think he's straight. . . . I know he's involved in LGBT stuff, so I'm not sure exactly what his orientation is. . . . And then the other guy, he's probably a few years older, but I'm not totally sure. So maybe he's thirty-ish, White, male." What is significant here is the effort invested by Hackbright to provide male and female career and technical mentors to students so that they have sources of support in all three areas, including their technical skills, career development, and personal issues.

Celeste described an example of how the geek sisterhood operates. An engineer at Uber who is an alumna of Hackbright eagerly set up a site visit for the graduating class: "We went on site for both of those, and the Uber one we worked with a few Uber engineers because one of our alumni works there and she set the whole thing up. . . . Hackbright has a bunch of mentors and people working in the industry that they match up with current students and to help you with . . . interview prep, everything. So they invited all the mentors whether or not they worked for [company name] to come to that, so there was more of a mixture there. Those were really fun."

For women like Isabella and Celeste, accelerated coding boot camps have created an alternative pathway into an engineering career. In a male-dominated occupation, all women coding boot camps enable university-educated women who have earned degrees in the arts, humanities, social sciences, or nontechnical professional degrees to "reset" their career goals. Coding boot camps produce a labor pool of female engineers who can be recruited and hired by companies like Uber that have had a "leaky pipeline" of women leaving and that need to improve their gender statistics.

Heidi: A High School Teacher Becomes an Engineer

The twenty-seven-year-old daughter of a German father and an Asian mother, Heidi is employed as a software engineer in one of the satellite offices of a firm, which is headquartered in San Francisco and has offices in Atlanta, New York, London, and Tokyo. Born in Germany, Heidi, who identifies as bisexual, grew up in the United States and is now a naturalized US citizen. After teaching biology at an international school for six years in Latin America, Heidi drifted into a career as a software engineer. She recalled what led to her career change:

> I had some very gifted students who were interested in computer science, but that was not something that was offered at the school I was teaching at. I spoke to the principal, and I tried to petition to get CS offered at the school. But it was unfortunately not a possibility at the time. . . . We all got together, and we started to think about "How can we inject this into our existing classes and curriculum." . . . So, in order to feel like I could

do that well, I wanted to brush up and decided to take online courses on Python, which was a language similar to my previous experience, but I had never coded in it before. So I was going to start with the basics. I did that with the motivation of just being ready to instruct young minds if it should be related to computer science. . . . I started taking those classes. I was really, really enjoying them. Started taking more and more classes— took several classes on Coursera in machine learning and data analytics. And eventually was, "I think this is what I want to do." I took the plunge. I attended a coding boot camp.

When Heidi was asked to describe her experience at an all-women boot camp, she recalled what the boot camp experience provided beyond the technical skills. Her descriptions of her experiences reflect a pattern across the interviews, in which the boot camps enhanced women's confidence and provided a geek network that enabled them to successfully transition to a new career. Heidi described what the boot camp experience provided: "I think what boot camps can offer . . . is help getting into the industry. That's not to say I didn't learn a great deal technically while I was there! I also chose one that required a background knowledge in coding. . . . I felt like I lacked confidence in moving into the job market. And I also was anxious about 'Do I actually know what I need to know?'"

After completing a one-course preparation program at home, Heidi had to pass a technical entrance exam. Then she was admitted to the program and attended an on-site three-month program. At the boot camp, her cohort included one Indian, two Blacks, four East Asians, and nine Whites. There were a number of competing coding boot camps that were coed, but Heidi chose one that was female only. Explaining her decision, she recalled,

The [boot camp] I actually choose was called Grace Hopper. It's entirely for women. The largest motivation for me was this particular boot camp—you didn't have to pay tuition until you have landed a software engineering position. That was really comforting as well because they can be quite pricey. But I ended up finding out that I loved the all-female environment. I had never been in a learning environment that was all female. And I didn't really expect that I would benefit from it. . . . It was great. The months that I learned there and then worked there were very, very happy months for me. I really enjoyed my time.

Being a member of an all-female cohort was a transformative experience for Heidi. She has remained in contact with all but one woman in her class. This is evidence of how her enrollment in this all-women boot camp provided her with a professional network that continues to support her. She meets regularly with her former classmates, who now work in other tech organizations. She described the women in her cohort:

> My cohort was sixteen women. . . . There was nineteen of us that started, but only sixteen of us graduated. In my cohort, there was a very wide set of ages and experiences. One of the women I worked with most closely there was in her forties. She had actually been a full-time software engineer in her twenties and maybe early thirties. But once she had children, she became a stay-at-home mom. And now she wanted to reenter the work field. . . . She went to the boot camp to refresh her skill set. . . . She was probably the one who had the most experience. And then there were several people kind of like me who were self-taught but had chosen another career for the time being. On the other end of the spectrum, there were a few people who had very little experience early on but had decided this is what they wanted to do.

Heidi noted that the most talented member of her cohort was Ayesha, a Black woman, who was from a working-class background. Reflecting on the challenges that Ayesha faced, Heidi recalled, "Ayesha was the most hard-working out of all of us and the most creative. . . . The last couple of months are just building things. I can think of some of the things she built. It was amazing. She was the one it took the longer time to find a job. Just based off ability, she should have been one of the first people to find a job." Despite being one of the most talented students in her cohort, Ayesha received the most rejections, and it took her the longest time of anyone in the cohort to receive a job offer . It took Ayesha so long to secure a job that she was forced to move back home and live with her parents in Florida while she searched for employment because she could not afford to remain unemployed.

When Heidi compared the experiences of her Black, Asian, and White peers who graduated with her from the boot camp, the role of race, class privilege, and family capital became apparent. Heidi later compared Ayesha to the other woman in her class whom she identified as Black, who was the daughter of an Asian and Black parent and the second generation of her family to attend Yale University. This biracial Black women secured a job quickly, while Ayesha, who has two Black parents and did not come from a privileged background, struggled for almost a year before securing employment.

What Heidi suggested is that despite Ayesha's demonstration of her excellent technical skills and a creative mind, anti-Black racism and the stigma that can attach to women who are from a working-class background worked against her, the sole Black woman from a working-class background in Heidi's program cohort. When Ayesha is compared to her peers including a Black woman of multiracial heritage, the daughter of middle-class parents, it is clear that her class background and her exclusion from elite alumni networks mattered. Her post-boot-camp experience differed from the multiracial Black woman, who was quickly hired and had a smooth pathway into the technology job market. Ayesha's experiences provide a cautionary tale regarding homogenizing the experience of women who may be socially classified as "people of color" but have distinct histories that are separated by class background and educational credentials, and symbolic capital to attaches to women who have an Ivy League degree.

Conclusion

Isabella, Anastasia, Celeste, and Heidi all argued that intensive or accelerated coding boot camps not only provided them with technical training but more importantly integrated them into a supportive network of career mentors, technical mentors, and recruiters who opened doors for them and provided them with key introductions that facilitated their entry into the technology labor force. With the support of male and female mentors in the industry, they repositioned themselves in the labor market and "reset" their career goals.

Women who had completed a coding boot camp curriculum and quickly secured full-time jobs as programmers identified several forms of geek capital that all-women coding boot camps provided. First, they described being assigned to and receiving support from gender-diverse mentors in the industry, who served as a form of social capital that is known as "bonding capital" as well as "bridging capital." Bridging capital provided women from nontechnical backgrounds with weak ties that allowed them to secure the respect that led to interviews and job offers. These credentials also provided what has been called "linking capital"— that is, it integrated networks of corporate actors who were interested in increasing their numbers of women engineers. Coding boot camps provided women with introductions to recruiters, managers, and people in decision-making positions who could hire them. Mentors provided career support, technical advice, and emotional support. They opened doors and provided crucial introductions to employers. All-women coding boot camps provided social relationships that opened doors to socially closed and, in some cases, ethnic-based networks. Boot camp credentials are a ticket to a network of central industry actors and decision-makers in Silicon Valley.

Second, women argued that coding boot camps allowed them to reskill, reset their careers, increase their salaries by at least 25 percent, and become socially integrated into San Francisco Bay Area technology networks. In this chapter, I have paid careful attention to the social capital that coding boot camps provide beyond training in coding and computer fundamentals. In my analysis of the occupational trajectories of women who had earned their degrees in the arts, humanities, and social sciences, coding boot camps did not replace college, but instead they provided a network, bonding capital, and offered a certification that this person has the technical skills necessary to culturally fit in and succeed as an engineer.

All-women coding boot camps are part a growing industry that offers skills training, mentors, and access to corporate recruiters for those who are trying to (1) enter the industry for the first time, (2) change careers, (3) reenter the technology industry after having taken leave to give birth and care for young children, or (4) upgrade their skills. Interviews with graduates of intensive engineering academies who are now employed as software engineers revealed that coding boot camps provide much more than technical skills. They also provide a built-in community of mentors (male and female), access to a network of alumna engineers employed in Silicon Valley, and a community of recently minted women engineers who can offer one another ongoing support as they apply for and secure jobs.

Among the White, university-educated women in this study, their gender, Whiteness, and class background were a form of currency that they leveraged. Writing about the role of credentials in engineering, McIlwee and Robinson summarize what has been called a "hidden agenda" in the sociology of education: "Educational requirements, argue the theorists of credentialism, function not merely as a means of creating a technically competent labor force, but as a means of controlling access to high paying occupations. . . . This process of creating educational barriers to middle-class jobs is at the heart of credentialism. Professional education is as important for the people it excludes as for the knowledge it imparts. It is a means, above all else, of controlling a labor market."[25]

Coding boot camps provide a credential that enables university-educated White women who already have strong social ties to the tech industry through their spouses, domestic partners, and friends to change careers and enter the technically skilled labor force.[26] There are currently no qualitative or quantitative studies that provide a rigorous comparative analysis across regional technology labor markets by gender, race, age, and class background. The findings in this chapter contribute an important case study to ongoing debates about the value of the emerging for-profit tech educational market. It departs from research that has focused on the "lower-education" for-profit schools that primarily serve less economically privileged groups of low-income women who are parents.[27]

The experiences of the university-educated White women in this chapter who switched into technical careers in a four-month period, provide a cautionary tale regarding who may benefit from this new postsecondary educational market. White women who completed a ten- or twelve-week accelerated engineering certification program already possessed immense forms of geek capital—as well as economic, social, cultural, and marital capital. All were university educated. All were young, White, middle-class, and either heterosexually married to or in a domestic partnership with a White male engineer who was embedded in a technology network.

The White women in this study who had completed the curriculum at all-women coding boot camps possessed the social and economic resources to follow this alternative pathway. They enrolled in coding boot camps equipped with the information needed to make decisions. Among the White women in this study who became software engineers, 80 percent were "digitally literate"; that is, they had taken a number of massive online open courses (MOOCs) and had already mastered some basic programming with the assistance and support of lovers, spouses, or friends. In other words, they were not total "beginners" in the sense of having had no experience with computing. In addition to being from middle-class backgrounds, they reported having savings or financial resources from family members, so they did not have to take out loans that are available to some segments of the coding boot camp market. Women who possess racial, class, and marital capital have been able to change careers, but it is not yet clear whether for-profit coding boot camps will fundamentally restructure the racial, class, and gender structure of the executives and decision-makers in Silicon Valley.

This chapter provides the first sociological analysis of a cohort of White software engineers who used coding boot camps as route into a technically skilled position. For White, university-educated, middle-class women, the limited quantitative date available, combined with the current study, demonstrates that coding boot camps can serve as an on-ramp to a fast-track six-figure job as a software engineer. This emerging market has not yet replaced traditional four-year university degrees; however, it has created a new credential that has allowed a cohort of women without degrees in computer science or engineering to reskill and reset their careers.

This is a dynamic market, and more research is needed on the role that these academies play in placing their graduates and on the postgraduate occupational experiences of these female engineers. All-women coding boot camps are a potential change agent in the postgraduate educational market. They could also represent the first phase of deskilling in one area of the technology sector. Once again, we see women who did not follow a linear pipeline into technically skilled jobs in Silicon Valley.

Conclusion

The Tech Sisterhood and a New Movement for Equality

What I see happening is a whole new level of sisterhood.
—Sukhinder Singh Cassidy, quoted in Cabot and Walravens, *Geek Girl Rising*

On November 1, 2018, roughly twenty thousand people, 20 percent of the Google workforce, staged a global walkout that included employees in eighteen cities including nine locations in Silicon Valley and the company's offices in Atlanta, Austin, Chicago, New York, and Portland, among other cities. Although the largest walkouts were in California and New York, workers in Brazil, Canada, Japan, India, Singapore, and Australia also walked out. Photographs posted for the media on #GoogleWalkout Press Photo Book included images of female employees holding handwritten signs that read, "I deserve to feel safe at work," "End Rape Culture," "Happy to Quit for $90 Million," "Believe Women," and "Worker's Rights Are Women's Rights."

This twenty-first-century walkout by Google employees, which was described as "largely women-led," was organized in less than a week. This mobilization was in response to a *New York Times* article that reported that Andy Rubin, a Google executive, had been handed an "exit package of $2 million per week for four years," an amount totaling $90 million.[1] After a sexual harassment investigation. Google concluded that allegations that he had coerced a woman to perform oral sex on him in a hotel room were credible.[2] These allegations were kept quiet, and he was given millions in exchange for his resignation. This article was further evidence that Google had a toxic organizational culture that allowed male executives to treat women like sexual toys, rewarded them with a large payout, and then invested in their next start-up. Men who engaged in abusive behavior toward women were rewarded, promoted, and protected even in cases when they had been credibly accused of sexual misconduct.[3]

This global walkout was stunning in its resemblance to twentieth-century labor-union protests in its demand for real structural changes. The organizers of the Google walkout presented a list of five demands that could produce real change in corporate practices and an occupational culture rooted in accountability, transparency, and equity:

1. An end to Forced Arbitration in cases of harassment and discrimination.
2. A commitment to end pay and opportunity inequity, for example, making sure there are women of color at all levels of the organization, and accountability for not meeting this commitment. This must be accompanied by transparent data on gender, race and ethnicity, compensation gap, across both level and years of industry experience, accessible to all Google and Alphabet employees and contractors.
3. A publicly disclosed sexual harassment transparency report.
4. A clear, uniform globally inclusive process for reporting sexual misconduct safely and anonymously.
5. A commitment to elevate Chief Diversity Officer to answer directly to the CEO, make recommendations directly to the Board of Directors, and appoint an Employee Representative to the Board.[4]

Both affluent and low-wage technology workers have, until recently, not been politically active.[5] However, as more and more revelations come to light regarding the behavior of the titans of technology, who can violate their employment contracts, sexually harass employees, and then be paid millions to start another company, a collective rebellion is brewing. Reporting for the *New York Times*, Naomi Scheiber analyzed the impact of the November walkout of the Google employees, which represented a radicalization of a workforce that until recently had not collectively organized:

For decades, Silicon Valley has been ground zero for a vaguely utopian form of individualism—the idea that a single engineer with a laptop and an internet connection could change the world, or at least a long-established industry. . . . But the issues that contributed to the walkout at Google—the company's controversial work with the Pentagon on artificial intelligence, its apparent willingness to build a censored search engine for China and above all its handling of sexual harassment accusations against senior managers—proved too large for any worker to confront alone, even if that worker made mid-six figures. They required a form of solidarity that would be recognizable to the most militant 20th century labor organizers.[6]

Within months of the walkout, four of its organizers were fired or left Google. Meredith Whittaker, one of the organizers, a Google veteran, and the cofounder with Kate Crawford of the AI Now Institute at New York University was one of the casualties. In July 2019, writing for *Wired*, Nitasha Tiku reported, "Four of the seven Google employees who organized a 20,000-person walkout in November have resigned from the company, including two women who claimed Google retaliated against them for their internal activism. The latest to leave Meredith Whittaker, who ran Google Open Research and has emerged in the past couple of years as a prominent voice demanding increased accountability from tech companies around uses of artificial intelligence."[7] Whittaker announced her departure in an internal post that was subsequently published on *Medium*, writing about the dangers of Google's growing and dominant role in artificial intelligence (AI):

> July 10th was my 13-year Google anniversary, and today is my last day. . . .
> I'm committed to the AI Now Institute, to my AI ethics work, and to orga-
> nizing for an accountable tech industry—and it's clear Google isn't a place
> where I can continue this work. . . . Google, in the conventional pursuit
> of quarterly earnings, is gaining significant and largely unchecked power
> to impact our world (including in profoundly dangerous ways, such as
> accelerating extraction of fossil fuels and the deployment of surveillance
> technology). . . . How this vast power is used—who benefits and who bears
> the risk—is one of the most urgent social and political (and yes, technical)
> questions of our time. And we have a lot of work to do. The AI fields is
> overwhelmingly white and male, as the Walkout highlighted, there are sys-
> tems in place keeping it that way. . . . I have tried hard to offer evidence and
> pathways for positive structural change, but over time I realized that my
> presence "at the table" was more about the appearance of an inclusive de-
> bate, rather than seriously contending with the problems in the company.[8]

Whittaker concluded by thanking her coworkers and encouraging them to continue to push for structural changes. She argues for a need to build more powerful organizing structures. Whittaker provides a clear set of strategies for tech workers that emphasizes building alliances with people outside the tech industry and transparency. Her major suggestions for the future of tech labor activism include the following:

- Unionize—in a way that works
- Protect conscientious objectors and whistleblowers
- Demand to know what you're working on, and how it's used
- Build solidarity with those beyond the company[9]

Two years after Whittaker's resignation, Google employees sucessfully organized a union in Silicon Valley's anti-union climate. On January 2, 2021, more than four hundred engineers and other employees formed a new union called the Alphabet Workers Union, named after Google's parent company, Alphabet. Reporting for the *New York Times*, Kate Conger writes that this development at "one of the world's largest companies" presented "a rare beachhead for labor organizers in staunchly anti-union Silicon Valley." The union's creation is highly unusual for the tech industry, which has long resisted efforts to organize its largely white-collar workforce.

> Organized in secret for the better part of a year, . . . the group is affiliated with the Communications Workers of America, a union that represents workers in telecommunications and media in the United States and Canada. But unlike a traditional union, which demands that an employer come to the bargaining table to agree on a contract, the Alphabet Workers Union is a so-called minority union that represents a fraction of the company's more than 260,000 full-time employees and contractors. Workers said it was primarily an effort to give structure and longevity to activism at Google, rather than to negotiate a contract.[10]

One reason that it has been difficult to organize workers in Silicon Valley is that labor unions tend to focus on wages, and this is a field where, for technically skilled women, the wages are relatively high. Moreover, many women in the tech industry not only are well paid but do not see gender inequality—or prioritize it—as their struggle. For example, Marissa Mayer, the former vice president at Google, has "never been interested in the conversation surrounding 'women in tech.' . . . She stressed that her interest is, and always will be, putting the most qualified technical talent to work regardless of gender."[11] As we have seen, the amount, form, and degree of employment discrimination that women face vary greatly, based on their racial, caste, and class position. White women, as a group, have been moving into management at higher rates, when compared to Asian women, while Black and Latinx women are barely visible except as "diversity representatives." This is an example of what Harvey Wingfield describes as "equity work."[12] The struggles facing technology workers, who are an elite and highly paid group of workers, are different from the earlier labor struggles of poorer, less educated generations of domestic and immigrant blue-collar workers.

Google Strikes Back: Retaliation against Renegades

On December 2, 2020, Timnit Gebru, an Ethiopia-born engineer and former coleader of Google's Ethical Artificial Intelligence Team, was ordered by Megan Kacholia, an executive, to remove her name from a research paper that she coauthored on racial and gender biases embedded in commercial facial-recognition software. This paper debunked claims of the technology's accuracy.[13] A cofounder of the nonprofit organization Black in AI, Gebru is widely recognized as a pioneer in the field of facial-recognition software and algorithmic discrimination. The daughter of an economist and electrical engineer, Gebru followed her mother to the US after being granted status after the war between Ethiopia and Eritrea. Gebru is a second-generation engineer who followed the "family major" of electrical engineering. After immigrating to the US, she earned a degree in electrical engineering from Stanford. Black women data scientists like Gebru make up 1.1 percent of women employed in technical positions at Google.

Gebru was fired after posting a series of tweets about "silencing marginalized voices" and dismissing Google's internal diversity program as a "waste of time."[14] She posted to "a listserv for women who worked at Google Brain, the company's most prominent AI lab and home to Gebru's Ethical AI teams."[15] Within twenty-four hours of her firing, more than fifteen hundred workers had signed a letter demanding that she be rehired and promoted. Reporting on Gebru's departure, Tom Simonite wrote,

Gebru's tweet lit the fuse on a controversy that quickly inflamed Google. The company has been dogged in recent years by accusations from employees that it mistreats women and people of color, and from lawmakers that it wields unhealthy technological and economic power. Now Google had expelled a Black woman who was a prominent advocate for more diversity in tech, and who was an important internal voice for greater restraint in the helter-skelter race to develop and deploy AI. . . . Gebru claimed in tweets and interviews that she'd been felled by a toxic cocktail of racism, sexism and censorship. Sympathy for Gebru's account grew as the disputed paper circulated like samizdat among AI researchers, many of whom found it neither controversial nor particularly remarkable. Thousands of Googlers and outside AI experts signed a public letter castigating the company.[16]

Gebru's research on bias in facial-recognition software aligns with research by Black scholars in the field of critical technology studies. Ruha Benjamin and Safiya Umoja Noble, Black critical technology scholars, have innovated the fields of science and technology studies and critical race studies. Safiya Umoja Noble has studied the impact of the "digital decisions" made by search engines. In *Algorithms of Oppression: How Search Engines Reinforce Racism*, Noble uses a Black feminist lens to theorize the ways that technology can reinforce racism while appearing to be "neutral."[17] Noble, a veteran in the digital marketing sector of the technology industry, whose job was to advertise to Black and Latinx customers, is a pioneering researcher in the field of critical technology studies. She describes the goals of her research this way: "to highlight cases of such algorithmically driven data failures that are specific to people of color and women and to underscore the structural ways that racism and sexism are fundamental to what I have coined algorithmic oppression."[18] In her analysis of Google's search engine, Noble explains, "I am building on the work of previous scholars of commercial search engines such as Google but am asking new questions that are informed by a Black feminist lens concerned with social justice for people who are systemically oppressed."[19]

The firing of Gebru is important not only because it provides further evidence of the forms of discipline and retaliation that technically skilled women in Silicon Valley face if they challenge corporate practices and advocate for underrepresented groups. Gebru's experience also underscores why it is important to have Black women and women from underrepresented groups studying AI and involved in the production of apps. Her experiences are relevant to Safiya Noble's analysis of the role of digital technologies in the production of what she conceptualizes as *algorithmic oppression*. Noble argues that "racism and sexism are fundamental to . . . algorithmic oppression."[20]

In *Race after Technology: Abolitionist Tools for the New Jim Code*, Ruha Benjamin advances Michelle Alexander's concept of the "New Jim Crow" with her trenchant analysis of the ways that algorithms sort and rank us into moral categories. Posing the question, "What happens when this kind of cultural coding gets embedded into the technical coding or software programs?" Benjamin argues,

> when automated systems from employment, education, healthcare, and housing come to make decisions about people's deservedness for all kinds of opportunities, the tech designers are erecting a *digital caste system*, structured by existing racial inequities that are not just colorblind. I argue that tech fixes often hide, speed up, and even deepen discrimination, while appearing to be neutral or benevolent when compared to the racism of a previous era. This set of practices include that I call the New Jim Code encompasses a range of discriminatory designs—some that explicitly work to amplify hierarchies, many that ignore and thus replicate social divisions, and a number that aim to fix racial bias but end up doing the opposite.[21]

Given the consequences of the "codes" written, it is important to understand the struggles of women and Black women, in particular, to participate in the information technology industry not just as coders, writing algorithms, but as decision-makers at the executive level.

Experiential Gaps: Barriers to Mobilization for Intersectional Justice

One of the challenges to organizing that technically skilled women face is that their experiences vary greatly. Asian and White women employed on all-male technology teams have different experiences from Black women, who describe experiencing high rates of ethnic isolation and social marginalization and do not have family members embedded in the industry. Black women are also not perceived as desirable as tech workers due to imagined cultural deficiencies. The women's pathways to technology careers varies, and this creates experiential gaps between women who are positioned differently in the ethnic hierarchies in Silicon Valley. Asian American women, like Jade (see chapter 4) and Britney (see chapter 5), who were hired through social referrals and worked at start-ups, described having rewarding experiences. White women and White Latinas who identified as LGBTQ and were generally more invested in a more racially or ethnically inclusive workplace (as measured by the presence of Blacks and Latinx) expressed more frustration and were often looking for their next job.

Women employed on H-1B visas may be reluctant to call out caste discrimination or challenge discriminatory policies because they have secured high-paying jobs that they enjoy and most are on the pathway to permanent residency and citizenship. Other women are either unaware of or uninterested in the structural racism that US Blacks, Latinx, and other underrepresented ethnic minorities face because they believe that a meritocracy is operating. Their experiences differ from those of members of underrepresented groups such as Blacks or Latinx, with whom they do not share a culture, language, or religious faith.

In *Brotopia*, Emily Chang, a technology journalist for Bloomberg News, describes the experiential gap and variations in the forms of discrimination that divide women in Silicon Valley:

> In Silicon Valley, if you're not a white man, your identity is a ball and chain, from which you cannot escape. White women in tech have one kind of burden. Latina women have another. Black women, yet another. Asians are generally well-represented in the filed but underrepresented in leadership, adding another wrinkle to the story. . . . And aside from race, there are so many other facets of one's identity that can leave women feeling even more isolated. . . . Simply hiring more white women isn't going to solve Silicon Valley's diversity problem. If the industry is supposed to represent the future, there must be room for talented people who are not young, straight, white, well established, childless, and male.[22]

Two-thirds of the White women in this study did not report directly challenging the sexism or racism they witnessed in the tech industry. Among the White women interviewed, half reported observing or being told about racism and/or sexism on their team or in their workplace. Among the women who directly challenged racism, only a handful were White; several were multiracial (presented as White) or queer. None of the immigrant Indian women in this study described directly challenging anti-Black racism. One of the primary obstacles to organizing technology workers to fight for intersectional justice is that technology workers are differentially valued and segregated by race, caste, class status, national origin, religious faith, and/or occupational role.

Patterns of horizontal segregation within the same firm appeared to be relatively common for the women in this study: Spanish-speaking women from Mexico or Central America typically worked on Spanish-speaking teams, while immigrant Indian women described working with their coethnics who celebrate and share the same Indian holidays at work. Asian and White women were socially and culturally segregated from Black women. In striking contrast to Asian Indian women, Black women found themselves to be racial, gender, religious, and ethnic tokens, isolated from non-Black women.

In earlier chapters, women have described the ways that their caste, class, ethnic background, and social relationships have shaped the opportunities and forms of discrimination that they negotiated. Women were not equally valued, and their access to career opportunities and power was not equally distributed. The experiences of Black women diverged from those of Asian American, immigrant Indian, and White women. White women were given more opportunities to move up the corporate ladder into managerial positions, while Asian women often faced a "bamboo ceiling." Women who possessed high degrees of geek capital in the form of social ties to men in the industry (spouses, siblings, parents, friends) were able to leverage their familial and social relationships to secure jobs and enter the industry.

A lack of cross-ethnic solidarity and awareness of anti-Black racism was found among a segment of the Asian American and immigrant Indian workers. This was due, in part, to their social and familial segregation from non-Indians at home and work. Women described working on monocultural teams with other immigrant Indians, often from their home state and region in India. In some cases, they rarely even spoke English among their coworkers with whom they shared a language, religion, and caste background. One Indian American described working in an occupational environment where her coworkers spoke Malayalam and celebrated Hindu religious holidays and rituals at work (see chapter 2).

The degree of vulnerability that technically skilled women experienced varied greatly. For immigrant Indian women, when they discussed their vulnerability, it was most often in relation to their immigration status. In striking contrast to Black women, they did not describe feeling isolated culturally, and in most cases, they worked alongside people who speak one of their native languages and are from the same region in India. In striking contrast to the Black women, the struggles they focused on were planning their pathways into the United States, with the economic and social support of their parents and extended families.

Among the White women who were first generation, they described having to negotiate working on all-male teams, but 40 percent of them reported having the support of White family members in the industry (parents or siblings). Like the Asian Indian women, they described the support that they received as children and adults from family members and friends in the industry. Women with family members in the industry had more social and cultural resources to manage the forms of discrimination that they may face.

Some of the Asian American and Asian Indian women had worked in the industry for decades, without relinquishing a belief in meritocracy, despite their observing the rejection and absence of Black and Latina women applicants at their firms. Ellen Pao describes the ethnic makeup of the employees at her first job out of Harvard business school: "Looking back I don't think I worked with a single Latinx or Black employee the whole time I was there."[23] Pao has since become a force for change as a cofounder of Project Include. She describes her interpretation of the failure of her company to hire a single Black or Latinx person or member of another underrepresented group during her tenure at her venture capital firm: "I believed CEOs when they said they were committed to hiring candidates from underrepresented groups. . . . I nodded when they explained how they'd turned down a nonwhite or woman candidate simply because of 'personality mismatch': in other words, they just wouldn't fit in with the hard-charging, high-stakes culture. I believed that their 'diversity' initiatives were sincere and that each initiative's failure was just temporary or 'bad luck' or due to 'bad actors.'"[24]

Elissa Shevinsky, a White veteran of the technology industry, reflects on why gender inequality had not been a priority for her during her early years in Silicon Valley. She recalls why she did not initially challenge the bro culture in her Silicon Valley networks: she did not want to lose the rewards she received. Her analysis demonstrates how both cisgender and LGBTQ women make calculated decisions that enable them to survive in this male-dominated industry. To retain the jobs that are rewarding and give them pleasure, in many cases, they do not directly challenge the status quo or cultural norms in Silicon Valley. Shevinsky describes her change in perception:

> I'd also been in tech since 2001. I wasn't seeing the problems clearly because I'd been part of the technology industry for too long. I also wanted to focus on getting things done rather than on feminist-inspired activism. So I made the bros-only atmosphere work for me. I overcompensated by picking a frat boy to cofound a company with me. . . . I had the greatest time drinking Scotch at Google I/O with some of the best CTOs [chief technology officers] in the media industry. They treated me like a bro. I didn't want to lose those moments. . . . My year living and working with younger Silicon Valley startup guys in the SoMA district of San Francisco was an onslaught of misogyny, penis jokes, porn references, and general lack of common courtesy. . . . Despite all this, I continued to defend the status quo. I wanted to just drink Scotch with my guy friends and build software. . . . I didn't want to think about gender issues but the alternative is tits and dick jokes at our industry's most respected events.[25]

Women like Shevinsky, who are veterans of the technology industry, have increasingly begun to adopt a "feminist/intersectional" perspective as they reflect on their experiences in Silicon Valley technology firms. A comparative analysis of the occupational trajectories of the White engineers in this study revealed that there are many pathways into technically skilled jobs in Silicon Valley. And these opportunities and pathways are shaped by a number of factors unrelated to merit. The Asian Indian, Asian American, and Anglo-American women were better able to convert their educational credentials into jobs due in part to the degree to which their parents, spouses, siblings, and others in their network were embedded in the technology ecosystem. First-generation technology workers who were Black or Black Latinx and not from middle-class families faced "glass walls" and struggled to convert their educational credentials and technical skills into full-time jobs.

Second-generation engineers—the daughters, spouses, or siblings of engineers—benefited from their access to decision-makers and gatekeepers. What distinguished the second-generation Asian American and White women is not educational credentials or technical skills but rather economic resources, social capital, access to alumni networks, and built-in-mentors—that is, family members and friends employed in the tech industry who could provide guidance and key introductions to decision-makers. Their proximity to male engineers (husbands, fathers, siblings) who smoothed their pathways into technology careers enabled women with diverse educational credentials and experiences to secure positions as software engineers. For example, Anastasia, whose husband was an engineer and provided $10,000 for her to attend a ten-week coding boot camp, would otherwise not have been able to quit her job and devote three months to an accelerated engineering curriculum.

In this study, Black natives of the United States were not favored in hiring, retention, or promotion and were more likely to be treated as disposable. Black women were also occupational renegades because they had to forge their own paths into the industry, rather than following an established trail already forged. When compared to their non-Black peers, Black women endured extreme cultural isolation and described feeling that they had to constantly overperform. In chapter 3, we met Maya, a twenty-nine-year-old Black women, a former entrepreneur who had to overwork and endure fifteen interviews to secure a position that some women got after one or two interviews after receiving a social referral. In contrast to the White female engineers who secured full-time positions as engineers after completing an intensive twelve-week curriculum, Maya did not have a mentor—that is, no one to sponsor her or provide her with the social referrals that the veterans of coding boot camps possessed.

Women who have worked in the tech industry for more than a decade have proposed a number of solutions that could help to improve the climate for women working in the industry. Most are fairly straight-forward and involve establishing a transparent accountability infra-structure. One proposal is to address the funding gap in venture capital, which would support more women-led founders. Increasing the number of firms founded by women could help change the culture in Silicon Valley and provide more access to women from underrepresented groups.

Landmark Gender Discrimination Settlement at Pinterest

On April 2, 2020, Francoise Brougher, a fifty-five-year-old French-born engineer and its first chief operating officer (COO), was fired by Pinterest. A thirty-year veteran in the tech industry, Brougher remotely managed a team of 750 people when she was fired. Brougher sued Pinterest for gender discrimination and won. Describing what happened to her on *Medium*, Brougher related the events that led to her sudden departure. "I believe that I was fired for speaking out about the rampant discrimination, hostile work environment, and misogyny that permeates Pinterest. What happened to me at Pinterest reflects a pattern of discrimination and exclusion that many female executives experience, not only in the tech industry, but throughout corporate America."[26]

Brougher won a $22.5 million settlement, which is the largest gender discrimination settlement in US history. Brougher, the "most senior executive to file a lawsuit against a company worth $122 billion," has created a foundation to distribute a portion of the settlement money to organizations and projects that support diversity in the technology industry.[27] Among the organizations that her foundation is supporting are /dev/color, a professional network of Black engineers, and Last Mile Education Fund, which supports low-income students and brings them from graduation into the technology industry.

During the same month that Brougher was fired, two Black women employed as public policy and social impact managers, also left Pinterest over racial and gender discrimination in pay. Ifeoma Ozoma, the daughter of Nigerian immigrants, and Aerica Shimizu Banks, a Black-Japanese woman on her team, negotiated their departure packages after learning that they were paid less than others in their job category. Banks was replaced by a White man. Reporting for *Time* magazine, Janice Min wrote, "[Ozoma] hired a lawyer after she concluded that she and another experienced woman on her team, . . . who is Black and Japanese American, were being paid less than what their job descriptions indicated per Pinterest guidelines. Ozoma's salary disparity—about $64,000 annually—was significant but not as meaningful as the stock grant given every employee based on position, and hers appeared to be 33,675 shares short of what her job description merited."[28]

After leaving Pinterest, Ozoma and Banks went on to draft legislation for the California state senate that would abolish NDAs (nondisclosure agreements) around racial discrimination. In March 2021, they testified before the California legislature. SB331, a Senate bill sponsored by the California senator Connie Leyva and known as the Silenced No More Act was introduced on February 8, 2021. This bill would expand protections against secret workplace settlements and further prohibit the use of confidentiality agreements for workers leaving a company.[29] NDAs have had devastating effects on the victims of discrimination and harassment, preventing victims from speaking about their experiences. Ozoma described her motivation to get this legislation passed: "In addition to legal and financial restrictions, NDAS also have a substantial emotional effect. . . . People experiencing harassment are further isolated being unable to share their experiences even with those close to them. Imagine leaving your job and not being able to tell anyone—even your spouse—why. . . . It's trauma on top of the initial discrimination that you faced."[30] The bill has received support from a number of labor and human rights organizations, including AI Now Institute, Color of Change, Time's Up!, and Equal Rights Advocates. If passed, the bill would spark a wave of change in the tech world and beyond, affecting all workers in the nation's most populous state.[31] These two cases at Pinterest are evidence of a growing number of women who are beginning to develop strategies that lead to changes in legislation, new organizations, and funding agencies with the goal of creating new mechanisms to dismantle economic, social, and cultural barriers to support underrepresented groups.

The Venture Capital Gap

Kathryn Finney, a Black former fashion blogger and now a venture capitalist, founded digitalundivided in 2013 as a social enterprise with the goal of creating pathways for Black and Latina women in the innovation economy. Finney has identified a weakness in diversity initiatives that may account for the failure of such initiatives within technology firms that are run by Asian and White men, who continue to be overrepresented in leadership positions. In her analysis, Finney concludes, "Little attention has been given to the role of intersectionality in tech entrepreneurship. In fact, the majority of the discussion focuses on either women (mostly White) or Black (mostly men), but rarely on those who are both women and Black (or Latinx). It seemed Black women founders, who own a majority of Black businesses and are in the greatest position to have an immediate impact on entrepreneurship and innovation in Black communities, are invisible in the start-up world."[32]

In 2018, digitalundivided launched ProjectDiane, the first study of the entrepreneurial experiences of Black and Latina women founders in the United States.[33] ProjectDiane's 2020 report found that the majority of Black and Latina women-led start-ups were founded in three states: California, Georgia, and New York. ProjectDiane takes its name from Diane Nash, a cofounder and student organizer for SNCC (Student Nonviolent Coordinating Committee). Nash, a Black Catholic from a middle-class family in Chicago, played a key role in the student movement for racial justice in the 1960s.[34] ProjectDiane's second report, published in 2020, drew on a database of 650 sources. According to this report, "For Black and Latinx women, having a background in STEM is not the primary pathway to founding or funding a company. The majority of ProjectDiane founders (70%) do not have a STEM degree at the undergraduate or graduate level, suggesting that Black and Latinx women founders find their way to entrepreneurship through a variety of educational backgrounds and pathways."[35] This suggest that sociologists interested in gender inequality have neglected the venture capital gap and the access to investors needed by entrepreneurs founding women-led start-ups. An analysis of female founders calls attention to how many entrepreneurs did not major or earn degrees in STEM fields. The industry engages in what is called "pattern matching"—a reference to the way investors fund people who look like them or resemble college dropouts like Mark Zuckerberg, confirming the stereotype of the "male genius."

A small number of Asian and White men control which start-ups receive venture capital—that is, the funds provided by investors that are the lifeblood of Silicon Valley.[36] Peter Thiel and the men who founded

Paypal sold it for a profit to eBay, and then they became venture capitalists known as the "Paypal Mafia." Describing the venture capital monopoly, Emily Chang notes,

> After the sale of eBay, the Paypal Mafia unfurled like an octopus and deployed its tentacles all over Silicon Valley. Members were forever bonded by what they'd shared. . . . And as these men dispersed, their relationships became the currency in which they traded. They joined one another's companies, funded each other's ventures, defended one another's controversial public statements and more. For Founders Fund, Thiel partnered with two less prominent Paypal cofounders, Ken Howery and Luke Nosek, The partners invested in their old PayPal buddy Elon Musk's space venture, SpaceX (Musk also founded Tesla). . . . The PayPal Mafia became so dominant that in 2017 Adam Pisoni—an entrepreneur who never worked at PayPal but was recruited by Sacks to be his Yammer co-founder—cited what he called the Mafia's "dynastic privilege" as "one of the major contributors to the lack of diversity" in Silicon Valley.[37]

Katy Levinson proposes reasonable changes that would not require millions of dollars in "anti-bias" training:

> What needs to change is three-fold. The first thing is pretty simple: in all organizations there exists a code and conduct and clear method to report misconduct. . . . Second, while there will always be truly malicious people, most people just don't realize the harm of their action. There needs to be correction without punishment for people who are not malicious. . . . It allows those who are doing things wrong to learn in a safe environment. . . . The goal is simple here: help your well-intentioned friends figure out they are hurting people without making it seem like a threat or shaming. . . . Third, and most important, is making a serious personal commitment to solving this. . . . Making a personal commitment means forming an opinion on more than just broad concepts. It also requires learning about specific instances of harassment. Make sure the systems to handle malicious abuses of power against women have teeth, and that they seek to let the disenfranchised blow the whistle, rather than simple "keeping stuff under control."[38]

A recurring theme in interviews with White heterosexual, cisgender, and LGBTQ women is the requirement that they adapt to the "bro" work culture in order to maintain their relationships with their male coworkers and keep their jobs. Some women described employing "job-hopping" as a strategy to manage issue. This strategy required social and cultural capital—that is, one needed to be embedded in a tech network to secure another position. This was challenging for women who were trying to secure their first jobs.

White women varied in their experiences but in unexpected ways. White women who identified as LGBTQ, especially those who were nonbinary or queer, established rewarding and productive relationships with the men on their all-male teams. They avoided the forms of sexual harassment and gender discrimination that their cisgender peers described. Middle-class White women married to or in a domestic partnership with White male engineers, like their immigrant Indian peers, benefited from familial and/or social embeddedness in the technology ecosystem. This gave them informal mentoring and access to information and introductions to gatekeepers. Thus, 40 percent of the White women and 90 percent of the Asian Indian and Indian American women had access to social and familial capital that provided entry into the industry. The exclusion of Black and Latina women was perceived and discussed as normative, unremarkable, and a reflection on their skill level, motivation, and merit, rather than structural racism.

A Tech Sisterhood Mobilizes

Women in Silicon Valley have begun to organize female networks of investors, connectors, and mentors. They are establishing networking events in gender-segregated spaces where women nourish interracial, intergenerational, and multiethnic collaborations between founders, investors, and serial entrepreneurs.[39] Women in Silicon Valley are mobilizing to change the gender structure of the industry and build more gender-inclusive power structures. They are achieving this goal in several ways:

- Data activists produce data that provides transparency and demands accountability in the industry.
- Angel investors provide funding for start-ups led by women innovators.

- Connectors organize events and organizations that create networks that connect women investors, innovators, and mentors to support women.
- Founders create women-led start-ups that hire women from diverse backgrounds.

Women are developing new strategies that place emphasis on building a women-led financial and social tech infrastructure. It is too early to know how successful this will be, but there has been a growing recognition that men are not going to just give women the reins.

As we enter the third decade of the twenty-first century, Silicon Valley technology firms continue to use recruiting practices such as social referrals that reinforce and reproduce ethnic, racial, and gender inequalities. As an industry that is generating billions of dollars in wealth, Silicon Valley has not been a vehicle for economic and social mobility into the middle class for Blacks, Latinx, Native Americans, and other underrepresented groups.

In 2020, the United States witnessed a multiracial coalition come together to support the Black Lives Matter movement, a twenty-first-century civil rights movement for racial and economic justice. Asian American, Latinx, and White women and men marched in solidarity with Blacks in the ongoing fight for racial justice. The technology sector is injust and not yet a vehicle for economic justice and social mobility for everyone. It is my hope that a decade from now, this book will be read as history—a bygone moment in time before geek girls mobilized alongside workers across occupations and won their fight for racial, economic, and gender justice in Silicon Valley's technology sector.

APPENDIX A

Timeline of Notable Women in Computer Science and Engineering and Struggles against Discrimination

1815   Augusta Ada Byron, the first conceptual programmer and daughter of the English poet Lord Byron (George Gordon Byron) and Anne Isabella Milbanke, is born.

1833   Ada Byron and her mother attend a demonstration by Charles Babbage, a British mathematician, of a prototype of his Difference Engine.

1843   Ada Byron (now the Countess of Lovelace) publishes a set of notes that are the first algorithm—a set of instructions intended to program the first general-purpose computer, designed by Charles Babbage, a British mathematician.

1883   Edith Clarke is born in Maryland. After studying mathematics and engineering at Vassar College, she will become the first professionally trained female engineer in the United States.

1906   Grace Hopper (née Murray) is born. She helped develop the first programming language for business machines (COBOL).

1908   Mary Golda Ross, the first known Native American engineer and citizen of the Cherokee Nation, is born in Oklahoma.

1912   Edith Clarke is hired as a human "computer" by American Telephone and Telegraph (AT&T). She begins studying electrical engineering at Columbia.

1918   Edith Clarke becomes the first woman to earn an MS in electrical engineering from Massachusetts Institute of Technology (MIT).

1918   Katherine Johnson (née Coleman), a Black mathematician, is born in West Virginia. She will become the first Black woman to work as a NASA scientist. Between 1953 and 1988, Johnson calculated many orbital missions for NASA and National Advisory Committee for Aeronautics (NACA), the predecessor of NASA.

1921   Gender discrimination prevents Edith Clarke from securing a job as an engineer, so she begins to work at General Electric as a supervisor.

1925   Edith Clarke, a White woman, is granted a patent for her invention of the Clarke Calculator, a device that solves equations involving electrical currents, voltage, and impedance in power transmission lines.

1926   Edith Clarke becomes the first woman to deliver a paper at the annual meeting of the American Institute of Electrical Engineers (AIEE).

1928   Grace Murray, a White woman, receives a bachelor's degree in mathematics and physics from Vassar.

1930   Grace Murray Hopper earns a PhD from Yale University.

1932   Katherine Coleman, a fourteen-year-old Black teenager, enters West Virginia State, a historically Black college.

1936   Sally Hacker, a pioneer in feminist technology studies, is born in Illinois. She later serves as chair of the National Organization for Women's AT&T task force.

1937   Katherine Coleman earns degrees in mathematics and French at age eighteen.

1942   Hedy Lamarr (née Hedwig Eva Maria Kiesler), a European American actress and inventor, is born in Austria. She is granted a patent for a frequency-hopping signal for radio communications that cannot be tracked or jammed.

1942   Mary Ross, the first known Native American engineer (Cherokee Nation), is hired by Lockheed Space and Missiles to work on classified aerospace projects.

1944   Grace Hopper is one of three programmers assigned by the US Naval Reserve to a computation project in which she works on the Harvard Mark I—the first digital computer built for the US Navy, also known as the IBM Automatic Sequence Controlled Calculator (ASCC).

1946   Grace Hopper joins the Harvard faculty as a research fellow in engineering sciences at the Computational Laboratory.

1947   Edith Clarke, an Anglo-American, joins the faculty in the Department of Engineering at the University of Texas at Austin, becoming the first female professor of electrical engineering in the United States.

1949   Anita Borg, a White computer scientist, is born in Chicago, Illinois.

1951   Ekaterina Dylaneevna Shkabara, a Russian female senior researcher, codesigns the Small Electronic Calculating Machine (MESM), the first Soviet computer,

1953 Katherine Coleman Johnson, a Black mathematician, is hired as a human "computer" at the National Advisory Committee for Aeronautics (the predecessor to NASA).

1955 Grace Hopper creates the first programming language, called B-O. This language becomes the model for the first truly standard programming language, Common Business-Oriented Language (COBOL).

1961 Katherine Coleman Johnson, a Black aerospace technologist at NASA, calculates the trajectory for the May 5 space flight of Alan Shepard, the first American in space.

1962 John Glenn, the first man to orbit the Earth, asks Katherine Johnson to verify the flight-path calculations, when electronic computers are used for the first time.

1964 Lynn Conway joins IBM Research as a cisgender male.

1967 Grace Murray Hopper is recalled to the US Naval Reserve to standardize COBOL.

1968 Lynn Conway is fired by IBM for her male-to-female gender transition. She takes on a new secret identity as Lynn.

1969 Grace Murray Hopper receives the first Computer Science "Man of the Year" award from the Data Processing Management Association.

1969 Katherine Johnson calculates the trajectory for the Apollo 11 flight to the moon.

1970 A landmark sex-discrimination case is filed against AT&T by fifteen thousand women.

1972 Sandy Kutzig, an innovator and entrepreneur who earned her bachelor's in mathematics in 1968, as a young mother founds ASK, an inventory-tracking company, in her bedroom.

1973 Lynn Conway, an innovator and pioneer in supercomputing technologies, is recruited by Xerox Palo Alto Research Center (PARC), where she launches a revolution in microchip design in the 1970s, including very large-scale integration methods (VLSI). She is fired when she begins a gender transition.

1975 Marissa Mayer, the first woman engineer hired by Google, is born in Wisconsin.

1980 Lynn Conway publishes *Introduction to VLSI Systems*, the bible of microprocessor chip design.

1981 Judith Estrin, an innovator, an entrepreneur, and the daughter of two computer scientists, cofounds Bridge Communications (with her then husband), which manufactures network routers, bridges, and communication servers. It becomes a publicly traded company in 1985 and merges with 3Com in 1987.

1982   Susan Kare, a White woman, born in 1954 in Ithaca, New York, is hired by Apple to design the visual elements (typeface, fonts, icons) that users interact with on the original Macintosh.

1983   Sally Ride becomes the first White American woman astronaut to travel to space on a NASA mission.

1984   Sandy Lerner is part of a team that invents the router, a device that helps computers talk to each other. She cofounds Cisco Systems while working at Stanford's Graduate School of Business.

1987   Anita Borg founds Systers, the first email network for women in technology, to create a supportive space for women to seek input and share advice.

1987   Inspired by Sally Ride, Mae Jemison, a Chicago-born physician and engineer trained at Stanford, becomes the first Black woman selected to join NASA's astronaut corps. She becomes the first Black woman to go into space in 1992.

1987   Joan Higginbotham, a Black electrical engineer, is hired by the Kennedy Space Center as a payload engineer. She is the second Black woman astronaut selected by NASA to travel to space. A crew member of the space shuttle *Discovery*, she travels to the International Space Station in 2006.

1990   Carly Fiorina (née Cara Sneed) enters the management-trainee track at AT&T (American Telephone and Telegraph).

1992   Mattel Inc. begins to sell Barbie dolls that say, "Math class is tough." Systers plays a role in getting Mattel to remove that phrase from Barbie's microchip.

1992   Mary Ross, a citizen of the Cherokee Nation, is recognized by the Silicon Valley Engineering Council Hall of Fame.

1992   Mae Jemison is the first Black woman astronaut to travel to space, as a member of the crew of the space shuttle *Endeavor*.

1994   Anita Borg cofounds the Grace Hopper Celebration of Women in Computing.

1995   Judith Estrin cofounds Precept Software, an internet video-streaming company. Cisco buys it for $84 million in 1998 and names her chief technology officer.

1997   Marissa Mayer studies artificial intelligence and earns a degree in symbolic systems from Stanford University.

1997   Anita Borg begins work as a researcher in the Office of the Chief Technology Officer at Xerox PARC in Silicon Valley.

1997   Anita Borg founds the Institute for Women and Technology (after her death, it is renamed the Anita Borg Institute for Women and Technology).

1998   Diane Greene, an innovator and technology entrepreneur, founds VMWare, a mainstream virtualization company, which refers to creating a virtual, rather than actual, version of something, including computer hardware platforms, storage platforms, and computer network resources. Virtualization includes the act of creating a virtual machine that acts like a real computer with an operating system.

1998   Meg Whitman is named chief executive officer (CEO) of eBay, an internet firm founded in 1995 that has thirty employees.

1999   Marisa Mayer, an engineer, is hired at Google as its first female engineer and twentieth employee. As vice president of search products and user experience, she is responsible for developing the Google search engine.

1999   Susan Wojcicki, a cofounder of Google, is named as its first marketing manager. She is in charge of Google's original video service.

1999   Carly Fiorina is named chief executive officer of Hewlett-Packard and becomes the first woman to lead a top-twenty Fortune 500 firm.

2001   Sheryl Sandberg is hired by Google as vice president of its global online sales and operations, following a career as a management consultant.

2003   Anita Borg dies of brain cancer.

2006   Meredith Whittaker, cofounder of the AI Institute, is hired by Google.

2006   Joan Higginbotham becomes the third Black woman astronaut to travel to space, as a member of the crew of the space shuttle *Discovery*. She participates in fifty-three space shuttle launches during her career at the Kennedy Center.

2008   Facebook hires Sheryl Sandberg for the role of chief operating officer.

2011   Kimberly Bryant, a Black engineer, founds Black Girls Code in San Francisco to provide technology education for African American girls. She revises an MIT curriculum and begins running workshops for Black girls.

2011   Meg Whitman is named CEO of Hewlett-Packard.

2011   Marissa Mayer, age thirty-seven, leaves Google for Yahoo and becomes the youngest person to serve as a CEO of a Fortune 500 company.

2012   Ellen Pao files a $16 million gender-discrimination lawsuit against her former employer, Kleiner Perkins Caufield & Beyers, for gender discrimination in promotion.

2015   Katherine Johnson is awarded the Presidential Medal of Freedom by Barack Obama at the age of ninety-seven, for her pioneering work as a mathematician.

2015   Tina Huang, a former employee, sues Twitter for gender discrimination.

2015   Katherine Moussouris, a computer security researcher, files a gender-discrimination lawsuit against Microsoft, alleging that she was passed over for promotions while less-qualified male colleagues were promoted.

2016   In July, Qualcomm, a smartphone chipmaker, agrees to pay $19.5 million to settle a class-action lawsuit representing thirty-three hundred workers before the case is even filed. It was accused of pay disparities and not promoting women.

2016   On May 5, the Katherine G. Johnson Computational Research Facility, a new four-hundred-thousand-square-feet building, is dedicated to Katherine Johnson in Hampton, Virginia, at the Langley Research Center. It opens in September 2017.

2017   Susan Fowler, an engineer and former employee at Uber, publishes a three-thousand-word blog post that details her experiences of sexual harassment. It goes viral and leads to the resignation of Travis Kalanick, Uber's founder and CEO.

2017   Tesla is accused by a former female Asian employee of ignoring complaints of sexual harassment, paying her less than men, and firing her in an act of retaliation.

2017   In April 7, the US Department of Labor accuses Google of "systematic compensation disparities" against women "across the entire workforce."

2017   Meredith Whittaker and Kate Crawford cofound the AI Now Institute at NYU, an institute studying the social implications of artificial intelligence. The AI Institute focuses on four issues: bias and inclusion, labor and automation, rights and liberties, and safety and civil infrastructure.

2018   Mattel announces a Barbie doll in the likeness of Katherine Johnson, with a NASA badge, for its Inspiring Women series.

2018   In a gender-bias case against Twitter, a California judge denies class-action status to the plaintiffs. Twitter argued that the women did not show proof that managers used a common set of practices to decide promotions.

2018   The *New York Times* publishes a report, based on an analysis of court and corporate documents, that documents that Google had given large payouts to men accused of sexual misconduct.

2018   On November 1, more than twenty thousand Google employees stage a worldwide walkout to protest the company's handling of sexual harassment claims. This walkout is organized in less than three days by Tanuja Gupta, Claire Stapleton, Meredith Whittaker, and others.

2019   Meredith Whittaker, a research scientist at New York University, resigns from Google.

2019   The US Mint issues a dollar coin that honors Mary Ross. The first Native American mathematician and engineer, Ross worked on the first manned and unmanned orbiting flights for the defense industry.

2019   On November 8, Katherine Johnson (née Coleman) is awarded the Congressional Medal of Honor at the age of one hundred.

2020   IBM apologizes to Lynn Conway, a transwoman, for firing her fifty-two years ago and gives her a lifetime achievement award for her "pioneering work."

2021   More than two hundred employees at Google form the Alphabet Workers Union. On January 8, 2021 it represented 600 employees.

APPENDIX B

Timeline of Significant Moments in Technology
Innovation and in Silicon Valley

1885　Herman Hollerith invents the tabulator, which is used to punch cards
to process statistical information and is used in the 1890 US Census.

1891　Leland and Jane Stanford found Stanford University.

1897　Guglielmo Marconi sends the first long-distance radio transmissions.

1909　Cyril Elwell founds the Federal Telegraph Corporation in Palo Alto.

1911　Hollerith's Tabulating Machine Company is bought, and the name is
changed to International Business Machine (IBM).

1924　Fred Terman, a native of Palo Alto and the son of a Stanford faculty
member, joins the faculty at Stanford after earning his degree in engineering at MIT.

1939　Bill Hewlett and Dan Packard, Stanford University engineering students who are mentored by Fred Terman, found Hewlett-Packard.

1943　IBM establishes a punch-card plant in San Jose.

1943　The Electronic Numerical Integrator Computer (ENIAC), the first fully
electronic programmable digital computer, is built at the University of
Pennsylvania. It is completed in 1945.

1943　Colossus, a series of ten electronic computers, is built at the top-secret
code-breaking facility at Bletchley Park, the headquarters for British
Intelligence.

1944　The first electronic computers operate at Bletchley Park, outside of
London.

1945　IBM funds the Watson Scientific Computing Lab at Columbia
University.

1946　First academic credit courses in computer science are offered at
Columbia University.

1946　The Institute of Electrical Engineers (AIEE) is founded.

1947　The Association for Computing Machinery (ACM) is founded.

1949   The first operational stored-program computer is built at Cambridge University.

1951   The Institute of Radio Engineers (IRE) is founded.

1951   Stanford Research Park, a joint initiative between Stanford University and the city of Palo Alto, is established as the first industrial technology park in the United States.

1953   Cambridge University establishes the first computer science degree program in the world.

1956   Lockheed Aerospace Company sets up a laboratory in the Stanford Industrial Park.

1957   Fairchild Semiconductor Company is founded in Silicon Valley, with financing from the Fairchild camera shop in New York.

1958   NASA opens a research center in Mountain View, California.

1958   NASA disbands the "colored computing pool" when digital computers are adopted.

1959   Computer Business Oriented Language (COBOL), a computer programming language, is designed for business use by a committee representing the US government and the computer industry. Grace Hopper plays a key role in the design.

1962   Purdue University establishes the first Computer Science Department in the United States.

1963   The Institute of Radio Engineers (IRE) and the American Institute of Electrical Engineers (AIEE) merge and form the IEEE computer society.

1971   Don Hoefler, a writer for *Electronic News*, is the first person to use the term "Silicon Valley" in print in reference to the Santa Clara Valley, in a series of articles.

1976   Steve Jobs and Steve Wozniak found Apple Computer in Cupertino.

1992   Intel becomes the world's largest semiconductor manufacturer.

1995   Amazon.com is launched on the web as the "world's largest bookstore," except that it is a website.

1995   eBay, an e-commerce corporation, is founded by Pierre Omidyar in San Jose.

1998   Max Levchin, Peter Thiel, and Luke Nosek found Palm Pilot Payments and Cryptography, which creates the company now known as PayPal.

2001   Apple launches the iPod.

2003   FaceMash is founded in a college dorm room by Mark Zuckerberg, Eduardo Saverin, and others.

2004   The Facebook replaces FaceMash, and Zuckerberg moves to Palo Alto, California, in June. It is now available to Stanford and Ivy League university students.

2005   Skype is acquired by eBay under Meg Whitman's tenure.

2005   Facebook expands to twenty-one universities in the United Kingdom.

2005   More than 50 percent of all jobs outsourced by Silicon Valley companies go to India.

2006   YouTube is acquired by Google for $1.6 billion. Susan Wojcicki is credited for handling this acquisition.

2008   The 23andMe genome test kit is named "Invention of the Year" by *Time*.

2008   The Silicon Valley has 2.4 million people (less than 1 percent of the US population) generating more than 2 percent of the US GDP, with a GDP per person of $83,000.

2008   Google owns almost 70 percent of the internet search market.

2010   Apple introduces the tablet computer iPad. It sells one million units in one month.

2010   The smartphone market grows 55 percent, with 269 million units sold worldwide.

2012   Hackbright Academy launches an all-women engineering academy with a ten-week immersive engineering curriculum for $10,000.

2013   Facebook hires 7 Black people out of 1,231 new hires. Facebook employs a total of 45 Black staff out of a total US workforce of 4,263 employees.

2014   Blacks represent 1.5 percent of Facebook employees.

2014   Google pays Andy Rubin (inventor of the Android) a $90 million exit package in installments of $2 million monthly after an investigation concludes that a sexual harassment complaint by a female employee was credible.

2015   Ellen Pao's trial begins in San Francisco Superior Court. On March 27, Pao loses her lawsuit. The jury rules in favor of Kleiner Perkins on all counts.

2016   The National Labor Relations Board files a complaint against Google for unlawful surveillance and interrogation to chill and restrict employee rights.

2016   Hackbright Academy, a San Francisco–based all-women immersive coding school, is bought by Capella University for $18 million.

2017   In January, the US Department of Labor sues Oracle for paying White men more than their peers with the same job title and for preferring Asian men and discriminating against non-Asian workers when filling technical roles.

2017   Palantir agrees to pay $1.7 million over accusations that it discriminates against Asian employees, one week after the Department of Labor accuses Google of systematically underpaying women.

NOTES

PREFACE

1. See Hollings, Martin, and Rice 2017, 224.
2. See Fuegi and Francis 2003, 17.
3. The Analytical Engine was never built due to a lack funding, but it was a proto-type for the first computing machine with integrated memory.
4. Hollings, Martin, and Rice 2017, 230–31.
5. Misa 2015, 16.
6. Gürer 2002, 175.
7. Fuegi and Francis 2003, 16.
8. Thompson 2019.
9. Matthews 2003, 187–188.
10. Matthews 2003, 188.
11. Matthews 2003, 188.
12. Matthews 2003, 187.
13. With the falling off of military spending after the end of the Cold War and with Lockheed merging with Martin Marietta in 1994 to become Lockheed Martin, those Lockheed employees who were lucky enough to hold onto their jobs began to feel the pinch. At century's end, Lockheed Martin employed only 7,850 people in the Valley, a big reduction from the high-water mark of 25,000 (Matthews 2003, 190).
14. In 2018, Ross was chosen by the US Mint to be depicted on a 2019 one-dollar gold coin, as part of the Mint's celebration of Native Americans in the space program.
15. Floum 2013.

INTRODUCTION

1. See Boyd 2011; Weisberg 2013.
2. In an interview in *Vogue*, Jacob Weisberg (2013) described Mayer as "an unusually stylish geek . . . wearing a red Michael Kors dress with a gold belt and a brown Oscar de la Renta cardigan." See Goel 2017: "A standout among Silicon Valley's male CEOs, Mayer worked very hard during her five years as Yahoo's CEO. Mayer resigned in 2017, after Verizon purchased Yahoo. Martha Josephson, a partner at a headhunting firm used by Mayer to recruit senior executives argued, 'As hard as the job was, she didn't get a break. If she were an ugly man, she'd be a hero.'"

3. See Sorkin and Rusli 2012. Chris Saca, a venture capitalist who had worked with Mayer, described her as having "geek cred."

4. Miller 2012.

5. Boyd 2011, 82.

6. Marissa Mayer was one of the angel investors who put her personal money into launching Mint.

7. Varma 2007, 361.

8. Boyd 2011, 82.

9. Boyd 2011, 87.

10. Broyles and Fenner 2010; Jacobson 2014; Isaac 2016; Kolhatkar 2017; Levin 2017a, 2017b, 2017c, 2017d, 2018a, 2018b; Varathan 2017; Luckie 2018; Kim and Rangarajan 2018.

11. Gee and Peck 2016; Dickey 2016a, 2016b; Fowler 2017; Neate 2015; Mundy 2017; Pao 2017; Wong, 2017a, 2017b; Kamble 2020; Sohrabji 2018.

12. Gee and Peck 2016.

13. Covert 2019; Somerville 2017.

14. See Chou 2013.

15. Dickey 2016a; Vassallo et al. 2015.

16. Isaac 2016.

17. Four percent identified as multiracial. McGregor 2014; Beasely 2017; Baron 2018.

18. *PBS NewsHour* 2014; Jacobson 2014.

19. Sassler, Michelmore, and Smith, 2017.

20. Funk and Parker 2018; Bui and Miller 2016; US Census Bureau 2016.

21. Funk and Parker 2018; US Census Bureau 2016.

22. Dickey 2016a, 2016b; Beasely 2017; Funk and Parker 2018.

23. Bhuiyan, Dean, and Hussain 2020.

24. See Acker 2006, 443. For intersectional studies of women in tech or STEM fields that do not include transgender and LGBTQ women, see Alegria 2016; Alegria and Branch 2015; Tao and McNeeley 2019.

25. Sahoo, Sangha, and Kelly 2010; Fernandez 2018.

26. Safiya Noble uses the term "algorithmic discrimination," which is synonymous with "digital discrimination." See Daniels 2015, 2016; Noble 2018; Benjamin 2019; Nopper 2019; Brock 2020; Gray 2020; Chrispal, Bapuji, and Zietsma 2020; Tiku 2020. Intersectional analyses that have provided important insights on race, gender, and citizenship in the technology industry have not considered caste or marital status. See Alegria 2019; Wynn 2020.

27. Ajaya, Sangha, and Kelly 2010; Baas 2009; Banerjee 2006; Biao 2007.

28. Putnam 2000; Woolcock and Sweetser 2002.

29. Abbate 2012, 41.

30. Luckie 2018; Min 2021.

31. Hepler 2018; Harkinson 2014; Tiku 2020.

32. With two exceptions, all of the women who participated in this study were employed in Silicon Valley at the time of their interview.

33. Four interviews were not recorded at the request of the interviewees; instead, detailed notes were taken.
34. Emerson, Fretz, and Shaw 1995.
35. The two Baby Boomers in this study were born in India and Bangladesh.
36. Among the US-born participants, there were no Baby Boomers. One participant who was born in Bangladesh could be characterized as a Baby Boomer in age, but he did not identify as a Boomer.
37. Most participants who were US nationals had changed jobs every two years and had worked at three or more start-ups and publicly traded companies.
38. Alegria and Branch 2015; Tao and McNeely 2019.
39. Digital job boards are online sites where jobs are advertised. They are typically only accessible to current students or alumni. They are accessible only to "eligible" members of a university or alumni community. These have replaced physical job boards that were common in the twentieth century.
40. Pearlstein 2014.
41. Of the women who took the immigration pathway, two immigrated on family visas as the spouse of an engineer or technical worker. They shifted to full-time employment after a period of being full-time housewives and mothers.
42. Berlin 2017, 73.
43. Berlin 2017, 406.
44. Sturgeon 2000, 47, 16.
45. Rao 2013; Kenney 2000; Saxenian 1994.
46. Saxenian 1994, 25.
47. Matthews 2003, 136.
48. Geha 2020.
49. See OpenDoors 2019.
50. Gray and Suri 2019; Pellow and Park 2002; Gray 2020.
51. Pellow and Park 2002, 3.
52. US Census Bureau 2015; Raj 2012.
53. Nakaso 2012; Data from US Census Bureau's 2011 American Community Survey (ACS), the US Department of Homeland Security's (DHS's) Office of Immigration Statistics (OIS) 2012.
54. Banerjee 2006, 430.
55. US Department of State 2019.
56. Banerjee 2006, 430.
57. Banerjee 2006; Biao 2007; Purkayastha 2005, 2010; Radhakrishnan 2011; Park, J. S. 2018.
58. Baas 2009; Banerjee 2006; Bhatt 2018; Biao 2007; Purkayastha 2005, 2010; Raghuram 2004, 2005; Radhakrishnan 2011.
59. Luthra 2009, 229.
60. Pager, Bonikowski, and Western 2009; Quillian et al. 2017; Ridgeway 2014.
61. Roohi 2017.
62. Fernandez and Nichols 2002.

63. Kanter 1977.
64. Reskin and Roos 1990; Reskin 1993.
65. Acker 1990, 1992, 2004, 2006.
66. Acker 2006, 443.
67. Acker 2006, 443.
68. Kanter 1977, 207.
69. See Alfrey and Twine 2017; Schilt 2011. Lauren Alfrey and I found that gender-fluid women who identify as LGBTQ and who are not Black are not treated as gender tokens but, instead, are treated as social males if they do not challenge the sexist and racist workplace culture on their all-male teams. In this study, I found that male-to-female transgender engineers established their careers while presenting as men and then transitioned to presenting as female, which enabled them to avoid some of the discrimination that cisgender women experienced early in their careers.
70. Kanter 1977; Bielby and Baron 1984; Bielby 2000; Acker 1990, 1992, 2004, 2006; Reskin and Roos 1990; Reskin 1993, 2000.
71. Abbate 2010; Cockburn 1985; Wajcman 1991, 2007, 2010; Woodfield 2000; Ensmenger 2010, 2012; Faulkner 2001; Hayes 2010; Misa 2010; Schlombs 2010.
72. Banerjee 2006; Embrick 2011; Bielby and Baron 1984; Browne and Misra 2003; Pager and Quillian 2005; Royster 2003; Rivera and Tilcsik 2016; Shih 2006; Rivera 2012a, 2012b; Pager and Pedulla 2015.
73. Alegria 2016; Alegria and Branch 2015; Aneesh 2006; Banerjee 2006; Biao 2007; Kamat, Mir, and Mathew 2004; Radhakrishnan 2011; Purkayastha 2005.
74. Petersen, Saporta, and Seidel 2000.
75. Some contractors are employed while full-time employees take maternity leave or need additional help for a project.
76. Pearlstein 2014.
77. Harding 1986, 1991; Cockburn and Ormrod 1993; Hacker 1979, 1981, 1983, 1989, 1990; Wajcman 1991.
78. MacKenzie and Wajcman 1995.
79. Faulkner 2000, 2001, 2007, 2009.
80. Wajcman 1991, 14–15.
81. See Nakamura 2008; Daniels 2009; Noble 2018; Benjamin 2019; Gray 2020.
82. Schlombs 2010.
83. Hicks 2017, 233.
84. Ensmenger 2012, 29.
85. Ensmenger 2012, 5. In *The Computer Boys Take Over*, Ensmenger clarifies that in the 1950s, "software was not something that was purchased off-the-shelf, nor was it a single application or product. Rather, it was a bundle of systems, services and support" (6).
86. Harding 1986.
87. Woodfield 2000, 8.

88. Woodfield 2000, 1.
89. Ensmenger 2012, 238.
90. Abbate 2012, 66–67.
91. During the birth of the commercial computing industry in the 1960s, the practice of segregating and listing job advertisements by gender was still common for US and British newspapers. Janet Abbate points out that "technical job categories such as engineering appeared only in the men's sections, so that even if an individual employer wanted to run a gender-neutral ad, it would have been difficult" (2012, 65).
92. Murray 1993, 66–67.
93. Ensmenger 2012, 35.
94. Abbate 2012; Cockburn 1985, 1988; Hicks 2010; Ensmenger 2010, 2012.
95. Hicks 2017, 20.
96. Haigh 2010, 56.
97. Gürer 2002.
98. Rupp 1978; Milkman 1987.
99. Light 1999, 458.
100. Gee and Peck 2016.

CHAPTER 1. THE SILICON VALLEY CASTE SYSTEM

1. Primack 2014; Shevinsky 2015c; Reed 2016; Vara 2016; Pao 2017; Molla 2017, 2018; Wong 2017; Pardes 2020.
2. Fowler 2017; Pao 2017; US Department of Labor 2017; Varathan 2017.
3. Acker 2006.
4. Fowler 2017; Chang 2018; Pao 2017; Chou 2015; Joy 2015; Shevinsky 2015c; Isaac 2016, 2017a, 2017b, 2017c.
5. US Census Bureau 2016.
6. See Facebook's first annual *Diversity Report*, released in 2015.
7. Vara 2016; Alfrey and Twine 2017.
8. Ashcraft, McLain, and Eger 2016.
9. Dean and Bhuiyan 2020.
10. Vara 2016; Alfrey and Twine 2017.
11. Anand and McBride 2020.
12. Anand and McBride 2020.
13. See US Equal Employment Occupation Commission 2014.
14. Tiku 2017; Vara 2016; Rangarajan and Evans 2017; Funk and Parker 2018.
15. Vara 2016.
16. Tiku 2020.
17. Dickey 2016a.
18. Erica Joy also writes under the names Erica Joy and Erica Baker.
19. Lacy 2007, 76.
20. See Baker 2016.
21. Karake 2020.

22. Grant 2018.
23. Amrute 2016; Banerjee 2006; Kamat, Mir, and Mathew 2004; Purkayastha 2010; Raghuram 2004, 2005.
24. Radhakrishnan 2011, 35.
25. Upadhya 2007; Shanker 2008.
26. Shanker 2008, 192.
27. Radhakrishnan 2011, 34–35.
28. Aneesh 2006; Radhakrishnan 2011; Shanker 2008.
29. Fernandez 2018; Radhakrishnan 2011.
30. Radhakrishnan 2011, 42–43.
31. Dutt 2020.
32. Cal. Dept. Fair Empl. & Hous. v. Cisco Systems, Inc., et al. (N.D. Cal. 2020), https://regmedia.co.uk/2020/07/01/cisco.pdf.
33. Acker 1990; Reskin and Roos 1990.
34. Royster 2003; Quillian et al. 2017; Pager, Bonikowski, and Western 2009.
35. Massey and Denton 1988; Royster 2003.
36. Tiku 2020.
37. Equality Labs, n.d.
38. Gibbs 2014; Rodriguez 2015; E. Rosenberg 2018; Tiku 2020.
39. Berreman 1960; Cell 1981; Fredrickson 1981.
40. For a history of unfree labor and enslaved labor in California, see Smith 2013.
41. Allen 1994; Smedley 1993; Fredrickson 1981.
42. Williams, Muller, and Kilanski 2012.
43. Wilkerson 2020, 70–71.
44. Anti-Black racism and white supremacy, segregation in labor markets, segregated housing markets, and access to education have been durable features of US life for most of the country's history (Fredrickson 1981; Cell 1981; Massey and Denton 1988; Hamilton and Ture 1992). The end of de jure (legal) segregation was replaced by de facto (in fact) segregation in education, housing, and social life. The lifelong effects of this segregation are evident today in Northern California and, by extension, in the Silicon Valley labor market, which continues to deny underrepresented groups—especially Blacks and Latinx—entry into higher-paid, higher-status occupations in this industry.
45. Chrispal, Bapuji, and Ziestma 2020; Tiku 2020. Scholars of the Indian IT sector have found that the caste system remains intact and is disguised by a discourse of merit (Fernandez 2018).
46. Steinberg 1995.
47. See Frankenberg 1993, for her concept of race, color, and power-evasive discourses.
48. Noble and Roberts 2019, 118.
49. Rivera 2012b; Royster 2003.
50. Bourdieu 1984; Rivera 2012b; Rivera and Tilscik 2016.
51. McPherson, Smith-Lovin, and Cook 2001.

52. Lata used the term "American" when referring to White people in the industry and also confirmed a preference at her company for hiring Asian Indian workers, which has also been alleged as a form of discrimination at Oracle and other top technology firms in Silicon Valley.
53. Tiku 2017.
54. Levin, 2017c.
55. Levin 2017c.
56. President Trump rolled back Obama-era protections for female workers.
57. Levin 2017f.
58. Levin 2017d.
59. Levin, 2017f.
60. Acker 1990, 2006.
61. Acker 2006, 443.
62. Levin 2019a, 2019b.
63. Tiku 2019a.
64. Levin 2019a.
65. US Department of Labor 2017.
66. Levin 2019b.
67. Fowler 2017.
68. Farnsworth 2017.
69. See Wakabayashi 2018.
70. Levina and Hasinoff 2017, 490–91.

CHAPTER 2. IDEOLOGIES, MYTHOLOGIES, AND REALITIES

1. Chang 2018, 121. In *Brotopia*, Chang describes a gathering she held with a "dozen women engineers" at her home the same day that the *Atlantic* cover story titled "Why Is Silicon Valley So Awful to Women?" by Liz Mundy dropped. A male-to-female transgender engineer named Lydia Fernandez attended that event. An engineer at Uber, Fernandez began her career presenting and being seen as a man. After completing an internship at Code2040, a program that helps recruit Blacks and Latinx and places them at established tech companies, Fernandez came out as transgender and changed her name to Lydia.
2. Embrick 2011; S. Collins 2011.
3. Metcalfe 2010.
4. Metcalfe 2010, 2.
5. Ma and Liu 2017, 3.
6. Ma and Liu 2017, 4.
7. Wiener 2016; Williams 2016; Wells and Koh 2017.
8. Ahmed 2012, 54.
9. Jesse 2006; Ma 2009; Metcalfe 2010; Wynn 2020.
10. Shevinsky 2015b, 206.
11. Abbate 2012, 40.
12. Pao 2017, 44.

13. Fernandez 2018, 5.
14. Fernandez 2018, 9.
15. Fernandez 2018, 16–17.
16. Dwoskin 2020.
17. Smedley 1993.
18. Allen 1994; Smedley 1993.
19. Ohlheiser 2017; Matsakis 2017, 2018.
20. Ohlheiser 2017.
21. Tiku 2019c.
22. See Ohlheiser 2017.
23. See Damore 2017.
24. See Jaschik 2005; also see Goldenberg 2005.
25. Lewis 2017.
26. Damore 2017.
27. Matsakis 2018.
28. Vara 2016; Molla 2017; Rangarajan and Evans 2017.
29. Vara 2016.
30. Watters 2017.
31. Wynn (2020) interviewed thirty-seven people and observed eighty meetings. She gained access to high-level executives. This article focuses on interviews conduced with nineteen people.
32. Wynn 2020, 107.

CHAPTER 3. BLACK GEEK GIRLS
1. Chernikoff 2015.
2. Chernikoff 2015
3. Gee and Peck 2016; Chang 2018; Pao 2017; Evans and Rangarajan 2017; Funk and Parker 2018.
4. Anderson 2018.
5. Evans and Rangarahan 2017; Mundy 2017; Vara 2016.
6. Mundy 2017.
7. Durr and Wingfield 2011; Collins 1997.
8. Wingfield 2009, 2010; Durr and Wingfield 2011.
9. Kanter 1977.
10. Wingfield 2009, 2010; Wingfield and Alston 2014.
11. Shih 2006.
12. Reveal sought the EEO-1 reports from 211 of the Bay Area's biggest tech companies as part of an ongoing diversity data project. Of the 211 companies surveyed, only 23 released their reports. See Evans and Rangarajan 2017.
13. Evans and Rangarajan 2017.
14. Levin 2017a, 2017b.
15. Wynn 2020, 107–8.
16. Gee and Peck 2016, 17.

17. "Head count" means that there is no money in the budget for her to be full-time.
18. Lacy 2007, 88.
19. Lacy 2007, 84.
20. McIlwee and Robertson 1992.
21. Banerjee 2006.
22. Shih 2006.
23. Alfrey and Twine 2017; Vara 2016.
24. Shih 2006.
25. Feagin and Sikes 1992.
26. Kanter 2007, 219.
27. Shih 2006.
28. Wingfield 2010, 257.
29. Wingfield 2010, 257.
30. Wingfield 2010; Wingfield and Alston 2014.
31. Wingfield and Alston 2014, 275.
32. Durr and Wingfield 2011.
33. Joy 2015; Baker 2016; Chernikoff 2015; Levin 2017c; Vara 2016; Chang 2018.
34. Gerson, 2010.
35. Kanter 1977, 219.
36. Kanter 1977, 208.
37. Kanter 1977, 209.
38. Lacy 2007; Durr and Wingfield 2011.
39. Lacy 2007, 76.
40. Lacy 2007, 76.
41. Lacy 2007, 77.
42. Banks 2000.
43. Levinson 2015, 54.
44. Benner 2017a.
45. Benner 2017b.
46. Wingfield 2019.

CHAPTER 4. FIRST-GENERATION GEEK GIRLS
1. McPherson, Smith-Lovin, and Cook 2001.
2. "Assets" are any icon or image that you see on a website and that needs to be saved in a folder in the source file.
3. Bourdieu 1997.
4. Lin 2000, 786.
5. Cook 2014.

CHAPTER 5. SECOND-GENERATION GEEK GIRLS
1. Pao 2017, 14–15.
2. Pao 2017, 14.
3. Pao 2017, 16.

4. Alfrey and Twine 2017.
5. Reeves 2018, 12.
6. McIlwee and Robinson 1992.
7. Ma 2009; Ma and Liu 2017.

CHAPTER 6. TRANSNATIONAL GEEK GIRLS

1. McIlwee and Robinson 1992.
2. Amrute 2016; Banerjee 2006; Kamat, Mir, and Mathew 2004; Purkayastha 2010; Raghuram 2004, 2005; Roohi 2017; Roos 2013.
3. Radhakrishnan 2011, 8.
4. Radhakrishnan 2011; Bhatt 2018.
5. Baas 2009; Biao 2005; Radhakrishnan 2011.
6. Baas 2009; Banerjee 2006; Bhatt 2018; Biao 2005, 2007; Kamat, Mir, and Matthew 2004; Purkayastha 2005; Radhakrishnan 2011; Raghuram 2004, 2005; Varma 2007, 2009.
7. Bhatt 2018.
8. Bhatt 2018, 57.
9. Bhatt 2018, 65.
10. Bhatt 2018, 72.
11. Radhakrishnan 2011, 10.
12. Radhakrishnan 2011, 8.
13. Vara 2016.
14. Vara 2016.
15. Varma and Kapur 2015.
16. Gibbs 2014.

CHAPTER 7. CODE-SWITCHERS

1. Dev Bootcamp, which operated in six cities, closed its doors in 2017, four years after Bishay sold it to Kaplan.
2. Kessler 2017.
3. For an analysis of the coding boot camp market, see Arbeit et al. 2019.
4. "Full stack" means a course that covers both the front end (the part that the user sees) and the back end (the portion running on the server).
5. Lohr 2015.
6. See President's Council of Advisors on Science and Technology 2012; US Department of Education 2016.
7. White House 2015.
8. Funk and Parker 2018.
9. Eggleston 2018.
10. Writing for the *New York Times*, Tina Rosenberg (2018) presented an uncritical and glowing report of the opportunities that coding boot camps provide to nontraditional students who do not have the opportunities, resources, or time to

attend an expensive four-year university degree program at MIT, Stanford, Carnegie Mellon, or UC-Berkeley. In her profile of Access Code, Rosenberg writes, "Instead of demanding traditional credentials, the program evaluates applicants as they solve logic puzzles and spend two days learning basic coding. One in 10 is accepted. C4Q says that upon entering those students are earning an average of $18,000 per year, but when they graduate and find work in software engineering which almost all do—they make an average of $85,000. . . . Students pay nothing until they graduate and get a high paying tech job."

11. Lohr 2015.
12. Eggleston 2014, 2015a, 2015c, 2016a, 2016b, 2017a, 2017b, 2018.
13. Thompson 2017.
14. Wilson 2017, 70.
15. Acker 2006; Bourdieu 1997; Britton 2000; Granovetter 1973.
16. Charles and Brady 2002, 2006.
17. Margolis et al. 2008.
18. Hackbright Academy, "About," accessed August 2018, https://hackbrightacademy.com.
19. Due to the high up-front costs of boot camps, with an average cost of $11,900, some boot camps have begun to offer deferred tuition, loan programs, and income-sharing agreements (Eggleston 2018). While some coding boot camps offer scholarships to low-income applicants, women, military veterans, and ethnic minorities, others offer deferred tuition in what is called an "income-sharing agreement." In this agreement, applicants agree to pay either a flat monthly amount or a percentage of their monthly salary after they have secured a full-time job during their first years of employment.
20. A 2016 report published by Hackbright analyzed the employment outcomes of seventy-nine students who completed the curriculum during the first six months of 2016. Based on self-reports of alumnae, Hackbright concluded that within six months after completing their curriculum, 71 percent of its alumnae were employed in paid in-field positions. Of alumna in full-time positions, 83 percent earned more than $80,000 per year, with 37 percent earning more than $110,000. Hackbright alumna earned higher salaries when compared to those who had earned a bachelor's degree in computer science.
21. Hackbright 2018.
22. A 2018 Course Report market survey of 828 graduates of 41 coding boot camp schools that offered in-person classes found that the average coding boot camper was thirty years old, White, and a man who had six years of work experience and had never worked as a programmer. This annual study of coding boot camp outcomes by Course Report is based on self-reports of graduates of 41 schools and does not necessarily represent all students enrolled in coding boot camps. See Eggleston 2018.
23. The exception, Brielle, went to a coed coding boot camp in North Carolina because it offered her free tuition as an employee serving in a nontechnical role.
24. Granovetter 1973, 1974.

25. McIlwee and Robinson 1992, 26.
26. In a rigorous review of the coding boot camp industry, an RTI study found, "This evidence . . . may indicate that rather than providing a short-cut to a high-paying career for students who cannot afford the time or cost of a traditional 4-year institution, comprehensive career preparation programs are simply providing vocational training to well-resourced students who have already demonstrated their academic proficiency by earning a bachelor's degree" (Arbeit et al. 2019, 21).
27. Cottom 2019.

CONCLUSION
1. Hicks 2017.
2. Wakabayashi et al. 2018; Hicks 2017.
3. Fowler 2017; Wakabayashi et al. 2018; Chang 2018; Fowler 2017; Wong 2017.
4. Stapleton et al. 2018.
5. In the late twentieth century, sociologists began studying gender relations and organizing among high-tech workers in the US and Asia. See Hossfeld 1995. Sociologists began to produce a body of research on gender, stratification, and obstacles to organizing among high-tech workers. Also see McKay 2006.
6. Scheiber 2018.
7. Tiku 2019b.
8. Whittaker 2019.
9. Whittaker 2019.
10. Conger 2021.
11. Boyd 2011.
12. Wingfield 2019.
13. Hao 2020a.
14. According to media reports (Wong 2020), Google tried to "suppress her research." Also see Simonite 2021.
15. See Tim Simonite's (2021a) report on Gebru's forced exit from Google; Hao 2020b.
16. Simonite 2021b.
17. Noble 2018.
18. Noble 2018, 4.
19. Noble 2018, 31.
20. Noble 2018, 4.
21. Benjamin 2019, 8.
22. Chang 2018, 127.
23. Pao 2017, 44.
24. Pao 2017, 7.
25. Shevinsky 2015c, 64–65.
26. See Brougher 2020.
27. Griffith 2020.
28. Min 2021.
29. Paul 2021.

30. Paul 2021.
31. Paul 2021.
32. Finney 2016.
33. digitalundivided is intentionally spelled without spaces dividing the words "digital" and "undivided."
34. Nash was a student activist, a strategist, and a cofounder of the Student Nonviolent Coordinating Committee (SNCC). As an organizer, she played a central role in the 1963 desegregation campaign.
35. DigitalUndivided 2020.
36. Chang 2018.
37. Chang 2018, 84–85.
38. Levinson 2015, 56–57.
39. Cabot and Walravens 2017, 14–15; Zarya 2018.

REFERENCES

Abbate, Janet. 2010. "The Pleasure Paradox: Bridging the Gap between Popular images of Computing and Women's Historical Experiences." In *Gender Codes: Why Women are Leaving Computing* edited by Thomas J. Misa. Hoboken, 213–27. New Jersey: IEEE Computing Society.

———. 2012. *Recoding Gender: Women's Changing Participation in Computing*. Cambridge, MA: MIT Press.

Acker, Joan. 1990. "Hierarchies, Jobs, Bodies: A Theory of Gendered Organizations." *Gender & Society* 4 (2): 139–58.

———. 1992. "Gendered Institutions: From Sex Roles to Gendered Institutions." *Contemporary Sociology* 21:565–69.

———. 2004. "Gender, Capitalism and Globalization." *Critical Sociology* (1): 17–41.

———. 2006. "Inequality Regimes: Gender, Class and Race in Organizations." *Gender & Society* 20 (4): 441–64.

Ahmed, Sara. 2012. *On Being Included: Racism and Diversity in Institutional Life*. Durham, NC: Duke University Press.

Alegria, Sharla. 2016. "A Mixed Methods Analysis of the Intersection of Gender, Race, and Migration in the High-Tech Workforce." PhD diss., University of Massachusetts at Amherst.

———. 2019. "Escalator or Step-Stool? Gendered Labor and Token Processes in Tech Work." *Gender & Society* 33 (5): 722–45.

Alegria, Sharla, and Ebonong Hannah Branch. 2015. "Causes and Consequences of Inequality in STEM: Diversity and Its Discontents." *International Journal of Gender, Science and Technology* 7 (3): 321–42.

Alfrey, Lauren, and France Winddance Twine. 2017. "Gender-Fluid Geek Girls: Negotiating Inequality Regimes in the Tech Industry." *Gender & Society* 31 (1): 5–27.

Alicandri, Jeremy. 2020. "IBM Apologizes for Firing Computer Pioneer for Being Transgender . . . 52 Years Later." *Forbes*, November 18, 2020. www.forbes.com.

Allen, Theodore W. 1994. *The Invention of the White Race*. Vol. 1, *Racial Oppression and Social Control*. London: Verso.

Amrute, Sareeta. 2016. *Encoding Race, Encoding Class: Indian IT Workers in Berlin*. Durham, NC: Duke University Press.

Anand, Priya, and Sarah McBride. 2020. "For Black CEOs in Silicon Valley, Humiliation Is Part of Doing Business." *San Jose (CA) Mercury News*, June 16, 2020.

Anderson, Monica. 2018. "Black STEM Employees Perceive a Range of Race-Related Slights and Inequities at Work." Pew Research Center, January 10, 2018. www .pewresearch.org.

Aneesh, A. 2006. *Virtual Migration: The Programming of Globalization*. Durham, NC: Duke University Press.

Arbeit, Caren, Alexander Bentz, Emily Forrest Cataldi, and Herschel Sanders. 2019. *Alternative and Independent: The Universe of Technology-Related "Bootcamps."* Research Report RR-0033-1902. Research Triangle Park, NC: RTI Press.

Ashcraft, Catherine, Brad McLain, and Elizabeth Eger. 2016. "Women in Tech: The Facts." National Center for Women and Information Technology (NCWIT). www.ncwit.org.

Baas, Michiel. 2009. "The IT Caste: Love and Arranged Marriages in the IT Industry of Bangalore." *South Asia: Journal of South Asian Studies* 32 (2): 285–307.

Baker, Erica Joy. 2016. "It's Time for Tech to Make Racism a Fireable Offense." *Quartz*, April 11, 2016. https://qz.com.

Banerjee, Payal. 2006. "Indian Information Technology Workers in the United States: The H-1B Visa, Flexible Production and the Racialization of Labor." *Critical Sociology* 32 (2–3): 425–45.

Banks, Ingrid. 2000. *Hair Matters: Beauty, Power and Black Women's Consciousness*. New York: New York University Press.

Baron, Ethan. 2018. "H-1B: Foreign Citizens Make Up Nearly Three-Quarters of Silicon Valley Tech Workforce, Report Says." *Mercury News*, October 19, 2018. www.mercu rynews.com.

Barton, LeRon. 2019. "Is Silicon Valley Using Culture Fit to Disguise Discrimination." *Raconteur*, May 1, 2019.

Bazelon, Emily. 2015. "What's Really at Stake in Ellen Pao's Kleiner Perkins Lawsuit." *New York Times Magazine*, February 24, 2015.

Beasley, Maya. 2017. "There Is a Supply of Diverse Workers in Tech, So Why Is Silicon Valley So Lacking in Diversity." Center for American Progress, March 2017. https:// cdn.americanprogress.org.

Benjamin, Ruha. 2019. *Race after Technology: Abolitionist Tools for the New Jim Code*. Cambridge, UK: Polity.

Benner, Kate. 2017a. "Abuses Hide in the Silence of Non-Disparagement Agreements." *New York Times*, July 21, 2017. www.nytimes.com.

———. 2017b. "Women in Tech Speak Frankly on Culture of Harassment." *New York Times*, June 30, 2017. www.nytimes.com.

Bergen, Mark, and Ellen Huet. 2017. "Google Fires Author of Divisive Memo on Gender Differences." *Bloomberg News*, August 7, 2017. www.bloomberg.com.

Berlin, Leslie. 2017. *Troublemakers: Silicon Valley's Coming of Age*. New York: Simon and Schuster.

Berreman, Gerald. 1960. "Caste in India and the United States." *American Journal of Sociology* 66 (2): 120–27.

Bhatt, Amy. 2018. *High-Tech Housewives: Indian IT Workers, Gendered Labor, and Transmigration*. Seattle: University of Washington Press.

Bhuiyan, Johana, Sam Dean, and Suhauna Hussain. 2020. "Black and Brown Tech Workers Share Their Experiences of Racism on the Job." *Los Angeles Times*, June 24, 2020. www.latimes.com.

Biao, Xiang. 2005. "Gender, Dowry and the Migration System of Indian Information Technology Professionals." *Indian Journal of Gender Studies* 12 (2–3): 357–80.

———. 2007. *Global "Body Shopping": An Indian Labor System in the Information Technology Industry*. Princeton, NJ: Princeton University Press.

Bielby, William T. 2000. "Minimizing Workplace Gender and Racial Bias." *Contemporary Sociology* 29:120–29.

Bielby, William T., and James N. Baron. 1984. "A Woman's Place Is with Other Women: Sex Segregation within Organizations." In *Sex Segregation in the Workplace*, edited by Barbara Reskin, 27–55. Washington, DC: National Academy Press.

Bonilla-Silva, Eduardo, Carla Goar, and David Embrick. 2006. "When Whites Flock Together:
The Social Psychology of White Habitus." *Critical Sociology* 32 (2–3): 229–53.

Bourdieu, Pierre. 1984. *Distinction: A Social Critique on the Judgment of Taste*. Cambridge, MA: Harvard University Press.

———. 1986. "The Forms of Capital." In *Handbook of Theory and Research for Sociology of Education*, edited by J. Richardson, 241–58. Westport, CT: Greenwood.

Boyd, E. B. 2011. "Where Is the Female Mark Zuckerberg?" *San Francisco Magazine*, December 2011, 82–93, 106.

Britton, Dana. 2000. "The Epistemology of Gendered Organizations." *Gender & Society* 14:418–34.

Brock, André. 2020. *Distributed Blackness: African American Cybercultures*. New York: New York University Press.

Brougher, Francoise. 2020. "The Pinterest Paradox: Cupcakes and Toxicity." *Medium*, August 11, 2020. https://medium.com.

Browne, Irene, and Joya Misra. 2003. "The Intersection of Gender and Race in the Labor Market." *Annual Review of Sociology* 29 (1): 487–513.

Broyles, Phillip, and Weston Fenner. 2010. "Race, Human Capital, and Wage Discrimination in STEM Professions in the United States." *International Journal of Sociology and Social Policy* 30 (5–6): 251–66.

Bui, Quoctrung, and Claire Cain Miller. 2016. "Why Tech Degrees Are Not Putting More Blacks and Hispanics into Tech Jobs." *New York Times*, February 25, 2016. www.nytimes.com.

Burke, Quinn, Cinamon Bailey, Louise Ann Lyon, and Emily Green. 2018. "Understanding the Software Development Industry's Perspective on Coding Boot Camps versus Traditional 4 Year Colleges." *Proceedings of the 49th ACM Technical Symposium on Computer Science Education*, February 2018, 503–8.

Burleigh, Nina. 2015. "What Silicon Valley Thinks of Women." *Newsweek*, January 28, 2015.

Cabot, Heather, and Samantha Walravens. 2017. *Geek Girl Rising: Inside the Sisterhood Shaking Up Tech*. New York: St. Martin's.

Cain, Claire Miller. 2012. "In Google's Inner Circle, a Falling Number of Women." *New York Times*, August 22, 2012. www.nytimes.com.

Cell, John. 1981. *The Highest Stage of White Supremacy: The Origins of Segregation in South Africa and the American South*. Cambridge: Cambridge University Press.

Chang, Emily. 2018. *Brotopia: Breaking the Boys' Club of Silicon Valley*. New York: Portfolio/Penguin.

Charles, Maria, and Kim Bradley. 2002. "Equal but Separate? A Cross-National Study of Sex Segregation in Higher Education." *American Sociological Review* 67:573–99.

———. 2006. "A Matter of Degree: Female Undergraduate Representation in Computer Science Programs Cross-Nationally." In *Women and Information Technology: Research on Underrepresentation*, edited by J. McGrath Cohoon and Williams Aspray, 183–204. Cambridge, MA: MIT Press.

Chernikoff, Leah. 2015. "This One Story Illustrates Tech's Diversity Problem," *Elle*, July 14, 2015. www.elle.com.

Cho, Sumi. 2008. "Post-Racialism." *Iowa Law Review* 94:1589–1649.

Chou, Tracy. 2013. "Where Are the Numbers?" *Medium*, October 11, 2013. https://medium.com.

———. 2015. "The Uncomfortable State of Being Asian in Tech." *Medium*, October 18, 2015. https://medium.com.

Chrispal, Snehanjali, Hari Bapuji, and Charlene Ziestma. 2020. "Caste and Organization Studies: Our Silence Makes Us Complicit." *Organization Studies*, October 4, 2020.

Cockburn, Cynthia. 1985. *Machinery of Dominance: Women, Men and Technical Know-How*. London: Pluto.

———. 1988. "The Gendering of Jobs: Workplace Relations and the Reproduction of Sex Segregation." In *Gender Segregation at Work*, edited by Sylvia Walby, 29–42. Milton Keynes, UK: Open University Press.

Cockburn, Cynthia, and Susan Ormrod. 1993. *Gender and Technology in the Making*. London: Sage.

Collins, Sharon. 1997. *Black Corporate Executives: The Making and Breaking of a Black Middle Class*. Philadelphia: Temple University Press.

———. 2011. "Diversity in the Post Affirmative Action Labor market: A Proxy for Racial Progress." *Critical Sociology* 37 (5): 521–40.

Conger, Kate. 2017. "Exclusive: Here's the Full 10-Page Anti-Diversity Screed Circulating Internally at Google." *Gizmodo*, August 5, 2017. https://gizmodo.com.

———. 2018. "Ex-Google Employee's Memo Says Executives Shut Down Pro-Diversity Discussions." *Gizmodo*, January 11, 2018. https://gizmodo.com.

———. 2021. "Hundreds of Google Employees Unionize, Culminating Years of Activism." *New York Times*, January 4, 2021.

Conger, Kate, Daisuke Wakabayashi, and Katie Benner. 2018. "Google Faces Internal Backlash over Handling of Sexual Harassment." *New York Times*, October 31, 2018. www.nytimes.com.

Cook, Tim. 2014. "Tim Cook Speaks Up: 'I Don't Consider Myself an Activist, but I Realized How Much I've Benefitted from the Sacrifice of Others.'" *Bloomberg Business*, October 30, 2014. www.bloomberg.com.

Cottom, Tressie McMillan. 2019. *Lower ED: The Troubling Rise of For-Profit Colleges in the New Economy*. New York: New Press.

Covert, Bryce. 2019. "Even Google Can No Longer Hide Its Gender Pay Gap." *New York Times*, March 7, 2019. www.nytimes.com.

Cramer, Maria. 2020. "52 Years Later, IBM Apologizes for Firing Transgender Woman." *New York Times*, November 21, 2020. www.nytimes.com.

Crenshaw, Kimberlé. 1989. "Demarginalizing the Intersections of Race and Sex: A Black Feminist Critique of Antidiscrimination Doctrine, Feminist Theory and Antiracist Politics." *University of Chicago Legal Forum* 140:139–67.

Damore, James. 2017. "Google's Ideological Echo Chamber." Documentcloud.org, July 2017. https://assets.documentcloud.org.

Daniels, Jessie. 2009. *Cyber Racism: White Supremacy Online and the New Attack on Civil Rights*. Lanham, MD: Rowman and Littlefield.

———. 2015. "My Brain Database Doesn't See Skin Color: Color-Blind Racism in the Technology Industry and in Theorizing the Web." *American Behavioral Scientist* 59 (11): 1377–93.

———. 2016. "The Trouble with White Feminism: Whiteness, Digital Feminism, and the Intersectional Internet." In *The Intersectional Internet: Race, Sex, Class and Culture Online*, edited by Safiya Umoja Noble and Brendesha M. Tynes, 41–60. New York: Peter Lang.

Dastin, Jeffrey. 2018. "Amazon Scraps Secret AI Recruiting Tool That Showed Bias against Women." Reuters, October 8, 2018. www.reuters.com.

Dean, Sam, and Johana Bhuiyan. 2020. "Why Are Black and Latino People Still Kept out of the Tech Industry?" *Los Angeles Times*, June 24, 2020.

Dickey, Megan Rose. 2016a. "Elephant in the Valley: Survey Sheds Light on Issues Women Face in Tech." *TechCrunch*, January 11, 2016.

———. 2016b. "Equal Employment Opportunity Commission Says Tech Industry Is Underutilizing Diverse Talent Pool." *TechCrunch*, May 18, 2016. https://techcrunch.com.

DigitalUndivided. 2020. *The State of Black & Latinx Women Founders*. ProjectDiane. https://digitalundivided.com.

Duffin Karen, and Kenny Malone. 2018. "NDA Tell-All, Episode 834." *Planet Money*, NPR, April 6, 2018. Podcast. www.npr.org.

Duffy, Kate. 2020. "Pinterest Has Paid $22.5 Million to Settle a Gender Discrimination Suit from Former Executive Francoise Brougher, Who Claimed She Was Fired after Speaking Up." *Business Insider*, December 15, 2020. www.businessinsider.com.

Durr, Marlese, and Adia Harvey Wingfield. 2011. "Keep Your 'N' in Check: African American Women and Interactive Effects of Etiquette and Emotional Labor." *Critical Sociology* 37 (5): 557–71.

Dutt, Yashica. 2020. "The Specter of Caste in Silicon Valley." *New York Times*, July 14, 2020.

Dwoskin, Elizabeth. 2020. "Complaint Alleges That Facebook Is Biased against Black Workers." *Washington Post*, July 3, 2020. www.washingtonpost.com.

Edmund, John. 2016. "Silicon Valley Doesn't Care about Black People." *Mercury News*, July 6, 2016.

Eggleston, Liz. 2014. "2014 Coding Bootcamp Market Size Study." Course Report, April 30, 2014. www.coursereport.com.

———. 2015a. "Coding Boot Camps Alumni Outcomes and Demographic Study." Course Report. www.coursereport.com.

———. 2015b. "2015 Coding Bootcamp Market Size Study." Course Report, June 8, 2015. www.coursereport.com.

———. 2016a. "2016 Coding Bootcamp Market Size Study." Course Report, June 22, 2016. www.coursereport.com.

———. 2016b. "2016 Coding Boot Camps Alumni Outcomes & Demographics Study." Course Report, September 14, 2016. www.coursereport.com.

———. 2017a. "2017 Coding Bootcamp Alumni Outcomes & Demographics." Course Report. www.coursereport.com.

———. 2017b. "2017 Coding Bootcamp Market Size Study." Course Report, July 19, 2017. www.coursereport.com.

———. 2018. "Coding Bootcamp Alumni Outcomes & Demographics 2018." Course Report. www.coursereport.com.

Elson, Diane. 1999. "Labor Markets as Gendered Institutions: Equality, Efficiency and Empowerment Issues." *World Development* 27 (3): 611–27.

Embrick, David. 2011. "The Diversity Ideology in the Business World: A New Oppression for a New Age." *Critical Sociology* 37 (5): 541–56.

Emerson, Robert, Rachel I. Fretz, and Linda L. Shaw. 1995. *Writing Ethnographic Fieldnotes*. Chicago: University of Chicago Press.

Ensmenger, Nathan. 2010. "Making Programming Masculine." In *Gender Codes: Why Women Are Leaving Computing*, edited by Thomas J. Misa, 115–41. Hoboken, NJ: IEEE Computer Society.

———. 2012. *The Computer Boys Take Over: Computers, Programmers and the Politics of Technical Expertise*. Cambridge, MA: MIT Press.

Equality Labs. 2018. *Caste in the United States: A Survey of Caste among South Asian Americans*. www.equalitylabs.org.

———. N.d. "Caste in the United States." Accessed September 20, 2018. www.equalitylabs.org.

Evans, Will, and Sinduja Rangarajan. 2017. "Hidden Figures: How Silicon Valley Keeps Diversity Data Secret." Reveal: Center for Investigative Reporting, October 19, 2017. www.revealnews.org.

Facebook. 2015. *Diversity Report 2015*. Menlo Park, CA: Facebook.

Farnsworth, Meghann. 2017. "Read the Full Investigation of Uber's Troubled Culture and Management." Recode, June 13, 2017. www.recode.net.

Faulkner, Wendy. 2000. "Dualism, Hierarchies and Gender in Engineering." *Social Studies of Science* 30 (5): 759–92.

———. 2001. "The Technology Question in feminism: A View from Feminist Technology Studies." *Women's Studies International Forum* 24 (1): 79–95.

———. 2007. "Nuts and Bolts People: Gender-Troubled Engineering Identities." *Social Studies of Science* 37 (3): 331–56.

———. 2009. "Doing Gender in Engineering Workplace Cultures: Gender In/authenticity and the In/visibility Paradox." *Engineering Studies* 1 (3): 169–89.

Feagin, Joe R., and Melvin P. Sikes. 1992. *Living with Racism: The Black Middle-Class Experience.* Boston: Beacon.

Fernandez, Marilyn. 2018. *The New Frontier: Merit vs. Caste in the Indian IT Sector.* Oxford: Oxford University Press.

Fernandez, Marilyn, and Laura Nichols. 2002. "Bridging and Bonding Capital: Pluralist Ethnic Relations in Silicon Valley." *International Journal of Sociology and Social Policy* 22 (9–10): 104–22.

Finney, Kathryn. 2016. *The State of Black Women Founders: ProjectDiane2018.* digitalundivided. www.projectdiane.com.

Floum, Jessica. 2013. "Tech Women Find Opportunities at Girl Geek Dinners." *San Francisco Gate,* August 25, 2013. www.sfgate.com.

Fowler, Susan. 2017. "Reflecting on a One Very Very Strange Year at Uber." Susan Fowler's blog, February 19, 2017. www.susanjfowler.com.

Franceschi-Bicchierai, Lorenzo, and Jason Koebler. 2019. "Google Employee Alleges Discrimination Against Pregnant Women in Viral Memo." *Vice,* August 5, 2019. www.vice.com.

Frankenberg, Ruth. 1993. *White Women, Race Matters: The Social Construction of Whiteness.* Minneapolis: University of Minnesota Press.

———. 2001. "Mirage of an Unmarked Whiteness." In *The Making and Unmaking of Whiteness,* edited by Brigit Brander Rasmussen, Eric Klinenberg, Irene Nexica, and Matt Wray, 72–96. Durham, NC: Duke University Press.

Fredrickson, George. 1981. *White Supremacy: A Comparative Analysis in American and South African History.* Oxford: Oxford University Press.

Fuegi, John, and Jo Francis. 2003. "Lovelace & Babbage and the Creation of the 1843 'Notes.'" *IEEE Annals of the History of Computing* 25 (4): 16–26.

Funk, Cary, and Kim Parker. 2018. "Diversity in the STEM Workforce Varies Widely across Jobs." Pew Research Center, Social Trends, January 9, 2018. www.pewsocialtrends.org.

Gee, Buck, and Denise Peck. 2016. *The Illusion of Asian Success: Scant Progress for Minorities in Cracking the Glass Ceiling from 2007–2015.* New York: Ascend Foundation. www.ascendleadership.org.

Geha, Joseph. 2020. "Silicon Valley Pain Index Shows 'White Supremacy' Prevalent." *Mercury News,* June 23, 2020.

Gehl, Robert W., Lucas Moyer-Horner, and Sara K. Yeo. 2017. "Training Computers to See Internet Pornography Gender and Sexual Discrimination in Computer Vision Science." *Television & New Media* 18 (6): 529–47.

Gerson, Kathleen. 2010. *The Unfinished Revolution: How a New Generation Is Reshaping Family, Work and Gender in America*. New York: Oxford University Press.

Gibbs, Samuel. 2014. "The Most Powerful Indian Technologists in Silicon Valley." *Guardian* April 11, 2014. www.theguardian.com.

Glass, Jennifer, Sharon Sassler, Yael Levitte, and Katherine M. Michelmore. 2013. "What's So Special about STEM? A Comparison of Women's Retention in STEM and Professional Occupations." *Social Forces* 92 (2): 723–56.

Goel, Vindu. 2017. "Dissecting Marissa Mayer's $900,000-a-Week Yahoo Paycheck." *New York Times*, June 3, 2017. www.nytimes. com.

Goffman, Erving. 1959. *The Presentation of Self in Everyday Life*. Garden City, NY: Doubleday.

Goldenberg, Suzanne. 2005. "Why Women Are Poor at Science, by Harvard President." *Guardian*, January 18, 2005.

Google. 2020. *Diversity Report 2020*. https://diversity.google.

Granovetter, Mark. 1973. "The Strength of Weak Ties." *American Journal of Sociology* 78 (6): 1360–80.

———. 1974. *Getting a Job: A Study of Contacts and Careers*. Cambridge, MA: Harvard University Press.

Grant, Nico. 2018. "'Very Lonely': The Unsettling Hum of Silicon Valley's Failure to Hire More Black Workers." *Bloomberg*, June 8, 2018. www.bloomberg.com.

Gray, Kishonna L. 2020. *Intersectional Tech: Black Users in Digital Gaming*. Baton Rouge: Louisiana State University Press.

Gray, Mary L., and Siddharth Suri. 2019. *Ghost Work: How to Stop Silicon Valley from Building a New Global Underclass*. Boston: Houghton Mifflin Harcourt.

Greenfield, Rebecca, Nico Grant, and Sarah Frier. 2018. "Facebook Has a 'Black People Problem,' Ex-Employee Writes." *Bloomberg*, November 27, 2018.

Grier, David Alan. 1996. "The ENIAC, the Verb 'to Program' and the Emergence of Digital Computers." *Annals of the History of Computing* 18 (1): 51–55.

———. 2005. *When Computers Were Human*. Princeton, NJ: Princeton University Press.

Griffith, Erin. 2020. "Pinterest Settles Gender Discrimination Suite for $22.5 Million." *New York Times*, December 14, 2020. www.nytimes.com.

Guess, Megan. 2015. "Reddit CEO Ellen Pao Takes On Former Firm in Discrimination Case." *Ars Technica*, February 2015. https://arstechnica.com.

Gürer, Denise. 2002. "Pioneering Women in Computer Science." *SIGCSE Bulletin* 34 (2): 175–83. Reprinted from original 1995 article published in *Communication of the ACM* 38 (1): 45–54.

Hackbright Academy. 2018. "12 Outstanding Web Apps Built by Female Engineers." *Hackbright Academy Blog*, August 24, 2018. https://blog.hackbrightacademy.com.

Hacker, Sally, 1979. "Sex, Stratification, Technology and Organizational Change: A Case Study of AT&T." *Social Problems* 26 (5): 539–57.

———. 1981. "The Culture of Engineering: Women, Workplace, and Machine." *Women's Studies International Quarterly* 4 (3): 341–53.

———. 1983. "Mathematization of Engineering: Limits on Women in the Field." In *Machina ex Dea: Feminist Perspectives on Technology*, edited by Joan Rothschild, 38–58. New York: Pergamon.

———. 1989. *Pleasure, Power and Technology*. Boston: Unwin Hyman.

———. 1990. *Doing It the Hard Way: Investigations of Gender and Technology*. Boston: Unwin Hyman.

Haigh, Thomas. 2010. "Masculinity and the Machine Man: Gender in the History of Data Processing." In *Gender Codes: Why Women Are Leaving Computing*, edited by Thomas J. Misa, 51–71. Hoboken, NJ: Wiley.

Hamilton, Charles, and Kwame Ture. 1992. *Black Power: The Politics of Liberation*. New York: Vintage. Originally published in 1967 under the title *Black Power: The Politics of Liberation in America*.

Hanna, Alex, and Meredith Whittaker. 2020. "Timnit Gebru's Exist from Google Exposes a Crisis in AI." *Wired*, December 31, 2020. www.wired.com.

Hao, Karen. 2020a. "'I Started Crying': Inside Timnit Gebru's Last Days at Google and What Happens Next." *MIT Technology Review*, December 16, 2020. www .technologyreview.com.

———. 2020b. "A Leading AI Ethics Researcher Says She's Been Fired from Google." *MIT Technology Review*, December 3, 2020. www.technologyreview.com.

———. 2020c. "We Read the Paper That Forced Timnit Gebru out of Google: Here's What It Says." *MIT Technology Review*, December 4, 2020. www.technologyreview.com.

Harding, Sandra. 1986. *The Science Question in Feminism*. Ithaca, NY: Cornell University Press.

———. 1991. *Whose Science, Whose Knowledge? Thinking from Women's Lives*. Ithaca, NY: Cornell University Press.

Harkinson, Josh. 2014. "Silicon Valley Firms Are Even Whiter and More Male than You Think." *Mother Jones*, May 29, 2014. www.motherjones.com.

Hayes, Caroline Clarke. 2010. "Computer Science: The Incredible Shrinking Woman." In *Gender Codes: Why Women Are Leaving Computing*, edited by Thomas Misa, 25–49. Hoboken, NJ: Wiley.

Hempel, Jessi. 2016. "A Woman's History of Silicon Valley." *Wired*, June 30, 2016. www .wired.com.

Hepler, Lauren. 2018. "Menial Tasks, Slurs and Swastikas: Many Black Workers at Tesla Say They Faced Racism." *New York Times*, November 13, 2018. www.nytimes.com.

Hicks, Marie. 2010. "Meritocracy and Feminization in Conflict: Computerization in the British Government." In *Gender Codes: Why Women are Leaving Computing*, edited by Thomas Misa, 95–114. Hoboken, NJ: Wiley.

———. 2017. *Programmed Inequality: How Britain Discarded Women Technologists and Lost Its Edge in Computing*. Cambridge, MA: MIT Press.

Hiles, Heather. 2015. "Silicon Valley Venture Capital Has a Diversity Problem." *Recode*, March 18, 2015.

Hiltzik, Michael. 2000. "Through the Gender Labyrinth." *Los Angeles Times*, November 19, 2000.

Hoge, Patrick. 2012. "Coder Boot Camp Grads Snapped Up." *San Francisco Business Times*, December 11, 2012. www.bizjournals.com.

Hollings, Christopher, Ursula Martin, and Adrian Rice. 2017. "The Early Mathematical Education of Ada Lovelace." *Journal of the British Society for the History of Mathematics* 32 (3): 221–34.

Hossfeld, Karen J. 1995. "Why Aren't High-Tech Workers Organized? Lessons in Gender, Race, and Nationality from Silicon Valley." In *Working People of California*, edited by Daniel Cornford, 405–32. Berkeley: University of California Press.

Isaac, Mike. 2016. "Women in Tech Band Together to Track Diversity after Hours." *New York Times*, May 3, 2016. www.nytimes.com.

———. 2017a. "Inside Uber's Aggressive Unrestrained Workplace Culture." *New York Times*, February 22, 2017. www.nytimes.com.

———. 2017b. "Uber Fires 20 amid Investigation into Workplace Culture." *New York Times*, June 6, 2017. www.nytimes.com.

———. 2017c. "Uber Releases Diversity Report and Repudiates Its Hard-Changing Attitude." *New York Times*, March 28, 2017. www.nytimes.com.

Jacobs, Jerry. 1989. *Revolving Doors: Sex Segregation and Women's Careers*. Stanford, CA: Stanford University Press.

Jacobson, Murrey. 2014. "Google Finally Discloses Its Diversity Record, and It's Not Good." *PBS NewsHour*, May 28, 2014. www.pbs.org.

Jarmon, Renina. 2013. *Black Girls Are from the Future: Essays on Race, Digital Creativity and Pop Culture*. Washington, DC: Jarmon Media.

Jaschik, Scott. 2005. "What Neil Summers Said: Remarks at NBER Conference on Diversifying the Science and Engineering Workforce." *Inside Higher Education*, February 18, 2005. www.insidehighered.com.

Jesse, Jolene Kay. 2006. "The Poverty of the Pipeline Metaphor: The AAAS/CST Study of Nontraditional Pathways into IT/CS Education and the Workforce." In *Women and Information Technology: Research on Underrepresentation*, edited by J. McGrath Cohoon and William Aspray, 239–78. Cambridge, MA: MIT Press.

Joy, Erica. 2015. "The Other Side of Diversity." In *Lean Out: The Struggle for Gender Equality in Tech and Start-Up Culture*, edited by Elissa Shevinsky, 153–63. New York: OR Books.

———. 2016. "Humans of Silicon Valley." *Medium*, April 12, 2016. https://medium.com.

Kamat, Sangeeta, Ali Mir, and Biju Mathew. 2004. "Producing Hi-Tech: Globalization, the State and Migrant Subjects." *Globalisation, Societies and Education* 2 (1): 1–39.

Kamble, Maya. 2020. "It's Time to End Caste Discrimination in the Tech Industry." *Al Jazeera*, July 27, 2020.

Kanter, Rosabeth Moss. 1977. *Men and Women of the Corporation*. New York: Basic Books.

Karake, Mark. 2020. "We Existed in a Parallel Universe—What It's Like to Be Black in Silicon Valley." WeForum, June 10, 2020. www.weforum.org.

Kenney, Martin, ed. 2000. *Understanding Silicon Valley: The Anatomy of a Region*. Stanford, CA: Stanford Business Books.

Kessler, Sarah. 2015. "Where Are the Women in Tech? Coding Bootcamps." *Fast Company*, August 24, 2015. www.fastcompany.com.

———. 2017. "The Future of Coding Bootcamps, According to the President of One That Is Shutting Down." *Quartz*, July 27, 2017. https://qz.com.

Kim, Cristina, and Sinduja Rangarajan. 2018. "What Women of Color in the Tech Industry Want." *Center for Investigative Reporting Blog*, April 14, 2018. www.reveal news.org.

Kolhatkar, Sheelah. 2017. "Letter from Silicon Valley: The Disrupters: The Women of Tech Call Out Workplace Sexism." *New Yorker*, November 20, 2017, 52–63.

Lacy, Karyn. 2007. *Blue-Chip Black: Race, Class and Status in the New Black Middle-Class*. Berkeley: University of California Press.

Larson, Eric. 2017. "Google Sued by Women Workers Claiming Gender Discrimination." *Financial Post*, September 14, 2017. http://business.financialpost.com.

Levin, Sam. 2017a. "Accused of Underpaying Women, Google Says It's Too Expensive to Get Wage Data." *Guardian*, May 26, 2017.

———. 2017b. "Black and Latino Representation in Silicon Valley Has Declined, New Study Shows." *Guardian*, October 3, 2017. www.theguardian.com.

———. 2017c. "Google Accused of 'Extreme' Gender Pay Discrimination by US Labor Department." *Guardian*, April 7, 2017. www.theguardian.com.

———. 2017d. "Google 'Segregates' Women into Lower-Paying Jobs, Stifling Careers, Lawsuit Says." *Guardian*, September 14, 2017. www.theguardian.com.

———. 2017e. "Sexism, Racism and Bullying Are Driving People out of Tech, US Study Finds." *Guardian*, April 27, 2017. www.theguardian.com.

———. 2017f. "Women Say They Quit Google Because of Racial Discrimination: 'I Was Invisible.'" *Guardian*, August 18, 2017.

———. 2018a. "Google Gender Pay Gap: Women Advance Suit That Could Affect 8,300 Workers." *Guardian*, October 26, 2018.

———. 2018b. "Google Sees Major Claims of Harassment and Discrimination as Lawsuits Proceed." *Guardian*, March 28, 2018.

———. 2019a. "Oracle Systematically Underpaid Thousands of Women, Lawsuit Says." *Guardian*, January 18, 2019.

———. 2019b. "US Government v Silicon Valley: Oracle Said to Owe $400m to Women and Minorities." *Guardian*, January 23, 2019.

Levina, Marina, and Amy Adele Hasinoff. 2017. "The Silicon Valley Ethos: Tech Industry Products, Discourses and Practices." *Television and New Media* 18 (6): 489–95.

Levinson, Katy. 2015. "Sexism in Tech." In *Lean Out: The Struggle for Gender Equality in Tech and Start-Up Culture*, edited by Elissa Shevinsky, 47–58. New York: OR Books.

Lewis, Paul. 2017. "'I See Things Differently': James Damore on His Autism and the Google Memo." *Guardian*, November 17, 2017. www.theguardian.com.

Light, Jennifer. 1999. "When Computers Were Women." *Technology and Culture* 40 (3): 455–83.

Lin, Nan. 2000. "Inequality in Social Capital." *Contemporary Sociology* 29 (6): 785–95.

———. 2002. *Social Capital: A Theory of Social Structure and Action.* Cambridge: Cambridge University Press.

Lin, Nan, and Mary Dumin. 1986. "Access to Occupations through Social Ties." *Social Networks* 8:365–85.

Lohr, Steve. 2015. "As Tech Booms, Workers Turn to Coding for Career Change." *New York Times,* July 28, 2015. www.nytimes.com.

———. 2017. "A New Kind of Tech Job Emphasizes Skills, Not a College Degree." *New York Times,* June 28, 2017.

Luckie, Mark. 2018. "Facebook Is Failing Its Black Employees." Facebook posting, November 8, 2018. www.facebook.com/notes/mark-s-luckie/facebook-is-failing-its-black-employees-and-its-black-users/1931075116975013/.

Luthra, Renee Reichl, 2009. "Temporary Immigrants in a High-Skilled Labour Market: A Study of H-1Bs." *Journal of Ethnic and Migration Studies* 35 (2): 227–50.

Ma, Yingyi. 2009. "Family Socioeconomic Status, Parental Involvement, and College Major Choices—Gender, Race/Ethnicity and Nativity Patterns." *Sociological Perspectives* 52:210–34.

Ma, Yingyi, and Yan Liu. 2017. "Entry and Degree Attainment in STEM: The Intersection of Gender and Race/Ethnicity." *Social Sciences* 6 (3): 89. www.mdpi.com.

MacKenzie, Donald, and Judy Wajcman, eds. 1995. *The Social Shaping of Technology.* Milton Keynes, UK: Open University Press.

Mandel, Lois. 1967. "The Computer Girls." *Cosmopolitan,* April 1967, 52–56.

Margolis, Jane, Rachel Estrella, Joanna Goode, Jennifer Holme, and Kimberly Nao. 2008. *Stuck in the Shallow: Education, Race and Computing.* Cambridge, MA: MIT Press.

Margolis, Jane, and Allan Fisher. 2002. *Unlocking the Clubhouse: Women in Computing.* Cambridge, MA: MIT Press.

Massey, Douglas S., and Nancy Denton. 1998. *American Apartheid: Segregation and the Making of the Underclass.* Cambridge, MA: Harvard University Press.

Matsakis, Louise. 2017. "Google Employee's Anti-Diversity Manifesto Goes 'Internally Viral.'" *Motherboard,* August 5, 2017. www.vice.com.

———. 2018. "Labor Board Rules Google's Firing of James Damore Was Legal." *Wired,* February 16, 2018. www.wired.com.

Matthews, Glenna. 2003. *Silicon Valley, Women and the California Dream: Gender, Class and Opportunity in the Twentieth Century.* Stanford, CA: Stanford University Press.

McBride, Sarah. 2013. "In Silicon Valley Start-Ups World, Pedigree Counts." Reuters, September 12, 2013. www.reuters.com.

McCall, Leslie. 2005. "The Complexity of Intersectionality." *Signs: Journal of Women in Culture and Society* 30 (3): 1771–1800.

McGirt, Ellen. 2017. "Apple Shareholders Take on Diversity." *Fortune,* February 9, 2017. http://fortune.com.

McGregor, Jena. 2014. "Google Admits It Has a Diversity Problem." *Washington Post,* May 29, 2014.

McIlwee, Judith S., and J. Gregg Robinson 1992. *Women in Engineering: Gender, Power, and Workplace Culture.* Albany: State University of New York Press.

McKay, Steve. 2006. "Hard Drives and Glass Ceilings: Gender Stratification in High-Tech Production." *Gender & Society* 20 (2): 207–35.

McKindreck, David, Richard Doner, and Stephan Haggard. 2000. *From Silicon Valley to Singapore: Location and Competitive Advantage in the Hard Disk Drive Industry.* Stanford, CA: Stanford University Press.

McLeannan, Sarah. 2012. "When the Computer Wore a Skirt: Langley's Computers, 1935–1970." *NASA History Program News* 29 (1): 25–32.

McPherson, Miller, Lynn Smith-Lovin, and James Cook. 2001. "Birds of a Feather: Homophily in Social Networks." *Annual Review of Sociology* 27:415–44.

Metcalfe, Heather. 2010. "Stuck in the Pipeline: A Critical Review of STEM Workforce Literature." *InterActions: UCLA Journal of Education and Information Studies* 6 (2): 1–20.

Milkman, Ruth. 1987. *Gender at Work: The Dynamics of Job Segregation by Sex during World War II.* Chicago: University of Chicago Press.

Miller, Claire Cain. 2010. "About Face: Most Companies Say They Want to Attract a Diverse Workforce, but Few Deliver." *New York Times Magazine*, February 28, 2010.

———. 2012. "In Google's Inner Circle, a Falling Number of Women." *New York Times*, August 22, 2012. www.nytimes.com.

———. 2014. "Google Releases Employee Data, Illustrating Tech's Diversity Challenge." *Bits* (blog), *New York Times*, May 28, 2014. https://bits.blogs.nytimes.com.

Min, Janice. 2021. "Pinterest and the Subtle Poison of Sexism and Racism in Silicon Valley." *Time*, March 22, 2021. www.time.com.

Misa, Thomas J. 2010. "Gender Codes: Defining the Problem." In *Gender Codes: Why Women Are Leaving Computing*, 3–23. Hoboken, NJ: IEEE Computer Society.

———. 2015. "Charles Babbage, Ada Lovelace, and the Bernoulli Number." In *Ada's Legacy: Cultures of Computing from the Victorian to the Digital Age*, edited by Robin Hammerman and Andrew Russell, 11–32. New York: ACM / Morgan and Claypool.

Molla, Rani. 2017. "Square and Pinterest's Latest Available Employment Data Reveals a Lack of Diversity in Top Ranks." *Recode*, October 19, 2017. www.recode.net.

———. 2018. "How Facebook Compares to Other Tech Companies in Diversity." *Vox*, April 11, 2018. www.vox.com.

Mundy, Liza. 2017. "Why Is Silicon Valley So Awful to Women?" *Atlantic*, April 2017. www.theatlantic.com.

Murray, Fergus. 1993. "A Separate Reality: Science, Technology and Masculinity." In *Gendered by Design: Information Technology and Office Systems*, edited by Eileen Green, Jenny Owen, and Den Pain, 64–81. London: Taylor and Francis.

Nakamura, Lisa. 2008. *Digitizing Race: Visual Cultures of the Internet.* London: Routledge.

Nakaso, Dan. 2012. "Asian Workers Now Dominate SV Tech Jobs." *Mercury News*, November 29, 2012.

Neate, Rupert. 2015. "Facebook Only Hired Seven Black People Last Year Despite Diversity Pledge." *Guardian*, June 25, 2015.

Noble, Safiya Umoja. 2018. *Algorithms of Oppression: How Search Engines Reinforce Racism*. New York. New York University Press.

Noble, Safiya Umoja, and Sarah T. Roberts. 2019. "Technological Elites, the Meritocracy, and Post-Racial Myths in Silicon Valley." In *Racism Postrace*, edited by Roopali Mukherjee, Sarah Banet-Weiser, and Herman Gray, 113–30. Durham, NC: Duke University Press.

Nopper, Tamara K. 2019. "Digital Character in 'The Scored Society': FICO, Social Networks, and Competing Measurements of Creditworthiness." In *Captivating Technology: Race, Carceral Technoscience, and Liberatory Imagination in Everyday Life*, 170–87. Durham, NC: Duke University Press.

Ohlheiser, Abby. 2017. "How James Damore Went from Google Employee to Right-Wing Internet Hero." *Washington Post*, August 12, 2017. www.washingtonpost.com.

OpenDoors. 2019. "2019 Fast Facts." https://opendoorsdata.org.

Ozkazanc-Pan, Banu, and Susan Clark Muntaen. 2018. "Networking towards (in) Equality: Women Entrepreneurs in Technology." *Gender, Work & Organization* 25 (4): 379–400.

Pager, Devah, Bart Bonikowski, and Brue Western. 2009. "Discrimination in a Low-Wage Labor Market: A Field Experiment." *American Sociological Review* 74 (5): 777–99.

Pager, Devah, and David S. Pedulla. 2015. "Race, Self-Selection and Job Search Process." *American Journal of Sociology* 120:1005–54.

Pager, Devah, and Lincoln Quillian. 2005. "Walking the Talk? What Employers Say versus What They Do." *American Sociological Review* 70:355–80.

Pao, Ellen. 2017. *Reset: My Fight for Inclusion and Lasting Change*. New York: Spiegel and Grau.

Pardes, Arielle. 2020. "Black Investors Call on VCs to Fix Hiring and Funding." *Wired*, June 9, 2020.

Park, John S. W. 2018. *Immigration Law and Society*. Cambridge, UK: Polity Press.

Parrish, Charlie. 2014. "Meet the PayPal Mafia, the Richest Group of Men in Silicon Valley." *Business Insider*, September 20, 2014. www.businessinsider.com.

Paul, Kari. 2021. "California Bill Targets NDAs That Prevent Workers from Speaking about Discrimination." *Guardian*, February 10, 2021. www.theguardian.com.

PBS NewsHour. 2014. "Google's Diversity Record Shows Women and Minorities Left Behind." May 28, 2014. www.pbs.org.

Pearlstein, Joanna. 2014. "The Schools Where Apple, Google and Facebook Get Their Recruits." *Wired*, May 22, 2014. www.wired.com.

Pellow, David Naguib, and Lisa Sun-Hee Park. 2002. *The Silicon Valley of Dreams: Environmental Injustice, Immigrant Workers, and the High-Tech Global Economy*. New York: New York University Press.

Petersen, Trond, Ishak Saporta, and March-David L. Seidel. 2000. "Offering a Job: Meritocracy and Social Networks." *American Journal of Sociology* 106 (3): 763–817.

Portes, Alejandro. 1998. "Social Capital: Its Origin and Applications in Modern Sociology." *Annual Review of Sociology* 24 (1): 1–24.

President's Council of Advisors on Science and Technology. 2012. "Engage to Excel: Producing One Million Additional College Graduates with Degrees in Science, Technology, Engineering and Mathematics." February 2012. www.whitehouse.gov.

Primack, Dan. 2014. "Venture Capital's stunning lack of female decision makers." *Fortune*, February 6, 2014. http://fortune.com.

Purkayastha, Bandana. 2005. "Skilled Migration and Cumulative Disadvantage: The Case of Highly Qualified Asian Indian Immigrant Women in the US." *Geoform* 36:181–96.

———. 2010. "Interrogating Intersectionality: Contemporary Globalization and Racialized Gendering in the Lives of Highly Educated South Asian Americans and Their Children." *Journal of Intercultural Studies* 31:29–47.

Putnam, Robert D. 2000. *Bowling Alone: The Collapse and Revival of American Community*. New York: Simon and Schuster.

Quillian, Lincoln, Devah Pager, Ole Hexel, and Arnfinn Midtbøen. 2017. "Meta-analysis of Field Experiments Show No Change in Hiring Discrimination." *Proceedings of the National Academy of Sciences* 114 (41): 10870–75.

Radhakrishnan, Smitha. 2011. *Appropriately Indian: Gender and Culture in a New Transnational Class*. Durham, NC: Duke University Press.

Raghuram, Pavarti. 2004. "The Differences That Skills Make: Gender, Family Migration Strategies and Regulated Labor Markets." *Journal of Ethnic and Migration Studies* 30 (2): 303–21.

———. 2005. "Migration, Gender and the IT sector: Intersecting Debates." *Women's Studies International Forum* 27:163–76.

Raj, Aditya. 2012. "The Indian Diaspora in North America: The Role of Networks and Associations." *Diaspora Studies* 5(2): 107–23.

Rangarajan, Sinduja, and Will Evans. 2017. "How We Analyzed Silicon Valley Companies' Diversity Data." Reveal: Center for Investigative Reporting, October 19, 2017. www.revealnews.org.

Rao, Arun. 2013. *A History of Silicon Valley: The Greatest Creation of Wealth in the History of the Planet, 1900–2013*. CreateSpace.

Reed, Vanessa S. 2016. "Diversity in Tech Remains Elusive Due to Racism, Lack of Representation and Cultural Differences." *Model View Culture*. https://modelviewculture.com.

Reeves, Richard. 2018. *Dream Hoarders: How the American Upper Middle Class Is Leaving Everyone Else in the Dust. Why That Is a Problem, and What to Do about It.* Washington, DC: Brookings Institution Press.

Reskin, Barbara. 1993. "Sex Segregation in the Workplace." *Annual Review of Sociology* 19:241–70.

———. 2000. "Getting It Right: Sex and Race Inequality in Work Organizations." *Annual Review of Sociology* 26:707–9.

Reskin, Barbara A., and Patricia Roos. 1990. *Job Queues, Gender Queues: Explaining Women's Inroads into Male Occupations*. Philadelphia: Temple University Press.

Ridgeway, Cecilia. 2014. "Why Status Matters for Inequality." *American Sociological Review* 79 (1): 1–16.

Ritcey, Alice, and Alistair Barr. 2018. "Google Staff in Rare Push Want Executive Pay Tied to Diversity." *Bloomberg Businessweek*, June 5, 2018. www.bloomberg.com.

Rivera, Lauren A. 2012a. "Diversity within Reach: Recruitment versus Hiring in Elite Firms." *Annals of the American Academy of Political and Social Science* 639:70–89.

———. 2012b. "Hiring as Cultural Matching: The Case of Elite Professional Service Firms." *American Sociological Review* 77 (6): 999–1022.

Rivera, Lauren A., and András Tilcsik. 2016. "Class Advantage, Commitment Penalty: The Interplay of Social Class and Gender in an Elite Labor Market." *American Sociological Review* 81 (December): 1097–1131.

Rodriguez, Salvador. 2015. "Silicon Valley Is Failing Miserably at Diversity, and What Should Be Done." *International Business Times*, July 11, 2015.

Roohi, Sanam. 2017. "Caste, Kinship and the Realisation of 'American Dream.'" *Journal of Ethnic and Migration Studies* 43 (16): 2756–70.

Roos, H. 2013. "In the Rhythm of the Global Market: Female Expatriates and Mobile Careers: A Case Study of Indian ICT Professionals on the Move." *Gender, Work & Organization* 20 (2): 147–57.

Rosenberg, Eli. 2018. "'Facebook Has a Black People Problem': Black Ex-Employee Spotlights Race Issues in Public Memo." *Washington Post*, November 27, 2018. www.washingtonpost.com.

Rosenberg, Tina. 2018. "A High Paying Job? Go to App Boot Camp." *New York Times*, April 17, 2018.

Rosenblatt, Joel. 2018. "California Judge Rules against Class-Action Status in Twitter Gender Bias Case." *Seattle Times*, July 3, 2018. www.seattletimes.com.

Royster, Deirdre. 2003. *Race and the Invisible Hand: How White Networks Exclude Black Men from Blue-Collar Jobs*. Berkeley: University of California Press.

Rupp, Leila. 1978. *Mobilizing Women for War: German and American Propaganda, 1939–1945*. Princeton, NJ: Princeton University Press.

Sahoo, Ajaya K., Dave Sangha, and Melissa Kelly. 2010. "From 'Temporary Migrants' to 'Permanent Residents': Indian H-1B Visa Holders in the United States." *Asian Ethnicity* 11 (3): 293–309.

San Francisco 2.0: Inside the City's Tech Boom. 2015. Directed and produced by Alexandra Pelosi. Color. 40 mins. HBO Documentary Films.

San Jose State University Human Rights Institute. 2021. *Silicon Valley Pain Index*. www.sjsu.edu.

Sassler, Sharon, Katherine Michelmore, and Kristin Smith. 2017. "A Tale of Two Majors: Explaining the Gender Gap in STEM Employment Among Computer Science and Engineering Degree Holders." *Social Science* 6 (3): 69.

Saxenian, AnnaLee. 1994. *Regional Advantage: Culture and Competition in Silicon Valley and Route 128*. Cambridge, MA: Harvard University Press.

Scheiber, Naomi. 2018. "Google Workers Reject Silicon Valley's Individualism in Walkout." *New York Times*, November 6, 2018. www.nytimes.com.

Schilt, Kristen. 2011. *Just One of the Guys? Transgender Men and the Persistence of Gender Inequality*. Chicago: University of Chicago Press.

Schlombs, Corinna. 2010. "A Gendered Job Carousel: Employment Effects of Computer Automation." In *Gender Codes: Why Women Are Leaving Computing*, edited by Thomas J. Misa, 75–94. Hoboken, NJ: IEEE Computer Society.

Shanker, Deepthi. 2008. "Gender Relations in IT Companies: An Indian Experience." *Gender, Technology & Development* 12 (2): 185–207.

Shevinsky, Elissa, ed. 2015a. *Lean Out: The Struggle for Gender Equality in Tech and Start-Up Culture*. New York: OR Books.

———. 2015b. "The Pipeline Isn't the Problem." In *Lean Out: The Struggle for Gender Inequality*, edited by Elissa Shevinsky, 203–16. New York: OR Books.

———. 2015c. "That's It—I'm Finished Defending Sexism in Tech." In *Lean Out: The Struggle for Gender Inequality*, edited by Elissa Shevinsky, 60–69. New York: OR Books.

Shih, Johanna. 2006. "Circumventing Discrimination: Gender and Ethnic Strategies in Silicon Valley." *Gender & Society* 20 (2): 177–206.

Simonite, Tim. 2021a. "The Exile." *Wired*, July–August 2021, 114–27.

———. 2021b. "What Really Happened When Google Ousted Timnit Gebru?" *Wired*, June 8, 2021. www.wired.com.

Singh, Vikash. 2018. "Myths of Meritocracy: Caste, Karma and New Racism, a Comparative Study." *Ethnic and Racial Studies* 41 (15): 2693–2710.

Smedley, Audrey. 1993. *Race in North America: Origin and Evolution of a Worldview*. Boulder, CO: Westview.

Smith, Stacey L. 2013. *Freedom's Frontier: California and the Struggle over Unfree Labor, Emancipation, and Reconstruction*. Chapel Hill: University of North Carolina Press.

Sohrabji, Sunita. 2018. "HCL Technologies Disproportionately Favors Indian Americans for Employment in U.S., Alleges Lawsuit." *India West*, August 23, 2018. www.indiawest.com.

Somerville, Heather. 2017. "Three Women at Uber in San Francisco Claiming Unequal Pay, Benefits." Reuters, October 25, 2017. www.reuters.com.

Sorkin, Andrew Ross, and Evelyn M. Rusli. 2012. "A Yahoo Search Calls Up a Chief from Google." *New York Times*, July 16, 2012. www.dealbook.nytimes.com.

Stapleton, Claire, Tanuja Gupta, Meredith Whittaker, Celie O'Neil-Hart, Stephanie Parker, Erica Anderson, and Amr Gaber. 2018. "We're the Organizers of the Google Walkout. Here Are Our Demands." *The Cut*, November 1, 2018. www.thecut.com.

Statista. 2020. "Distribution of Facebook Employees in the United States from 2014 to 2020, by Ethnicity." July 2020. www.statista.com.

Steinberg, Stephen. 1995. *Turning Back: The Retreat from Racial Justice in American Thought and Policy*. Boston: Beacon.

Strober, Myra. 1984. "Toward a General Theory of Occupational Sex Segregation." In *Sex Segregation in the Workplace: Trends, Explanations, Remedies*, edited by Barbara Reskin, 144–56. Philadelphia: Temple University Press.

Sturgeon, Timothy J. 2000. "How Silicon Valley Came to Be." In *Understanding Silicon Valley: The Anatomy of an Entrepreneurial Region*, edited by Martin Kenney, 15–47. Stanford, CA: Stanford University Press.

Tao, Yu, and Connie L. McNeely. 2019. "Gender and Race Intersectional Effects in the US Engineering Workforce. Who Stays? Who Leaves?" *International Journal of Gender, Science and Technology* 11 (1): 182–202. http://genderandset.open.ac.uk.

Thayer, Kyle. 2018. "Coding Bootcamps vs. Computer Science Degrees." *Medium*, March 2, 2018. https://medium.com.

Thayer, Kyle, and A. J. Ko. 2017. "Barriers Faced by Coding Boot Camp Students." Paper presented at the 13th annual ACM International Computing Education Research (ICER) Conference, Tacoma, WA.

Thompson, Clive. 2017. "The Next Big Blue-Collar Job Is Coding." *Wired*, February 2017. www.wired.com.

———. 2019. "The Secret History of Women in Coding." *New York Times Magazine*, February 13, 2019. www.nytimes.com.

Tiku, Nitasha. 2017. "Why Tech Leadership Has a Bigger Race than Gender Problem." *Wired*, October 3, 2017. www.wired.com.

———. 2019a. "Feds Also Say That Oracle Underpaid Women and Minorities." *Wired*, January 22, 2019. www.wired.com.

———. 2019b. "Most of the Google Walkout Organizers Have Left the Company." *Wired*, July 16, 2019. www.wired.com.

———. 2019c. "Three Years of Misery Inside Google, the Happiest Company in Tech." *Wired*, August 13, 2019. www.wired.com.

———. 2020. "India's Engineers Have Thrived in Silicon Valley, So Has Its Caste System." *Washington Post*, October 27, 2020.

Upadhya, Carol. 2007. "Employment, Exclusion and 'Merit' in the Indian IT Industry." *Economic and Political Weekly* 42 (20): 1863–68.

US Census Bureau. 2011. American Community Survey. Accessed October 2017. www.census.gov. The term "Hispanic" in this data set refers to both White and non-White Hispanics.

———. 2015. American Community Survey. Accessed October 2017. www.census.gov. The term "Hispanic" in this data set refers to both White and non-White Hispanics.

———. 2016. American Community Survey. Accessed October 2017. www.census.gov. The term "Hispanic" in this data set refers to both White and non-White Hispanics.

———. 2018. "Quick Facts: San Francisco." July 2018. www.census.gov.

US Department of Education. 2016. *Fact Sheet: ED Launches Initiative for Low-Income Students to Access New Generation of Higher Education Providers*. August 16, 2016. www.ed.gov.

US Department of Homeland Security. 2012. *2012 Yearbook of Immigration Statistics*. Office of Immigration Statistics. www.dhs.gov.

US Department of Labor. 2017. "US Labor Department Sues Oracle America Inc. for Discriminatory Employment Practices." January 2017. www.dol.gov.

US Department of State. 2019. *Open Doors 2019 Annual Data Release*. Institute of International Education, Bureau of Educational and Cultural Affairs.

US Equal Employment Opportunity Commission. 2014. *Diversity in High Tech: Executive Summary*. www.eeoc.gov.

Vara, Vauhini. 2016. "Why Doesn't Silicon Valley Hire Black Coders?" *Bloomberg Businessweek*, January 21, 2016. www.bloomberg.com.

Varathan, Preeti. 2017. "Silicon Valley's Gender Inequality Is Even Worse than Wall Street." *Quartz*, August 14, 2017. https://qz.com.

Varghese, Sanjana. 2019. "Ruha Benjamin: 'We Definitely Can't Wait for Silicon Valley to Become More Diverse.'" *Guardian*, June 29, 2019. www.theguardian.com.

Varma, Roli. 2007. "Women in Computing: The Role of Geek Culture." *Science as Culture* 16 (4): 359–76.

———. 2009. "Exposure, Training, and Environment: Women's Participation in Computing Education in the United States and India." *Journal of Women and Minorities in Science and Engineering* 15 (3): 205–22.

Varma, Roli, and Heiko Hahn. 2008. "Gender and the Pipeline Metaphor in Computing." *European Journal of Engineering Education* 33 (1): 3–11.

Varma, Roli, and Deepak Kapur. 2015. "Decoding Femininity in Computer Science in India." *Communications of the ACM* 58 (5): 56–62.

Vassallo, Trae, Ellen Levy, Michele Madansky, Hillary Mickell, Benneter Porter, Monica Leas, and Julie Oberweis. 2015. Elephant in the Valley. www.elephantinthe valley.com.

Villa-Nicholas, Melissa. 2016. "The Invisible Information Worker: Latinas in Telecommunications." In *The Intersectional Internet: Race, Sex, Class and Culture Online*, edited by Safiya Umoja Noble and Brendesha M. Tynes, 195–214. New York: Peter Lang.

Wadhwa, Vivek. 2012. "Why There Are So Few Black or Female Entrepreneurs in Silicon Valley." *TechCrunch*, August 19, 2012.

Waguespack, Leslie, Jeffrey Babb, and David Yates. 2018. "Triangulating Coding Bootcamps in IS Education: Bootleg Education or Disruptive Innovation?" *Information Systems Education Journal* 16 (6): 48–58.

Wajcman, Judy. 1991. *Feminism Confronts Technology*. University Park: Pennsylvania State Press.

———. 2007. "From Women and Gender to Gendered Technoscience." *Information, Communication & Society* 10 (3): 287–98.

———. 2010. "Feminist Theories of Technology." *Cambridge Journal of Economics* 34 (1): 143–52.

Wakabayashi, Daisuke. 2018. "Uber Eliminates Forced Arbitration for Sexual Misconduct Claims." *New York Times*, May 15, 2018.

Wakabayashi, Daisuke, Erin Griffith, Amie Tsang, and Kate Conger. 2018. "Google Walkout: Employers Stage Protest over Handling of Sexual Harassment." *New York Times*, November 1, 2018.

Watters, Audrey. 2012. "Top Ed-Tech Trends of 2012: Learning to Code." *Inside Higher Education*, December 16, 2012. www.insidehighered.com.

Weisberg, Jacob. 2013. "Yahoo's Marissa Mayer: Hail to the Chief." *Vogue*, August 15, 2013.

Wells, Georgia, and Yoree Koh. 2017. "Google Episode Sends a Message: Diversity Push Is a Hard Sell in Silicon Valley." *Wall Street Journal*, August 10, 2017, B4.

White House. 2015. "Fact Sheet: President Obama Launches New TechHire Initiative." Press release, Office of the Press Secretary. March 9, 2015. https://obamawhitehouse.archives.gov.

Whittaker, Meredith. 2019. "Onward! Another #Google Walkout Goodbye." Google Walkout for Real Change, July 16, 2019. http://googlewalkout.medium.com.

Wiener, Anna. 2016. "Why Can't Silicon Valley Solve Its Diversity Problem?" *New Yorker*, November 26, 2016. www.newyorker.com.

Wiessner, Daniel. 2017. "Tesla Hit by Class-Action Lawsuit Claiming Racial Discrimination." Reuters, November 13, 2017.

Wilkerson, Isabel. 2020. *Caste: The Origins of Our Discontents*. New York: Random House.

Williams, Christine, Chandra Muller, and Kristine Kilanski. 2012. "Gendered Organizations in the New Economy." *Gender and Society* 26 (4): 549–73.

Williams, Maxine. 2016. "Facebook Diversity Update: Positive Hiring Trends Show Progress." *Facebook Blog*, July 14, 2016. https://about.fb.com.

Wilson, Graham. 2017. "Building a New Mythology: The Coding Boot Camp Phenomenon." *ACM Inroads* 8 (4): 66–71.

Wingfield, Adia Harvey. 2009. "Racializing the Glass Escalator: Reconsidering Men's Experiences with 'Women's Work.'" *Gender & Society* 23 (1): 5–26.

———. 2010. "Are Some Emotions Marked 'White Only'? Racialized Rules in Professional Workplaces." *Social Problems* 57 (2): 251–68.

———. 2019. *Flatlining: Race, Work and Health Care in the New Economy*. Oakland: University of California Press.

Wingfield, Adia Harvey, and Renée Skeete Alston. 2014. "Maintaining Hierarchies in Predominantly White Organizations: A Theory of Racial Tasks." *American Behavioral Scientist* 58 (2): 274–87.

Wong, Julia Carrie. 2017a. "Facebook's Underclass: As Staffers Enjoy Lavish Perks, Contractors Barely Get By." *Guardian*, September 26, 2017. www.theguardian.com.

———. 2017b. "Segregated Valley: The Ugly Truth about Google and Diversity in Tech." *Guardian*, August 7. www.theguardian.com.

———. 2019. "Google Board Tried to Cover Up Sexual Misconduct, Shareholders Allege." *Guardian*, January 10, 2019. www.theguardian.com.

———. 2020. "More than 1,200 Google Workers Condemn the Firing of AI Scientist." *Guardian*, December 4, 2020. www.theguardian.com.

Woodfield, Ruth. 2000. *Women, Work and Computing*: Cambridge: Cambridge University Press.

Woolcock, Michael, and Anne Sweetser. 2002. "Bright Ideas: Social Capital—the Bonds That Connect." *Asian Development Bank Review* 34 (2): 26–27.

World Population Review. "San Francisco Population." Accessed December 10, 2018. http://worldpopulationreview.com.

Wynn, Alison T. 2020. "Pathways toward Change: Ideologies and Gender Equality in a Silicon Valley Technology Company." *Gender & Society* 34 (1): 106–30.

Wynn, Alison T., and Shelley J. Correll. 2018. "Puncturing the Pipeline: Do Technology Companies Alienate Women in Recruiting Sessions." *Social Studies of Science* 48 (1): 149–64.

Zarya, Valentina. 2018. "Female Founders Got 2% of Venture Capital Dollars in 2017." *Fortune*, January 31, 2018. https://fortune.com.

INDEX

Abbate, Janet: construction of skill, 8, 30, 234n29, 236nn65–67, 236n71
Acker, Joan: inequality regimes, 20, 56–58, 234n24, 238n33, 239nn60–61
administrative computing: the re-gendering or gender-flipping of occupations, 31–32
Ahmed, Sara, 66, 239n8
Alegria, Sharla, 234n24, 234n73
Alfrey, Lauren, 237n7, 241n23, 242n4
Algorithms of Oppression (Noble), 208
Alphabet Workers Union, 206, 227
alumni networks: value of, 119–121
American Community Survey, 36
American Dream: Indian realization of, 19
Anand, Priya, 237nn11–12
anti-black racism, 3, 36, 38–39, 67, 82–83, 105, 110, 199, 207, 211, 238n.44
artificial intelligence, x, 28, 205, 224, 226; racial bias in commercial facial recognition, 205; *See also* Gebru, Timnit
Ascend Report, 85
Atlantic, 82

Baas, Michael, 234n27
Babbage, Charles, ix
Baker, Erica Joy: anti-black racism, 40; stereotypes, 38
bamboo ceiling, 32, 85, 211
Banerjee, Payal, 17–18, 235n54, 235nn56–57

Banks, Aerica Shimizu: and California state legislation, 215
barriers to organizational change, 84
Barthes, Roland: 2
Beasely, Maya: 234n17
Benjamin, Ruha, 208, 209
Benner, Katie, 111
Berlin, Leslie, 235nn42–43
Bhatt, Amy,160, 242 nn7–10
biological essentialism: as myth, 73–76
Bishay, Shereef: Dev Bootcamp, 177
Blacks in Artificial Intelliegence. *See* Gebru, Timnit
Black women: as occupational ren-egades, 85, 214
Black Latina tech workers, 137–141, 157–58
Blue-Chip Blacks (Lacy), 89, 107
Bock, Laszlo, 5
Bonikowski, Bart, 235n60, 238n34
Bourdieu, Pierre, 182, 238n50
Boyd, E. B., 3
Brahmins, 43, 45–47, 162, 166–170. *See also* caste system
Brotopia: gendered caste system, 82, 239n1
Brougher, Francoise: gender discrimi-nation lawsuit against Pinterest, 215
Bryant, Kimberly (Black Girls Code), 80
employment discrimination, 215–216
Bureau of Indian Affairs, xi
Byron, Ada (Countess of Lovelace), ix–x

ABOUT THE AUTHOR

FRANCE WINDDANCE TWINE is Professor of Sociology at the University of California, Santa Barbara, a documentary filmmaker, and a visual artist. A native of Chicago, Twine is a citizen of the Muskogee-Creek Nation of Oklahoma and the author and co-editor of ten books and seventy-five articles and book chapters. Her publications include *A White Side of Black Britain* (2010), *Geographies of Privilege* (2013), and *Feminism and Antiracism: International Struggles for Justice* (2001). In 2020, Twine was awarded the Distinguished Career Award from the Race, Gender & Class section of the American Sociological Association. She divides her time between Santa Barbara and the San Francisco Bay Area.